Between Two Minds:

Healing from Depression
and
Anxiety for LDS Women

By

Dr. Judith Stay Moore

Published by:
Lowe-Izatt Enterprises
The Woodlands, TX

Cover design by Monica Strang
Page Layout and Design by Myrna Varga

ISBN: 978-0-9715287-5-8

Printed in the United States of America

Between Two Minds:

Healing from Depression
and
Anxiety for LDS Women

Acknowledgments

This book would not have been written without the ideas and encouragement from my son, Tom Moore. He told me this book was needed and inspired me to believe that I was the one to write it. He read and critiqued the first few chapters and encouraged me to keep going. I am also grateful for each of my other children, Jason, Tonya, Tina, Monica and Shane who have put up with me not being as available as I would like to have been for them and their families. They have always supported me in my work.

I will be forever grateful to Tracy Izatt, who had so much faith in the purpose of this book that she created her own publishing company to publish it. She had already been very generous in giving away many copies of my previous book after receiving her own gift of healing, and has spent much time and personal money to make this book happen. Tracy, you are amazing.

I am grateful to my four grandchildren, Derrick, Skyler, Collin and December, who lived with me for most of the time I was writing this book. They taught me so much.

I am very grateful to my parents, Helen and Jesse Stay, now inspiring me from the other side, who taught me the gospel of Jesus Christ from my youth, and were great examples of loving and serving.

I owe much to my brothers and sisters, Sharon Brown, Randy Stay, Linda Danielson, Larry Stay, Greg Stay and Tim Stay. They have been my heroes, always trying to be like Jesus, loving and giving to all, and have supported me in every way through my own dark times.

I also owe much to Tyler Mitchell, whose love and service and never-give-up attitude has taught me to love without judgment and to keep going when the going is tough, because "It's all good!"

Most of all I give great gratitude to my Heavenly Parents, who allowed me to be part of this great adventure called "The Plan of Happiness," and for my Savior, Jesus Christ, who, though a God, was born as a man of flesh and blood, suffering the pains of the world, to be a living example for mankind of what is possible for us. He descended from heaven to heal my sins that I may have joy. My heart is full of gratitude for His love, and I have prayed all throughout the writing of this book that it is His message I am giving.

Contents

**Note: This book is for informational purposes only. It is not
intended to be a substitute for professional medical advice,
diagnosis, or treatment. Always seek the advice of your physician or other qualified health provider with any questions you
may have regarding diagnosis or treatment for a medical or
emotional condition.**

Free from SAD: There is an Answer to Depression

For 30-plus years, I suffered from anxiety, depression, fibro-myalgia, and SAD (seasonal affective disorder) and searched in vain for a solution. Mired in my disordered state of mind, I imagined writing my story in a book, which I angrily titled *There Is No Answer*. My situation appeared to be hopeless, even life-threatening. Only in death, I surmised with great irony, would I find relief—only in death would I find life!

Miracles do happen. As of three years ago, I healed completely. Now the working title for my future book is *There Is an Answer!*

What is the answer? Can my answer also be your answer? I am convinced that healing from depression and anxiety can be the path to personal power and positivity.

In 1975, at the age of 18, I began feeling intense anxiety and depression. The reasons for this have never been fully understood, although it is likely a combination of nurture and nature. I grew up in a family with good and kind hearted parents. Despite their best efforts, there was still a great deal of disharmony, miscommunications, chaos, and lack of nurturing in my childhood and home. We also have a strong family history of emotional illness.

The consequences of this illness were severe as it impacted my personal relationships, ability to make and keep commitments, my work performance and, eventually, my role as a wife and mother.

My illness began with headaches, backaches and bouts of depression. However, as life happened, I was still able to successfully attend college, work part time, get married, and eventually had three children. I experienced overwhelming anxiety and feelings of responsibility with each pregnancy and child before they arrived. I prepared in every way I could possibly imagine to be the best wife and mother, reading numerous magazine articles and books. I also spent considerable time interviewing friends and family, striving to glean their counsel, as well as having excellent nutrition, adequate exercise and spiritual discipline. Despite all this, the anxiety seemed to generally worsen as time went on.

When I was 28, I read an article about SAD and realized that I had all the classic symptoms. My supportive husband and I then spent nearly three decades searching for cures and answers. I suffered from high anxiety, very unsociable behavior, low appetite, rapid weight loss and gain, hypomania etc. It was extremely difficult for me to do even basic tasks such as planning and preparing meals, family finances, and carrying on meaningful conversations.

In the spring and summer months, I experienced extreme anxiety. In the fall and winter I suffered with depression, self isolation, extreme cravings for simple carbohydrates, rapid weight gain and low libido. Nothing was easy. I spent the next couple of decades with the ups and downs of SAD. As many people with chronic illness do, I went from doctor to doctor, program to program, on and off numerous medicines—often with side effects—etc. I even had blessings of health from Church authorities and leaders for the purposes of healing and comfort.

But I never gave up. Neither did my husband and family. We all kept fighting to find answers. I feel it was the ability to never give up that helped save me and make me the much happier and emotionally stronger person I am today. One of the key answers I got from my journey is that people who face personal crises need to search always, never give up and persevere.

Day in and day out, year in and year out my husband and I prayed for a miracle. Several different winters I took my daughter out of school for two week periods and we went to Arizona, hoping and praying that the long hours of sun would alleviate the seasonal symptoms. I also spent winters in Florida, Aruba, Mexico, and Peru, which my neuropsychiatrist had recommended. His theory was that if I lived for a specified amount of time in a location close to the equator, then I would have relief; my symptoms would lessen.

Despite my best efforts, the symptoms usually worsened.

Through it all, I did my very best to be the head cheerleader for my children. I raised them with an attitude that if I was positive with them and encouraged them in all of their desires and goals, then they would be healthy and happy and balanced.

My goal was to give my children the nurturing, the love, the positive and balanced mom they needed and deserved; things that I never had growing up. I strove for this despite my tendency toward a negative, victim-like and guilt ridden state. However, though I had good intentions, and though my children knew they were loved, they had to deal with a lot as they suffered through my severe anxieties, and I usually felt like an inadequate mother and wife.

Sometimes during the formal spiritual prayers and blessings said in my behalf it was stated that I would be healed. After the blessing was said and done, my husband and I would wait, watch, and listen to see if my symptoms would lessen. NO SUCH THING, *except* for maybe one month every few years.

I tried almost everything, except for narcotics and admitting myself to long term hospital treatment, which would have added even greater expense to tens of thousands of dollars we had already spent.

Finally, in the year 2008, I decided to travel from my Texas home to Utah to see if I could develop trust with yet another doctor. Dr. Judith Moore was very kind, patient, and methodical. Key points about her skill as a physician included using both western medicine and osteopathic holistic medical care, special emotional work called psycho-kinesiology, counseling, and neurofeedback.

When I first came to Dr. Moore I was literally paralyzed with anxiety, from the time I went to bed until about 5 p.m. the next day. Then I would have a few better hours. It was extremely difficult for me to make any choice. I hated to go grocery shopping because there were too many choices, and it took hours and hours for me to decide what to pack when I went to Utah. I constantly compared what I couldn't do with what others were able to do, and always found myself lacking. Therefore I didn't like to be around other people, though I didn't want to be alone.

I went to Dr. Moore's office daily for two week periods. Fortunately my loving and supportive husband assisted me in arranging my trips between Texas and Utah over the next two years. Friends and family were also very supportive and helpful. I often didn't trust what Dr. Moore suggested because of my anxiety, and because of my fear that we would fail once again. I also had a hard time making myself do things to get better.

But I didn't give up, and neither did Dr. Moore. Searching until I found the best doctor and treatments was difficult, but my husband and I learned that being your own medical advocate is critical to healing. I allowed my husband to financially support my commutes to Utah for two years, and my husband and I were persistent and disciplined enough to work as a team doing neurofeedback at home for one straight year. During that year I went to a wonderful counselor in Texas, and had weekly phone visits with Dr. Moore. I also attended the LDS Addiction

Recovery Program, because it felt to me that my constant negative thinking was an addiction.

It took almost three years, but thank God, I was able to progress from those miserable days of feeling paralyzed to exquisite days of feeling free! One day I realized my anxiety was gone! And over the next few months all of my fibromyalgia symptoms and my persistent numbness went away.

I learned as I was healing that it was important for me to force myself to socialize, no matter how difficult it seemed. I recommend that as an ill person, you should do things you used to enjoy. For me, such activities as swimming and singing helped me become symptom free and led the way to getting back my life and my natural healthy, happy, genuine self.

My life has improved so much that I have now started a publishing and marketing business. The first book I am publishing is this book, *Between Two Minds: Healing from Depression and Anxiety for LDS Women*. I want others to be able to know that they can heal, and to experience the joy that I am experiencing in my life now. I believe that, through this book and the workbook, many women will be able to find their own answers to healing and be able to live in joy.

When my new business stabilizes, I will sit down and finally write my book, *There is an Answer!*

—Tracy Lowe Izatt

Preface

We each have to work things out between our two minds.

Much of the time we each deal with two minds. We may deal with the arguments between the mind of the natural man and the mind of the spirit. We may hear the ego mind chattering and strive to let the superego through. We act from the subconscious mind but only understand from the conscious mind. We may react from the proud adult mind but desire the humble mind of a little child. We may want to act from the loving and wise mind but the fearful mind, or what I call "The Beastie," takes over. We often deal with the angel on one shoulder and the devil on the other.

These terms may only be partially definable and may be somewhat interchangeable. But we recognize that there are often parts of our mind which seem to be at odds with each other. This fits with our LDS belief that "it must needs be, that there is an opposition in all things" (2 Nephi 2:11). This opposition begins in our own individual minds.

This opposition is especially intensified in those who suffer with depression and/or anxiety. As explained in the book, our *subconscious mind*, formed in childhood, holds our paradigm, or the beliefs from which we act in life. However, because we are not completely aware of the beliefs of the subconscious mind, we are often not aware of why we think, feel and act as we do. Our *ego mind*, or the mind of the natural man, may then tell us we are weak, stupid, worthless and unable to change. Our own mind lies to us.

One purpose of our life here on earth is to let go of the Mind of the Natural Man, or the Ego Mind, which is part of our mortal existence here on this earth, but which we often mistakenly believe is "The Real Me." Our purpose in part is to let go of that part of us that has been created for and in this mortal existence, that part of us with mortal weaknesses, and come to remember who we really are. As we come more into touch with our spiritual mind, that part of us that has always existed and always will, it is easier to come back into alignment with the Light, Love, Power and Truth within that has always been connected to God.

With the fall of Adam, the natural man was born. The mind of the natural man believes we are separated from God. That is our experience here on this mortal earth, that we are separated from our true selves as children of divine parentage, and that we are separated from God. But we have just forgotten. There is a piece of us, when connected to the Spirit, that knows all things, a piece of us that is true joy (see Moses 6:61).

When Lehi stated that *"Adam fell that men might be, and men are that they might have joy,"* he was speaking of the power of the atonement to bring all things back into oneness after learning from the opposition, or the duality, that was created by the Fall. As we partake of the atonement we begin to let go of the natural man, or the Ego Mind, and again remember the Love that is God, and in extension, is Us. Recognize that all joy is nothing but Self. When we truly know Self, the Real Self, that eternal part of us that came from Light and Love, we experience joy.

This book was written to assist LDS women suffering from depression and anxiety to learn how to recognize the difference between their own two minds, to pull themselves out of "The Beastie," and to come to be more habitually in the loving, wise and spiritual mind.

The examples of women in this book.

The stories of the women in this book, unless stated otherwise, are based on real situations, but the stories have been changed and are not about real women (so, please do not compare any of these stories to specific people). However, every story is typical of how depressed and anxious women may feel.

LDS women as a group are incredibly powerful.

I believe that there is no greater force that has the power to change the world than the combined women of the Relief Society of the Church of Jesus Christ of Latter-day Saints. LDS women are filled with desires to improve themselves, their families, their neighborhoods and the world. They desire to obey God and do what is for the highest good.

It is not for you to be led by the women of the world; it is for you to lead the…women of the world, in everything that is praiseworthy, everything that is God-like, everything that is uplifting and…purifying to the children of men (Joseph F. Smith). (1)

LDS women have the power to change the world.

If each LDS woman learns to let go of the limiting beliefs which keep her from being all of who she really is, if each LDS woman chooses to let go of judgment and guilt, if each LDS woman is able to hold in her heart true charity, the pure love of Christ, the love that God holds for each one of us, and be able to share that love in wisdom and power for herself, her family and each soul in the world, then the light and love of each of us combined together would have tremendous impact in changing the entire world towards love and peace.

> *Much of the major growth that is coming to the Church in the last days will come because many of the good women of the world (in whom there is often such an inner sense of spirituality) will be drawn to the Church in large numbers. This will happen to the degree that the women of the Church... are seen as distinct and different—in happy ways—from the women of the world....*

> *Thus it will be that female exemplars of the Church will be a significant force in both the numerical and spiritual growth of the Church [and the world] in the last days (Spencer W. Kimball). (2)*

The goal of this book.

The goal of this book is to assist each of us as LDS women in changing our minds from the control of the Mind of the Natural Man, or the Ego Mind, to the control of the Spiritual Mind, that part of us that is and always has been connected to God. This is done by becoming more consciously aware of the thoughts, beliefs, emotions and actions which limit us and keep us from being that beautiful source of love, light, wisdom and power that can change the world. By becoming more aware of what causes us to think, feel and act the way we do, we can learn and utilize techniques to be able to change and heal ourselves, with the help of God.

This book constitutes a discovery process to better understand what depression and anxiety are, and to assist in learning how we feel about ourselves and what our beliefs are that are keeping us from moving forward. Unless we become fully aware of where we come from, where we really are right now, what we are thinking and what we believe, it will be more difficult to use the techniques given in the accompanying workbook to change those thoughts and beliefs that are limiting us.

How to Use This Book

This book was written in a format to make it easier to read.

In writing this book, I have purposely kept the paragraphs short and added many subtitles because I have found that those who suffer from clinical depression and the various anxiety states have difficulty reading, focusing, and retaining what they read.

Therefore I have created this style so that you don't have to focus on too much at once. You can read it at your own pace and stop and ponder between paragraphs. You can stop reading when you can no longer focus without losing the whole chapter.

This is also why we have created CDs of the book. As you listen to the CDs, follow along in the book as much as possible. When you use both your ears and eyes to process the information, you will better retain it.

The chapters are best read in order, but can be interchangeable.

This book was written in a specific order, with each chapter providing information which assists with the following chapters. However, each chapter is also written to stand alone. Depression and anxiety often make it difficult to focus very long. There may be some chapters which you may feel drawn to read first, even if it is not the first chapter. You are welcome to do so.

The workbook assists you in making changes.

The workbook is an integral part of this book, and is only separate from the book to be able to have a format in which you can write and express yourself. The workbook can be started any time, and it will assist you whether you read the book or not. However, as you read the book, you may choose to go back and do some of the exercises over again, as you gain new insights.

Take your time.

In my reading of a self-help book, I like to get through it quickly so I can learn what I need to do to change. However, with this book, I encourage you to take your time. You might spend a few days or a week or a month on one chapter. You may choose to ponder on different principles until you can make them part of you.

Repetition is good.

After finishing the book, CDs and workbook, you may choose to go back and repeat various chapters and exercises many times as different problems arise in your life. We all need repetition. I was reminded over and over again of things I was doing or not doing which would keep me from being all I wanted to be even as I wrote this book. We often have the knowledge, but our weaknesses keep us from applying that knowledge and it is easy to forget.

Women with special circumstances can still learn even if their situation is not addressed.

Each woman is different and lives with different circumstances. You may be a single mother, or never married, or have no children. You may have a chronic debilitating illness, or are from a different culture, or be dealing with same sex attraction, etc. Not all of these concerns are addressed in this book. However, as women, our feelings are often very similar. Even if you don't fit the situations in the book, see if you have the same feelings. Deal with the feelings rather than the situation.

Change takes patience.

Remember that your mind and the problems of the mind were created over years. Although we hear of the miraculous stories of instant healing, be aware that most people heal over time. Just consider—if it takes six months to heal and you are better in six months, would it be worth the wait? How about a year? Or even two years?

If you are patient with yourself and keep working (hence the repetition), healing will come. I have seen it again and again. Each little thing you do is taking a baby step. And even a toddler taking baby steps can climb a mountain, given enough time, patience, and will.

Never measure the height of a mountain, until you have reached the top. Then you will see how low it was (Dag Hammarskjold). (3)

So be patient with yourself. Be kind to yourself. Encourage yourself. Be grateful for yourself. Find the best in yourself. Recognize your successes, no matter how small. Allow yourself to rest, just as a toddler would need rest in her climb up that mountain towards healing. Allow yourself to do the work, moment by moment, day by day, week by week, month by month. Even the weakest can do this work! Trust that the Lord will help you do it, too.

> *When the morning's freshness has been replaced by the weariness of midday, when the leg muscles quiver under the strain, the climb seems endless, and, suddenly, nothing will go quite as you wish—it is then that you must not hesitate (Dag Hammarskjold).* (4)

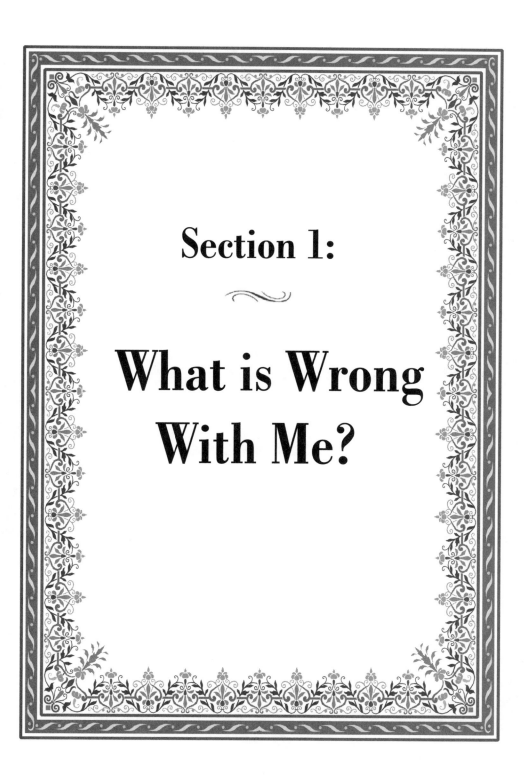

Section 1:

What is Wrong
With Me?

Chapter 1

Depression and Anxiety Are Real

Belle spoke to a Bishop once of her concerns about her persistent feelings of depression and anxiety. He was kind and told her to go home and look up the scriptures about joy, and pray that she could receive that joy through the Atonement of Christ. She followed his advice, but felt that she must be doing something wrong because the joy still wouldn't come. She felt very weak and sinful that she could not pray or will her depression away, increasing her self-hatred. It became hard for her to pray because she felt unworthy to receive His answers and His healing. Then she felt guilty, because she had been taught that it is important to pray when you feel least like praying. The prayer she does pray, like a mantra, is, "Please take this away! Oh God, please take this away!" But the prayers seem to go unanswered.

Belle is a woman in her early thirties that has been diagnosed with both major depression and general anxiety disorder. Over the years, since late high school, she has been on and off of medication and in and out of counseling, but she is still struggling.

Belle's life used to be fairly "normal," she thought, with times of anxiety and worry that she could push down, but in the last five or six years she has been filled with anxiety and depression that has been steadily taking over her life. She started anti-depressant medication five years ago which seemed to help at the time. However, she recently realized that it has been a long time since she has really felt any enjoyment or pleasure from life. Lately everything seems sluggish and grey. She has more and more periods where she feels no motivation to even get out of bed. She is either dealing with racing, obsessive worries about herself, her health or her family, or is in periods of feeling a bleak nothing, not caring about what happens to her.

Belle lives in a cloud of guilt. She feels very guilty because she believes that she is not a good wife or mother, and that she cannot be emotionally available for her children. She feels guilty because she believes that she is not a good church member. Lately she has turned down church jobs because the thought of doing one more thing is overwhelming. This makes her feel more guilty. She feels guilty about mistakes she made in the past. She feels guilty because she sees nothing but a bleak future for her and her family and it feels like her fault. She feels guilty simply because she is unhappy and a daughter of God should be happy.

Even though she is well versed in the gospel, and knows that God loves her, she doesn't feel it. It has been a long time since she has felt the Spirit. God feels far away; so far away that she feels she could never cross the bleak wasteland between them. At times she feels beyond the power of His love, and feels no hope for this life or the next, no matter how good she tries to be. She feels like she has ruined any chance she has for happiness, here or in the eternities. She worries and hurts inside about how this may affect her family. She feels doomed.

Belle is often filled with self-loathing, and can't stop the thoughts of how inadequate she is, all the mistakes she has made, and how she is ruining everyone's life. She constantly compares herself to others, and obsesses with thoughts of what others are thinking of her. She is afraid to become good friends with anyone because if they really knew her they may not like her. She hides most of her feelings even from her husband. She feels he wouldn't understand and wouldn't love her any more if he really knew everything she was thinking.

Belle has had times of feeling suicidal, and has even thought of ways that she could kill herself. The only thing that has kept her from suicide during those times is the knowledge of the effect that would have on her children, even though she believes they would be better off without her. She feels unfit for the Celestial Kingdom, and is ready to accept the life she deserves in the Telestial Kingdom. Certainly it would be infinitely better than how she is currently living on earth. She has prayed for forgiveness for thinking such thoughts, and is terrified every time they return, filling her with fear and sinking her deeper into the abyss of depression and anxiety.

Belle doesn't feel comfortable going to church, or talking about her problems with the "normal" sisters. She is afraid they will not understand. She assumes that others will think she has committed some sin or that she has in some way brought it upon herself. She worries constantly, when she does make it to church, that others will see how anxious and depressed she is feeling; that they will see that something is wrong with her. She is terrified that others will judge her, and would rather stay home than face that possibility.

Belle feels ashamed to be struggling with a mental illness in a church that in her mind appears to require perfection. She feels deeply flawed. She feels like a failure. Bella feels that being mentally ill has made her a disappointment to her family and to her God. She feels like she should be able to control this and hasn't been able to. She feels ashamed of not being able to meet the demands of life, and ashamed that she can't accomplish what she believes the other sisters are accomplishing. She believes that she can't fulfill her purpose on earth if she remains like this. She feels very much like a failure. Even though she knows mental illness is not a sin, it feels as if her thoughts and feelings, and her inability to do what has been asked of her, are sinful.

Belle's feelings are common.

Belle is a composite of many of my patients. Her feelings are common among them. Maybe Belle is your next door neighbor, or your Relief Society president, or your sister, or even you. You may not have every symptom that Belle has, or your symptoms may be worse, but if you suffer with depression or anxiety, you may relate to many of her feelings.

Depression and anxiety are very common, and are the leading cause of disability in the world. The National Alliance on Mental Illness (NAMI) states that "major depression is a serious medical illness affecting 15 million American adults, or approximately 5–8 percent of the adult population in a given year." (5) Anxiety disorders are the most common emotional illness in the U.S., affecting up to 18% of the population. (6)

Women with depression or anxiety often feel like they are the only one with problems like theirs.

This means that if you are suffering with depression or anxiety, possibly over fifteen percent of the people in your ward are suffering along with you. This doesn't even count the people that have low levels of depression, stress or nervousness that affect them and their families.

You are not alone. It is just that, in the LDS culture, we resist talking about our problems, so you probably *feel* very alone. You may feel that no one really understands what you are going through. You may feel that you are the only one with these problems and that you must be weak. This is false. This problem is real and it is common, both inside and outside of the church. You are far from alone, and many, many people experience the feelings you are experiencing.

Depression is real. Anxiety is real.

Many of Belle's feelings are common feelings among members of the LDS church. Being an active, believing member of the Church of Jesus Christ of Latter-day Saints does not protect us from depression or anxiety, just as it doesn't protect us from a broken arm or from cancer. Many church members, including some church leaders, are not completely aware of this.

I have had caring and well-meaning Priesthood leaders tell my patients suffering from depression: "Pray harder. Fast. Read the scriptures, and you will feel better." While this is good counsel, for someone with clinical depression and anxiety it may not be enough. I have seen those receiving that advice follow it more closely than most, and still some of them end up in the mental unit of their local hospital. That is because true clinical depression and anxiety disorders are not spiritual illnesses, but are physical illnesses of the physical brain.

This is not in any way a criticism of church leaders. They are good men and women doing the best they know how. Some of them are just not aware that clinical depression and generalized anxiety disorder are not simply because a person does not have enough faith. This book is to teach them as well.

Depression is not a spiritual illness, but a physical illness.

Depression and anxiety are real. Although depression and anxiety do cause one to believe in the lies the illness in her brain is telling her, and though I would imagine that Satan does prey on the weaknesses of the body, clinical depression and anxiety are *not* caused by, as many believe, giving in to and believing in Lucifer's lies.

On the contrary, depression and anxiety are illnesses of the body as real as multiple sclerosis and heart disease, and can be just as debilitating and deadly. The brain is part of the physical body, and depression and anxiety are diseases of the brain, related to over-activity in parts of the brain dealing with emotions. Depression and anxiety are physical illnesses of the mortal body (see chapter 2).

There is purpose to our earthly trials, weaknesses and illnesses.

Depression and anxiety are real. They, along with other physical illnesses, are part of the opposition that we came here to earth to experience. Clinical depression comes not because we did something wrong in the pre-existence. It is not because our spirits are flawed. It is not because we were not valiant in the war in heaven. It is not because we have sinned. Clinical depression is part of the mortal experience, a physical illness of the mortal body.

> *And his disciples asked him, saying, Master, who did sin, this man, or his parents, that he was born blind* [or depressed]?
>
> *Jesus answered, Neither hath this man sinned, nor his parents: but that the works of God should be made manifest in him (John 9:2–3).*

People with depression and anxiety judge themselves and are often judged by others.

Depression and anxiety are real. Most people are ashamed of their depression or anxiety and seek to hide it from others. Most people with depression feel judged and misunderstood, and often they are. Even though deep inside they know it is not their fault, the thoughts caused by the depression or anxiety make them believe they have done something wrong, and that it *is* their fault. It isn't. It is a physical illness of the physical brain, which manifests itself in mental and emotional changes.

Many good and great people have struggled with depression and anxiety.

You don't need to feel abnormal because you feel depressed or anxious. Some of the greatest leaders have suffered with the same struggles. Abraham Lincoln wrote in a letter to his friend at a very low point in his life, "*I am now the most miserable man living. If what I feel were equally distributed to the whole human family, there would not be one cheerful face on earth. Whether I shall ever be better I can not tell; I awfully forebode I shall not. To remain as I am is impossible; I must die or be better, it appears to me.*" (7) His friends hid his knife from him at that point because they were afraid he might commit suicide.

In fact, everyone in the world feels severe discouragement and stress at one point or another in their life. You are not alone. Probably most people you know struggle with this in one form or another. You are part of a group of amazing people that are going through the same struggles.

Because it is a real, physical illness, those with clinical depression and anxiety cannot "just snap out of it."

You would not say to someone with cancer, "Just snap out of it!" Many feel like they should be able to, and feel inadequate because they are unable to. This is really hard for family members and friends who have never suffered this way to understand. And so those who deal with depression and anxiety are constantly judging themselves, and often are also judged and feel judged by others.

Everyone has down times, times when they are sad, worried, unhappy.

Everyone deals with ups and downs in their lives. Sometimes these periods of sadness can last for days or even a few weeks. They are often in response to difficult times and experiences. Nephi experienced this, after his father had died and Laman and Lemuel were seeking to destroy him:

> ...*notwithstanding the great goodness of the Lord, in showing me his great and marvelous works, my heart exclaimeth: O wretched man that I am! Yea, my heart sorroweth because of my flesh; my soul grieveth because of mine iniquities.*
>
> *I am encompassed about, because of the temptations and the sins which do so easily beset me.*
>
> *And when I desire to rejoice, my heart groaneth because of my sins... (2 Nephi 4:17–19).*

Even Jesus, I believe, may have suffered at times from human loneliness and sorrow:

> ...*The foxes have holes, and the birds of the air have nests; but the Son of man hath not where to lay his head (Matthew 8:20).*

These down times are different than clinical depression and generalized anxiety disorder.

These are times that everyone experiences, these times of sadness when it is difficult to find light in the world, or times of worry when there are stressful events. These are generally situational, and usually end within a short time. They come and they go, and are part of the ups and downs of life. Of these times we can use the common euphuisms: "Fake it until you make it." "Turn lemons into lemonade." "Find solace in prayer and scripture reading." "Make a gratitude list." Or what President Hinckley's father told him when he was suffering from feeling homesick and worthless on his mission: *"Just forget yourself and go to work."* (8)

When people suffering from "down times" put these sayings into practice, they work. Therefore they often cannot understand why someone with true clinical depression or anxiety cannot pull themselves out of it by similar means. True clinical depression and generalized anxiety disorder are different than this. They can be so deep and debilitating that those suffering from them are unable to do what they and everyone else thinks they should be able to do.

There are varying stages of depression and anxiety.

Some people may be completely debilitated and non-functioning. Some may not be in the deeper stages; they may be able to function and go about their daily lives but still can never seem to feel happy. They feel like they live in a gray world where there is no joy even though they may be living a life in which they believe they should be happy.

Others are severe enough that they have a hard time even getting out of bed. They struggle to do their daily chores. They may be in and out of mental hospitals because their depression and anxiety are so severe. They fear they are crazy or going crazy.

Depression and anxiety have multiple causes, but can be healed.

Depression and anxiety can be genetic, environmental, biochemical, or related to personality traits—but that doesn't mean they have to be permanent. The brain can change, no matter what the cause and no matter what age we are. The brain has the capacity to change the pathways that have been created over the years simply by using the brain differently than it has been used. This ability of the brain to change is called *plasticity*.

The brain has the capacity to change.

The plasticity of the brain is what allows us to learn how to play the piano. In the beginning, as one learns to use each finger while reading the notes, the music is slow, simple and choppy, with lots of mistakes. However, with constant repetition and practice, new pathways are created in the brain which allows the piano playing to become more rapid and smooth. Everything that takes repetition to learn changes the brain to a degree.

Depression and anxiety are created and are healed by constant repetition of patterns of thought and feeling.

Even with genetic tendencies, depression and anxiety can be created in the brain by traumatic events, and by constant repetition of thoughts, beliefs, emotions and actions, which create habitual neuro-pathways in the brain. This constant repetition of negative thoughts, limiting beliefs and negative feelings creates pathways which allow the brain to jump into negative thinking and emotions in an instant.

To change those habitual "negative" pathways, it takes constant repetition of positive self-talk, changing limiting beliefs, and feeling positive emotions. No matter the cause of depression and anxiety, which is often multi-factorial, the brain has the capacity to change, and with the help of God one can improve and often heal one's self from these disorders.

The task of changing thoughts and emotions seems over-whelming and impossible to people with depression and anxiety.

The problem is, most people with clinical depression and anxiety don't know how to change their thoughts and feelings. They try and try, but nothing changes. Their brains can't figure it out. Their brains are not in a state where they *can* figure it out. They have never learned the tools necessary to make these changes.

The purpose of this book is to teach you how to change your brain.

My purpose is to address various causes of depression and anxiety, and the life experiences that may create the negative thoughts, beliefs and feelings that make them worse. As well, through the Workbook, exercises will assist you to learn how to heal from depression and anxiety, with or without medication, in a gospel setting.

Though reading scriptures, praying and believing in the gospel may not completely heal clinical depression or anxiety, the gospel of Jesus Christ offers many solutions if we open our hearts and know what to look for and how to utilize the information.

All healing comes through the atonement of Christ.

In truth, all healing *does* come through the atoning power of Jesus Christ, but often not until we learn what is important for us to learn from our experiences. This is usually a process of self-discovery. Not all people respond to the same things; however, I pray that in this book you will find ways to experience peace and healing.

The Savior teaches that we will have tribulation in the world, but we should "be of good cheer" because He has "overcome the world" (John 16:33). His Atonement reaches and is powerful enough not only to pay the price for sin but also to heal every mortal affliction. The Book of Mormon teaches that "He shall go forth, suffering pains and afflictions and temptations of every kind; and this that the word might be fulfilled which saith he will take upon him the pains and the sicknesses of his people... (Alma 7:11; see also 2 Nephi 9:21).

Healing blessings come in many ways, each suited to our individual needs, as known to Him who loves us best. Sometimes a "healing" cures our illness or lifts our burden. But sometimes we are "healed" by being given strength or understanding or patience to bear the burdens placed upon us"(Dallin H. Oaks). (9)

The radiation of our individual qualities has an effect on the entire world.

RADIATION

*"There is one responsibility which no man can evade
and that responsibility is his personal influence.
Man's unconscious influence is the silent,
subtle radiation of his personality—
the affect of his words and acts on others.
This radiation is tremendous!*

*Every moment of life, man is changing to a
degree the life of the whole world.*

Every man has an atmosphere which is affecting
every other man.
He cannot escape for one moment from this radiation of
his character, this constant weakening or strengthening of others.
Man cannot evade the responsibility by merely
saying that it is an unconscious influence.

Man can select the qualities he would permit to be radiated.
He can cultivate sweetness, calmness, trust,
generosity, truth, justice, loyalty, nobility,
and by these qualities he will constantly affect the world.
This radiation to which I refer comes from what a person really is,
not from what he pretends to be.
Every man, by his mere living, is radiating either sympathy, sorrow,
morbidness, cynicism, or happiness and hope—
or any of the hundred other qualities.
Life is a state of radiation and absorption.
To exist is to be the recipient of radiation.
To exist is to radiate."

—David O. McKay (10)

As we change our thoughts, feelings and beliefs from sadness, discouragement and fear to happiness, hope and love, we can radiate those qualities and affect the world. It is awe-inspiring to consider that one single woman, going through the process of healing by changing her own mind and heart can influence the entire world. What would happen if all LDS women were able to fill their hearts and minds with loving thoughts towards themselves and all around them? The power of women who know who they *really* are, love themselves and have true charity *can* change the world!

At the end of our mortal lives, as we pass through the veil, we are not going to be asked, "How many people hurt you? How were you mistreated? How often did you teach a lesson to others by getting back at them? How important was your job? How thin and pretty were you? How successful were your children?"

Rather, we will be asked, "How much did you love? How did you show compassion? Were you able to love your enemies? Did you treat others the way you wanted to be treated? How often did you smile at others? Say a kind word? Lift another? Forgive another?" The more we can let go of fear and be able to love, and the more we can inspire others to do the same, the more the world will change.

Chapter 2

Depression and Anxiety: What Are They?

M any people are suffering from depression and anxiety and don't know it. They don't realize that the problems in their lives stem from these issues. They just feel unhappy in many areas of their life, and may experience physical symptoms, and don't know why.

People with the following backgrounds in their personal histories have higher rates of anxiety and depression.

Do any of the following items apply to you or your life?

- Alcoholism or other addictions in the home

- Strict religious upbringing

- Parents that control through guilt and fear or frequent criticism

- Parents with high expectations

- Self or siblings parenting other siblings or parenting parents

- Feelings not easily expressed

- Negative emotional environment/depression or anxiety in other family members

- Lack of praise and approval

- Angry and/or over-reacting family members

- Separation from or loss of family members

- General unstable upbringing

- Being bullied, teased or excluded by other children

- Being the oldest child or responsible child

- Being the youngest child (not good enough to do what the older children do)

These situations often cause certain personality traits.

These traits are created by the child in order to survive, but they usually aggravate anxiety and depression. Note if you identify with any of these traits:

- Perfectionism

- Tendency to over-react with anger, depression or anxiety

- Inner constant nervousness that something bad will happen

- Low self-esteem/constant self-criticism

- Feeling constantly guilty over past and current behaviors

- Very sensitive to criticism

- Sensitive emotionally, including taking on other's emotions

- Unrealistic expectations of self and others

- Difficulty making decisions

- Obsessive thinking about past or future events

- Overly analytical

- Overly concerned with what others think of you

- Excessive worry over health problems

- Feeling like you don't belong

- Need to be in or appear to be in control

Because of these personality traits, people with anxiety and depression often have difficulty being alone, being able to drive, being able to go shopping, being able to socialize comfortably, and being able to make decisions. They often seek for other's approval and may seem to be very needy. They often appear to themselves and sometimes to others to be selfish, concerned only with themselves, but, the truth is, though their strongest desire may be to serve others, their minds are so occupied with obsessive thinking and fears that it is extremely difficult for their thoughts and actions to go outward towards others. Can you relate?

What is depression?

Clinically, depression is a common mental disorder that presents with depressed mood, loss of interest or pleasure, feelings of guilt or low self-worth, poor motivation to accomplish tasks, disturbed sleep or appetite, low energy, and poor concentration. These problems can become chronic or recurrent and can lead to substantial impairments in an individual's ability to take care of his or her everyday responsibilities. At its worst, depression can lead to suicide, a tragic fatality associated with the loss of about 850,000 lives globally every year. (11)

Symptoms of depression.

Some of the symptoms of depression include:

- Loss of pleasure in ordinary activities, including sex

- Decreased energy and fatigue

- Sleep disturbances (inability to go to sleep, early morning wakening, or oversleeping)

- Eating disturbances (loss of appetite or emotional eating, weight loss or gain)

- Feelings of guilt, worthlessness, and helplessness

- Thoughts of or desire for death, thoughts of suicide, attempting suicide

- Irritability

- Excessive crying

- Chronic muscle or joint aches and pains, headaches, stomach and/or abdominal pain that doesn't respond to treatment

Depression may result in:

- Lack of motivation and decreased productivity

- Difficulty cooperating with others

- Addictions (alcohol, drugs, pornography, eating disorders— eating too much or too little, or even addictive exercise)

Depression is the leading cause of disability in the world.

Depression accounts for more days in bed than the eight leading chronic illnesses. Depression occurs in persons of all genders, ages, and backgrounds, though it is diagnosed more than twice as often in women as it is in men. (12) Some of that may be because women seek for help more often than men, but the differences between the male and female brain also accounts for the increased depression in women (see chapter 3).

There is scientific evidence for brain changes related to depression.

Today, neuroscientists know that, in many cases, mental illness arises because of dysfunctions in particular brain structures. It has been shown through brain imaging techniques that the source of depression is in the deep limbic system of the brain, especially around the amygdala. (13) Recent evidence suggests that clinical depression might arise from the brain failing to grow new neurons in the amygdala and other specific areas. The amygdala has been shown to be smaller in women with depression. (14) It has been demonstrated that elevated levels of cortisol (the body's stress hormone) suppresses new cell growth and can even cause cell death in that area. It has also been shown that serotonin can enhance new cell growth in the amygdala. (15)

Through brain imaging techniques such as SPECT scans and functional MRIs, there is evidence that the deep limbic system is overactive in depression. Through quantitative electro-encephalograms (qEEGs), a form of brain-mapping that reads the brain wave patterns, it has been shown that people who experience depression often have an elevation of Alpha brainwaves in the central areas of the brain compared to normal, or they may have an imbalance of Alpha and Beta brainwaves between the right and left frontal lobes of the brain.

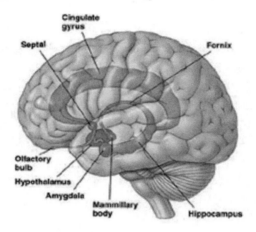

The limbic system shown above is overactive in depression, while the amygdala becomes activated with elevated levels of cortisol (the stress hormone).

A "chemical," or neurotransmitter imbalance may be involved.

The issue of depression being caused by a chemical imbalance in the brain is still in question. Although medications which change serotonin and other neurotransmitter levels in the brain have shown beneficial effects, there has not been overwhelmingly conclusive evidence that these chemicals are always out of balance in people that have depression and anxiety. It may not be so much an imbalance of neurotransmitters as the positive effect extra serotonin and dopamine may have on increasing new cell growth in the areas of the brain related to depression. However, the possibility of "chemical imbalance" is still a valid theory and continues to be investigated.

Depression and anxiety often go hand-in-hand.

Fifty-eight percent of those suffering from major depressive disorder also have an anxiety disorder. (14) Thirty-five percent have experienced at least one panic attack. One reason for this is because anxiety causes such stress in the body that the increased levels of cortisol from the anxiety lead to the changes in the brain that cause depression. I believe there is some level of anxiety in almost everyone who suffers from depression, and some depression in most people who suffer from anxiety.

What is anxiety?

Generalized anxiety disorder (or GAD) is characterized by excessive, exaggerated anxiety and worry about everyday life events. People with symptoms of generalized anxiety disorder tend to always expect the worst outcome and can't stop worrying about past events, health, money, family, work, school, or their own capabilities. In people with anxiety, the worry may become unrealistic or out of proportion for the situation. Daily life may become a constant state of worry, fear, and dread. Eventually, the anxiety may so dominate the person's thinking that it interferes with daily functioning, including work, school, social activities, as well as relationships. General anxiety may not be this severe or this obvious, but it can still have a dramatic and damaging affect on a person's life.

Physical symptoms of anxiety.

Anxiety affects the way a person thinks, but it often leads to physical symptoms as well, caused by stress chemicals that are released by the brain and the adrenal glands. Symptoms of anxiety can include:

- excessive and obsessive negative thoughts about the past or future

- an unrealistically negative view of problems

- restlessness and nervousness

- irritability

- muscle tension and pain

- headaches and migraines

- sweating

- difficulty concentrating

- nausea

- frequent urination

- frequent bowel movements

- stomach or abdominal pain

- chest pain

- heart palpitations

- numbness in one or many parts of the body

- startling easily

- difficulty breathing or catching the breath

- fatigue

- sleep difficulties

- trembling or shakiness, inside and/or outside .

These symptoms can be mild to very severe, leading to many fears that something is very wrong with their bodies.

Long term physical effects of anxiety.

People with anxiety can also have high blood pressure and high cholesterol, in response to the adrenaline overload that happens over time. Because of the constant adrenaline and cortisol release from the adrenal glands related to the stress of anxiety, the adrenals become stressed and eventually insufficient to deal with the constant stress. Often fatigue and depression will result. When the adrenals are out of balance there can be problems with blood sugar and insulin, the immune system, thyroid, sex hormones, increased inflammation, etc.

Anxiety and depression can make it difficult for people to heal physically.

When people have anxiety and depression it is harder for them to heal from physical illnesses. Their immune system becomes depressed and the chemicals released during the feelings of anxiety and depression keep the body from being able to reduce pain and induce healing. When a person has a chronic infection or has been in an accident and doesn't heal with good treatment in a normal amount of time, I look for signs of anxiety and depression.

Anxiety is related to and worsens other mental illnesses.

Increasing levels of anxiety can also worsen other mental illnesses, such as bipolar mania and schizophrenia. If those individuals are able to learn how to deal with anxiety in a different way, often their illness will be more controllable and not be as severe.

The physical symptoms of anxiety cause people to overuse the medical system because of their fears that something is physically wrong.

Many people with generalized anxiety disorder don't realize they have anxiety and go their doctor with many of the physical symptoms above. They are given many tests and various diagnoses depending on the symptom that is most prominent, and given medications to help those symptoms. If doctors were more knowledgeable about anxiety they would recognize the constellation of symptoms as being the symptoms of anxiety. Then the patient would be able to recognize the source of their physical problems, and receive help and treatment that would cure the physical symptoms as they were able to heal the anxiety and depression.

People with anxiety have obsessive thoughts and fears.

People with anxiety often have obsessive thoughts that circle around and around in their heads. They desire to know all the different angles of a situation before they make a decision, and decision making is very stressful for them. Some of the unrealistic fears they have related to their obsessive thoughts may include:

- fear of embarrassing themselves in front of others (social anxiety)
- fear of illness (cancer, heart attack, stroke, etc.)
- fear of dying
- fear of loved ones dying
- fear of losing control
- fear of going "insane"

- fear of hurting themselves or others

- fear of choking or losing their breath

- fear of driving

- fear for family members and loved ones

- a generalized fear that "something bad is going to happen"

The obsessive thoughts that won't quit may be about a recent conversation or about an event or meeting that may be coming up, with multiple scenarios about what should have been said or what should be said. The thoughts may be about a mistake that was made in the past, and the guilt associated with that mistake. The thoughts may include worry about a loved one and all the bad things that could happen. The anxious person may spend a good amount of their day in obsessive thinking.

People with anxiety feel the need for safety.

People with anxiety and panic attacks often "run away" to a safe place (usually home and/or bed) or a safe person (becoming very dependent), or find "safety" in medication or recreational drugs or addictions. They may reach a point where they have difficulty leaving their home (agoraphobia). In reality, there are no safe places, people, substance or activity, as this disorder is created from within and not from without. We will address this in future chapters.

Other disorders associated with anxiety.

In addition, people with generalized anxiety disorder often have other anxiety disorders (such as panic disorder, obsessive-compulsive disorder, and phobias), suffer from depression, and/or abuse drugs, alcohol, pornography, food, etc. A majority of people with addictions actually suffer from anxiety, and the addiction is used to "self-medicate," or reduce the anxiety. Until the anxiety is dealt with, it is very hard to rehabilitate from the addiction.

There is scientific evidence for brain changes in anxiety.

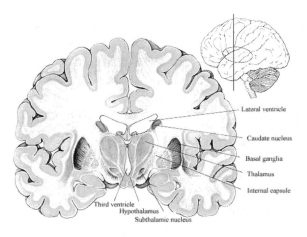

People with anxiety exhibit over activity of the basal ganglia.

It has been shown that the source of anxiety usually comes from the parts of the brain called the basal ganglia and amygdala. Over-activation of these areas can result in anxious and negative thinking. (17) Through qEEGs it has been shown that those with anxiety disorders often have an elevation of Beta, High Beta brainwaves over what is normally found.

Using medications for anxiety and depression.

In the last thirty years there have been many new medications which have often made depression and anxiety easier to live with. When medication works, it can be quite a miracle in changing lives. A person who was living in a black hole can begin to see the light of day.

However, for many people, medication is not always the answer. Studies show that anti-depressant medication works no better than placebo except in very severe depression. Some cannot deal with the side effects. Others have difficulty living with the "numbness" of emotions that sometimes comes from using anti-depressants and other psychotropic medications. Other people can't seem to find one that works for them. The class of drugs used for anxiety called benzodiazepines can be very addicting. Some people are simply anxious and fearful about using medications. And many find that after a few years they need more medicine, and eventually while on medication they feel almost as bad as they did without it. (See Appendix 1.)

Are you crazy?

It is important to understand that people with anxiety and depression are not "crazy." They are not living out of reality. They struggle with many aspects of their lives, but they are not "going insane." This is a major fear of those living with these problems, but it is not true.

Why a book about LDS women with anxiety and depression?

Because elevated levels of cortisol, the stress hormone, can cause brain changes that may lead to depression and anxiety, it is important to look at everything that may increase stress levels in a person's life, in both physical and emotional causes. The LDS culture creates a unique environment that may, at times, increase the risk for depression and anxiety.

Are mental illnesses caused by spiritual sin or weakness?

Some church members believe, in error, that...

- Depression and anxiety are spiritual illnesses brought upon members who are not living the gospel or who are sinning;

- Such emotional illnesses can best be cured by repenting and more fully following the gospel of Jesus Christ;

- Seeing counselors or using medication is a lack of faith.

This was the prevailing attitude of many conservative Christians who believed that mental illnesses were spiritual illnesses, sometimes caused by the devil or even by possession of evil spirits, rather than recognizing that they are physical illnesses of the brain. The belief that sin or spiritual possession is the cause of mental illness came because of a lack of scientific knowledge about what depression and anxiety really are.

It is true that sinning may increase stress, and therefore increase anxiety and depression, but sin *is not the root cause of these emotional struggles*. Everyone commits sin (no one is perfect) and yet not everyone suffers from clinical depression or anxiety.

People who are extremely obedient may also be very stressed because of the stress of trying to be obedient to every rule. People who are very obedient and striving not to sin may also suffer from the brain changes that lead to depression and anxiety. In other situations, a person with depression and anxiety may do things that are not acceptable because their brain is not in a healthy state, and their perception of how things are and should be is mixed up.

It is possible that evil spirits are attracted to those with depression and anxiety because of the prevalence of fearful and negative thoughts, but they are not the cause of the problem.

Attitudes and beliefs are changing.

The times and attitudes in the LDS Church and in the Christian community in general are changing as greater scientific knowledge and recognition of what mental illness really is has come forth. The Church has instituted the Social Service program which provides professional counselors for members.

However, this change of attitude has been slow, and the older beliefs often seep from one generation to the next, into and through talks and writings and counsel given to the members. Therefore, it is important for the LDS community to truly understand the physical nature of depression and anxiety.

Limiting beliefs add to depression and anxiety.

There are many limiting beliefs that LDS women hold as they come into my office that have been perpetuated by their interpretation of LDS traditions, such as the belief that they should do everything perfectly. These limiting beliefs increase their stress levels, which increases the possibility of depression and anxiety. These limiting beliefs are not the gospel of Jesus Christ, and they are not generally taught by the brethren, but individual interpretations have created cultural beliefs that are deeply rooted and hard to erase, increasing the feelings of depression and anxiety in our LDS population.

Strict religious teachings in the home can increase anxiety in children that may continue throughout their lives. It is important to learn how to be good LDS church members but not perpetuate the cultural beliefs that increase the anxiety and depression in ourselves and our children.

Depression and anxiety can improve and can even be cured.

The good news is that these problems can be treated, often even without medication. By learning various techniques to change beliefs and thoughts, by coming to a greater knowledge of the truth of the Gospel of Jesus Christ rather than centering on limiting cultural traditions, and by being able to feel the Spirit as the severity of depression and anxiety begin to lift, the LDS woman can change her brain, and therefore her life, to a point where depression and anxiety are no longer controlling her. She then can control what she chooses to think and feel. The depression and anxiety that comes from her physical body can change to the freedom and peace that radiates from spirit.

Chapter 3

The Brain of a Woman

When my first daughter was born, she acted very differently than her older brother had as an infant. As I would put her in her infant seat on the kitchen table she would follow me with her eyes, watching everything I did, listening to everything I said. My son, as an infant, hardly ever looked at me. His eyes were everywhere, exploring the world. As a young, unknowledgeable mother, I worried about her scrutiny of me. I felt that I was not a worthy person for her to be watching, to be learning from. What I didn't know was that she was simply following the dictates of her female brain, where even in infancy she was learning to create relationships and read the facial and body expressions of my emotions. The infant male brain is less focused on relationships and more on figuring the world out. As toddlers, even in play, little girls will create relationships between their dolls or cars or trains, having them all talk to each other, creating families or friends among them; while little boys just make noises and crash them.

The female brain and male brain have major differences.

To understand depression in women, it is important to understand the difference between the male and female brain. There is a greater than two-to-one ratio of depression in women compared to men. In the past the explanations have been political, religious and psychological, though not completely correct: "Women have been suppressed by men." "The Patriarchal nature of Western, or Christian, or LDS society must be the reason, as women are kept from leadership roles and from fulfilling their own needs." "The men of the church have kept women barefoot and pregnant."

The beliefs behind these sayings may be true in certain situations and marriages, and may certainly add to depression in women, but they are not universally true. I also don't believe they are the main root cause of depression in women, as the rates of male-vs.-female depression are the same worldwide, and among many cultures.

The "norm" may not be normal for you. We are each created differently.

When I write about "norms" or averages, please realize that *there are always exceptions to the norm*, in both men and women. Some of the differences in the brains of women and men are proven; others are theorized. So don't believe that if you don't fit the entire picture of the "typical" woman or "typical" man that you are abnormal. No one really fits every one of these descriptions, as there is a wide range of behavior within each gender. However, these gender differences are given to assist us in coming to a greater understanding of ourselves, of each other, and how this affects our lives and our relationships.

The hormonal changes of puberty change the body and the brain.

It is interesting to note that the discrepancy in the rates of depression between men and women doesn't start until the age of puberty—ages 12 to 13. (18) Hormones have incredible neurological effects that hormones have on the female brain during the different stages of life and the different hormonal balances of those stages. They affect her way of perceiving reality, her values and her needs. As the brain bathes in female hormones, with the "tide" going in and out, the brain actually changes during each fluctuation of the menstrual cycle. The fluctuations begin as early as three months old and last until after menopause. No wonder a man, whose hormonal state does not fluctuate throughout his life (though it is higher during teens and early twenties and may get lower in chronic illness, in severe stress and in older age), has a hard time understanding a woman who changes from month to month and year to year. Women have a hard time understanding themselves!

Men and women's brains respond differently to stress and conflict.

Men and women use different brain areas to solve problems, process language, and experience strong emotions. A woman's brain remembers more detail than a man's (holding onto the details of their first date or of the fights between them, of which the men often remember very little). Male and female brains use different circuits to accomplish the same tasks. Often, in studies, there are no performance differences between men and women at various tasks, but there are significant gender-specific differences in the brain circuits they activate to accomplish that task. Women also spend more time picturing the image in their minds, and therefore it may take them longer to get the same answer than it does men.

Why women talk more than men.

Women have 11% more neurons than men in the brain centers for language and hearing. The hippocampus, which processes and forms emotion and memory, is larger in women. No wonder women are better at feeling and expressing emotion and at remembering emotional events than men are. No wonder they are dying to talk when their husbands get home—they have all of that brain space that needs to be used! Whereas possibly the husband's brain space for talking was used up at work and he has nothing left to say.

Developing relationships is more important to women than to men.

As estrogen floods the young female brain at puberty, the young woman starts to focus more intensely on relationships, on emotions and on communication. At the same time, as testosterone floods the male brain, he becomes less communicative and less prone to intimate, emotionally connecting relationships, though more prone to desiring sexual relationships. The increase in the size of the aggressive part of the brain is shown through the young man's desire to conquer—in sports, with women, in the business world, in the car against every other car on the road, etc.

The lack of women in many professions in the past has not been due to the inability of women to perform those professions, and not even always to the suppression by males to keep women out, but possibly more because the female brain leads her to desire relationship and family more strongly than desiring a profession, and much more intensely than most men desire relationship and family. A woman today, because of cultural acceptance and sometimes cultural pressure, can often put those feelings on hold as she works up the ladder in her profession, but most women will feel that call of nature, or the call of their hormone-laden brains, for relationships and family quite strongly at some point in their lives.

Men have more sexual drive and thoughts than women do.

Women's brains have 2½ times less brain space devoted to sexual drive than men do. Where men may have sexual thoughts enter their brains many times a day, women may think of sex once, or when the hormones are right, up to a whopping three to four times a day. Because of these differences, in a strict religious society such as the LDS society, women often have a hard time understanding their husband's focus on sexual things, and may believe he is a "sex maniac." And husbands may believe their wife is "frigid," when both may be well within the normal range for their gender, though just not on the same page with each other. That is also why women may need to feel emotionally loved and have a loving relationship before they can truly enjoy sexual relations, and men often need to have sex in order to feel loved and be loving.

Men tend to be more aggressive and competitive than women.

Often men use that strong, competitive drive at work and in their professions, but can also use it at home with a need to dominate and conquer. Men have larger amygdalas, the part of the brain which processes fear and triggers aggression. In general, a man can easily get angry very quickly (and usually the anger leaves just as quickly). That anger is usually triggered by a subconscious fear, and is the way the man expresses that fear.

Women are wired to avoid conflict but remember details.

While a woman's brain is wired to avoid conflict, the stress effects and emotional results of that conflict remain and simmer in her brain much longer than a man's. A man will forget that he was angry very quickly, but the wife or the co-worker will be affected by that angry outburst for days, and often let him know about it, in detail that he doesn't even remember.

This results in another source of conflict between men and women, who usually don't realize that the difference between them originates in the brain. This doesn't give an excuse for anger that is directed at another person and hurts them. However, if why this happens is understood, it is easier to deal with, work through and change. It is not because the man is bad or the woman is too moody and can't let go of anything. It is because their brains make it easier for them to behave that way. When they understand this, it is easier not to point fingers and blame, but to rather work it through and work it out.

Women have to work to let go of worries to be able to enjoy sex.

Also, in sexual relations, men use the amygdala—their aggressive center (also housing fear and anxiety, which often "triggers" aggression in the male)—during sex as they "conquer" the woman (hopefully having learned tender and loving techniques for doing so). However, the woman must "turn off" the impulses from her amygdala—which is also the fear and anxiety portion of the brain—before she can experience orgasm. Any worry coming from the amygdala—about kids, about work, about health, about her schedule, about what is going to happen next, or even about sex itself—will stop the steps the body is taking toward orgasm.

This extra step the female brain must take to calm itself down and turn off may be why it takes women three to ten times longer to reach orgasm than men. If women do not know how to stop the thoughts and worries during that time, and if men do not know how to be patient and calming to their wives, it may be very difficult for the woman to experience orgasm. It is not uncommon for many women to not be able to have an orgasm for months following marriage because, among other reasons, their amygdala has been trained to avoid and react negatively to sex before marriage.

The female brain is much more expert at reading other's emotions than the male brain.

The part of the female brain that reads the emotional cues of a face, interprets the tone of voice, and assesses emotional nuances in body language is much more active than a male's. The "mother's intuition" is more than a myth. All of these things learned from infancy (an infant girl will look in the eyes and follow the face of those close to her much more often than an infant boy) add together to make the female a fairly accurate lie detector, which gives mothers and wives "eyes in the back of their heads," or "Mommy Power." They intuitively know what those close to them are feeling and going through because their brains' circuitry teaches them to know.

A woman may have problems when those around them are not honest with their feelings. When parents or spouses are not honest with their feelings and actions, the girls and women, who pick feelings up but don't really know where they are coming from, often begin to doubt themselves and lose trust in their own feelings. I often hear women say, "I knew it but I doubted myself."

Women tend to have more spiritual thoughts and desires.

The "spiritual" part of the brain, that part that relates to spiritual feelings and desires, is also larger in the female brain than in the male brain. Again, in a strict religious and patriarchal setting such as the LDS culture, this can be a source of conflict. The male is "supposed" to lead the family spiritually, but it is often the woman who is constantly pushing to have family prayer, family scripture reading and Family Home Evening. That does not necessarily mean that the man is failing in his duty. It is simply that his brain is not as spiritually developed as the woman's, and it takes more effort for him to reach that state than it does for her. She may think of spiritual things and have spiritual feelings more often than the man, and therefore tends to push for it more often in the family, as she desires all of her relationships to have those feelings.

This does not mean that the male brain cannot increase in its spiritual sensitivity. It just takes more time and effort to do so. It is important for the woman not to judge the man as being spiritually inferior, as it leads to self-righteousness. And it is important for the man not to see the woman as a "goody two shoes." She is just doing what comes naturally, especially when that part of her brain has been highly developed by the LDS culture.

> *Sisters, we, your brethren, cannot do what you were divinely designated to do from before the foundation of the world. We may try, but we cannot ever hope to replicate your unique gifts. There is nothing in this world as personal, as nurturing, or as life changing as the influence of a righteous woman (M. Russell Ballard).* (19)

The difference in the spiritual training of boys and girls.

As a simple example, look at the differences between Boy Scout summer camp and Girls' camp. Girls' camp is generally filled with many more spiritually uplifting events and activities than Scout camp. This is because the women planning it are spiritually directed to make it so, and the girls' brains lean towards enjoying those feelings. I have noticed recently that there is an increase in spiritually enhancing events in the Scout camps. This is good, as it will allow the young male brain to be able to increase in its spiritual capacity while it is still forming. However, if the Scout camps were as strongly geared toward spiritual activities as the Girls' camps are, many Young Men would probably not attend.

They are more interested in conquering: nature, boating, swimming, white water rapids, each other, etc. That is where their brains take them.

Missions assist young men to develop the spiritual part of their brain.

Missionary activity is somewhat of an equalizing experience which assists young men in developing their more spiritual nature. That part of their brain will actually change and grow as they have more spiritual experiences. However, when they return home it is very easy for them to lose that side of themselves as they focus on schooling and advancing in their careers, on "conquering," as the testosterone flooding their brains leads them to do. After returning, there are not as many spiritual experiences to keep that part of their brains active. Therefore, often women are considered more spiritual than men, and rightly so because of their brain make-up, but not because they are better than men. They are just different.

The female brain is at higher risk for anxiety and depression.

By understanding the female brain, we can see why a woman has a higher risk of depression than the man. Hormones and other chemicals flooding the brain change thoughts and emotions, and even the size and shape of various parts of the brain. An imbalance of hormones can create strong emotional pain in the woman (and often in those around her!). The hormonal, chemical and brain changes that come with puberty, falling in love, sexual relationships, the major hormonal changes with pregnancy, birthing, and nursing, caring for children, experiencing the empty nest, relationship break-ups, and, of course, menopause, can set a woman up for depression much more easily than her male counterpart.

Relationship problems lead to depression and anxiety more often in women than in men.

The misunderstandings that come in relationships because of these differences can lead a woman to feel inadequate and like a failure. Because of her strong emotional feelings she may feel out of control and also misunderstood. She may blame her husband because of his inability to communicate or be emotionally close. Men don't think in the same way and are not as emotionally invested because that part of their brain is not as active, and may not be able to give to their wives what the women believe they really need. This creates a perceived lack of love.

A perceived lack of love can cause depression and anxiety.

Because of past experiences, there is often created in the woman a belief that she has been or is unloved and unlovable. She may also have great difficulty loving herself. Because of this strong belief, she sees the world through negatively colored glasses. No matter how she is treated, even when she is loved, she may have a hard time perceiving that love. All she can focus on is those things that prove what she believes to be true, which is that she is unloved and unlovable.

The perceived lack of love is one of the strongest cause of depression in women, from childhood to old age. Because of the importance of relationships in the female brain, most often female depression and/or anxiety originates in relationship problems. Yes, a male can get depressed over relationship problems, but it happens much less often than with females, except with an actual break-up of that relationship or a death, in which the levels of depression are more equal.

Childhood experiences often cause a woman to have a perceived lack of love.

Usually, if a woman is depressed even though she has a healthy and loving relationship with her husband, it is often because of a perceived lack of love from her childhood through experiences with her parents, siblings and/or friends; or because of past abuse from any source. Or the child may create beliefs in her own mind, based on her experiences, which allow her to believe that she is not good enough, that she cannot please enough, that she has to be perfect to be loved.

These childhood experiences remain in the subconscious mind, all of which have a very profound effect on changing the brain and the deep limbic structures, the amygdala and the basal ganglia, which become overactive, creating sadness and anxiety.

Women attempt suicide more than men but men succeed at suicide more than women.

This perceived lack of love, and the need for loving relationships, causes women to attempt suicide two to three times more often than men. But men, when they are depressed, actually commit suicide four times more often than women. It is believed that women are actually subconsciously seeking for attention from their relationships and therefore subconsciously choose forms of suicide from which they can be "saved." Men, on the other hand, because of their more aggressive brains, tend to use more violent means for suicide, such as guns, hanging, jumping from heights, etc.

The chemicals released from constant stress cause brain changes which lead to depression and anxiety.

The constant stress from the areas of the brain called the deep limbic structures, the basal ganglia and the amygdala, through current and/or past feelings of perceived lack of love, results in negative thoughts and feelings. These negative thoughts and feelings cause changes in hormones and brain chemicals, which further aggravate the problem. The hormonal cycles of a woman's life then heightens the emotions and further changes the brain. Unless the perceived lack of love, from the past and/or the present, are dealt with, a vicious cycle develops chemically, hormonally, physically and spiritually which continues to deepen the depression or anxiety.

Often the cause of these beliefs is buried in the subconscious mind.

Sometimes a woman may believe that her life has been good, her marriage is good, and there seems to be no lack of love. She may feel that there is no reason for her depression and anxiety, and that something must be wrong with her. She may feel that it is totally genetic or totally a chemical imbalance which cannot be changed. But usually, in my office, through various techniques, we uncover many instances in the past that have caused or added to her feelings of not being good enough for those that are important to her. These belief-forming events may be small or large, but often they are buried in the subconscious mind and the woman is not consciously aware of them. Various techniques taught in this book will allow the reader to discover for themselves where their negative thoughts and feelings are coming from, and how to release them.

Remember, there are physiological reasons for the way you feel, think and act.

This doesn't mean that those parts in your brain that create problems in your life cannot be changed and improved, but it does help explain why you react and behave the way you do. I encourage spouses to read this together and discuss how the way they act and react with each other may relate to how their brain works.

Chapter 4

The Origin of Our Beliefs

*J*ulie was standing in line at the grocery store, when she started to feel sick to her stomach. Her heart started beating hard against her chest, and there was an overwhelming feeling that something was terribly wrong. Her chest felt tight and she had difficulty breathing. She felt like she was dying. She started shaking. She knew she had to get out of there.

Julie wheeled her cart out of line and left it in the aisle, rushing out of the store. Sitting in the car, afraid to drive, her mind too confused to call anyone, the symptoms finally started to subside. As Julie started being able to breathe normally again, she noticed that she was still nauseated, and though the outward shaking had subsided, she still felt an inner trembling. She debated about going to the hospital, but home felt safer, so she chose to go home and go to bed instead.

Julie just had her first panic attack. She didn't know what it was right away. During her third episode, her chest hurt so much that her husband took her to the emergency room. The tests showed nothing wrong, and the doctor suggested that she might be having anxiety or panic attacks. He suggested she see her primary care doctor and ask for medication. She was afraid to go. She didn't want her doctor to believe that she was crazy. She was also afraid of the medications. But her fear of having a panic attack while in public started limiting her life. She finally got the courage to talk to her doctor, and he prescribed an anti-depressant that was also supposed to help anxiety.

The medication seemed to help for a few months. She did feel better overall. But then, while on a cruise with her husband, she had another panic attack during one of the evening shows. She escaped to her room, and refused to come out for the rest of the cruise. She couldn't understand why she would be having panic attacks. They seemed to come out of the blue, with no pattern. Because she couldn't predict when they would happen, she became more and more housebound.

Comparison of depression and anxiety to an iceberg.

I often compare depression and anxiety to an iceberg. The part of the iceberg that can be seen above the ocean is the symptoms and causes of depression and anxiety that we are consciously aware of. We know we feel sad and unmotivated, we know we are worried about this thing that is interrupting our lives. But the part under the ocean, that is often much larger than what can be seen, is representative of the subconscious mind—those beliefs, thoughts, feelings, triggers and causes that we are not consciously aware of, but that have profound effect on our conscious thoughts, feelings, actions and reactions, and even our health.

The conscious and subconscious mind.

One of the common theories into the workings of the mind divides it into two parts: the conscious mind and the subconscious mind. The conscious mind is made up of the thoughts, beliefs, decisions, images and emotions we are completely aware of. We know we are thinking this thought, we can express this belief, we see that image in our mind, we make a decision by accepting or rejecting a thought, we know why we experienced this emotion.

The subconscious mind, on the other hand, harbors beliefs, thoughts, emotions and images that we are not consciously aware of, but from which we often react. This part of the mind seems to have an incredible power over us. While the conscious mind is creative, the subconscious mind keeps playing previously recorded programs. If the subconscious mind is not in alignment with our conscious desires for our life, we often seem to be unable to accomplish those desires.

The conscious mind.

The conscious mind uses judgment, intellect and critical thinking, and can accept or reject an idea as truth or untruth. It is rational and able to evaluate whatever it is faced with. It is the decision maker.

The conscious mind consumes energy. It needs to rest. It holds the temporary memory. It uses the five senses to take in the world around it. When a person has a conscious experience that produces strong emotions, the "critical factor," or the doorway into the subconscious mind, may open and cement a more permanent memory, which holds the emotions, thoughts and images of that experience in the subconscious mind. But the subconscious mind also holds a belief about self in relationship to the world that was formed from that experience, whether positive or negative.

The subconscious mind.

The subconscious mind cannot make a decision, but accepts everything put into it as truth. It reacts to emotions, and is emotional. It uses the imagination to work from. It does not think critically and cannot tell truth from falsehood. It takes things literally.

The subconscious mind stores long-term information and memories. It regulates involuntary body functions. It is continuously at work and never sleeps.

It is from the subconscious mind that our life "paradigm" is formed. One definition of paradigm is a pattern or model, a set of rules that we live our life from, or the glasses through which we look at and interpret our life experiences. Our subconscious mind contains the beliefs, created and recorded through past experiences, which form how we experience and live our life. If those beliefs are different from our conscious beliefs, we may find ourselves reacting to situations differently than how we want to act.

How our subconscious mind is formed.

When we are infants and young children, it is theorized that we have very little conscious mind, but our subconscious mind is wide open. Everything we hear, see and experience, repeated over and over by parents and those that care for us, becomes truth to the subconscious mind. Our own beliefs and reactions to what is said and how we are treated, which are the beliefs and reactions of a child, become truth to the subconscious mind.

What is put into the subconscious mind becomes the belief system that our unbidden thoughts come from, and from which we react. The subconscious mind is your child mind. It is open, receiving, believes everything and says yes to whatever comes into it. When we are dealing with strong emotional stressors, we often react from that child subconscious mind rather than from our adult conscious mind.

Constant repetition and traumatic events form the sub-conscious mind.

The beliefs stored in the subconscious mind are formed either by constant repetition or a traumatic event. Most commonly, constant repetition of the beliefs of our parents allows those beliefs to be planted and grown to create the way we view life.

A recent study reported in the Journal of the American Medical Association analyzed information from 26,229 adults concerning adverse childhood experiences (ACEs) which include verbal, physical, or sexual abuse, as well as family dysfunction (e.g. an incarcerated, mentally ill, or substance-abusing family member; domestic violence; or absence of a parent). Almost 60% of respondents reported having at least one ACE. (20)

This shows that it is not uncommon for us to experience trauma and repetitive negativity in our society, which when experienced by young children, forms negative thoughts and beliefs that reside in the subconscious mind.

Examples of teachings and experiences that may form our subconscious mind.

Critical parents or teachers

For example, a mother or father may believe that in order to teach their children what will make them happy, they must constantly point out everything their children are doing that is wrong. In some children, the subconscious mind may take that in as "I can't do anything right. I can't please my parents. I am not good enough. I am unlovable. I need to be perfect, etc." That becomes their belief, their paradigm. Then as they are older, even if they are intelligent and productive, they may have the underlying belief that they are stupid and not good enough.

Angry parents or family members

Children that live with parents and/or siblings who express a lot of anger, may have put into their subconscious mind the belief that life isn't safe. They never know from one day to the next what is going to set off the anger. They may find it difficult to make decisions because whatever decision they make can still be wrong, can still produce anger. They may believe that they have to do whatever they can to please someone so they won't get angry.

These children often live with an underlying nervousness or anxiety that something bad is going to happen, because the anger, directed at them or others they love, is "the something bad" that happens to them frequently. Or they may come to believe that anger is the only emotion that is acceptable, and become angry people themselves. All of these are beliefs about themselves that are locked into the subconscious mind. They may not be completely aware of these beliefs. However, they are the beliefs from which they react to their present life.

Bullies

Children who are bullied or teased by the other kids at school may form the paradigm that they are weak, that life isn't safe and they must be hypervigilant, that they aren't good enough, or that you need to be a bully to survive, or that you need to put down others to feel good about yourself. Each different personality creates their own individual paradigm.

High expectations

A family whose belief system creates high expectations for the children may have one or more children with anxiety because they believe they cannot fulfill those high expectations and are not good enough. Even if the parents don't put those expectations on their child, the child may learn it at church or school and place those expectations on herself.

Belief in scarcity

If children grow up with parents who never seem to have enough money, that becomes their paradigm. As adults, even if they have more than adequate amounts of money to live on, they may still feel like they don't have enough.

A friend of mine lived the first few years of his life in Germany at the end of World War II. His family never had enough food, and he had to go out as a very young child and pick stinging nettle for his mother to make soup with. "There is never enough food" became his belief about life, or his paradigm. As an adult, even though he was blessed with riches, he always had to have a stash of food with him, whether he ate it or not. If they went on vacation, the first stop after getting off of the plane was a grocery store so that he could always have food with him. This was a highly intelligent and successful man. It may seem silly to someone without that paradigm, but it was very real to him.

Trauma can also create a belief in the subconscious mind.

If a traumatic experience happens, it has a profound effect upon the subconscious mind. For example, if a child was in a car accident and thought she was going to die, she may then harbor a constant underlying fear of death. If a child was abused by a member of the household in the middle of the night, the adult woman may wake up in the middle of the night with anxiety or panic, unable to sleep, though she may not know why. Even adults are affected by traumatic events. That is what causes Post Traumatic Stress Disorder in soldiers. The trauma gets "stuck" in their subconscious mind and replays itself over and over again.

Understanding what formed our subconscious mind is not a game of blame. We can't change if we become a victim.

As we come to understand what created our paradigm, we aren't blaming anyone, even ourselves. We are simply gaining knowledge of why we act and react the way we do. Someone may have done something that created problems for us, but we were the ones that reacted to that problem the way we did and formed the beliefs that we did. As children, we didn't really know any other way to react or believe—we chose that way of reacting or believing from a child's mind, to be able to survive.

Once we realize that our past behaviors are based on the invisible operation of the subconscious mind, we can more easily forgive ourselves and others. It helps to know that our behaviors are caused by programs primarily derived from the beliefs of other people, who, in turn, were programmed by others, backward through time. Neither our parents nor their parents were aware they were acting out a pre-written script.

All the people with whom we have ever interacted were also acting out behaviors derived from programs downloaded into their subconscious minds since they were infants. Because of this they are usually unaware of how their words, actions and emotions impact our lives. Because of this, Jesus' plea on the cross to "forgive them, for they know not what they do" makes perfect sense.

However, if we now choose to put the blame on others, or even ourselves, we become the victim and can't change anything. Being a victim causes misery, because it creates the feeling that we have no control over our lives. But if we take accountability (not guilt or blame) for our choices, whether they were made consciously or not, we can change them, and change our subconscious beliefs. We *can* change our individual paradigm by discovering what it is, often by learning how it was created.

Where Julie's panic attacks came from.

At the age of six, Julie, from the story at the beginning of this chapter, had been sexually abused by a fourteen-year-old uncle who had lived with her family for a summer. It had happened several times, but she had told no one about it because he said her parents would be angry at her if she did. She was also embarrassed and ashamed about it. There was a part of her that believed that because she hadn't resisted, hadn't been able to say no, that it was her fault. She had kept it inside her for years, and had almost forgotten it.

Unresolved conflict and trauma that resides in the subconscious mind seems to have a need to be resolved.

When the beliefs of the subconscious mind cause reactions that interfere with the adult conscious mind, the body and mind start having symptoms. Until the beliefs or trauma are resolved the symptoms will continue through one avenue or another (see chapters 12 and 13).

How a panic attack is created.

The subconscious mind's reaction to trauma seems to be as if the little child or the adult that experienced that trauma has been walled off into a corner of the mind and is in a constant state of fear, not knowing when something bad will happen again. The memories that are locked in with that part can be almost as if the trauma was happening currently.

If this trauma is never worked through and dealt with, the experiences of that child or adult will begin to seep into the conscious mind more and more frequently, most often as feelings; but sometimes as dreams or pictures. When those feelings from the past are nervousness, fear and anxiety, then the levels of adrenaline increase, causing physical symptoms. When a rush of adrenaline is released, it often gives the feeling of impending doom, nausea, heart palpitations, chest pain, difficulty breathing or hyperventilation, brain fog or a "surreal" feeling, the desire to flee, etc. This constitutes a panic attack.

Often small events will "trigger" the memories held in the subconscious mind.

What Julie didn't know, because she was not consciously aware of it, was that the man in front of her in line at the store had some mannerisms that were similar to her uncle. That "little girl" inside of her subconscious mind which held onto the images of those mannerisms, reacted to that man with fear and panic. It was a "trigger" that caused a release of adrenaline, causing the symptoms of her panic attack. The panic attack was not caused by the man in line, but by the feelings and memories of that little girl trapped inside of the subconscious mind.

One panic attack triggers more panic attacks because people are afraid of them.

That part of the subconscious mind holding those horrible memories reached a point where it physically expressed some of the fear, releasing adrenalin and creating a panic attack. Because of the increase in Julie's levels of fear about having another panic attack, more and more triggers caused the rush of adrenaline, until it was simply fear of having another panic attack that caused them.

Julie may never know that the mannerisms of the man in line in front of her triggered her first panic attack, but there are things she can do to stop the rest of the panic attacks. By resolving conflict and trauma from the past and using various therapies to change the fears of her subconscious mind, and by using techniques during her panic attacks in the present, she can reduce the anxiety and stop the panic attacks.

Panic attacks are simply a release of chemicals, nothing more.

Once we can recognize what panic attacks are we can accept them and float through them without needing to fear them. No one has ever died from a panic attack. No one has ever "gone crazy" from a panic attack. There is no real "safe place" from a panic attack, because your own fears, or the fears of that traumatized part of you within, are creating them.

In the workbook (Technique 2), you will learn ways to deal with panic attacks, but the first step is to simply accept them for what they are: a release of chemicals into the body caused by certain "triggers," not impending death or doom or insanity. Accepting them and knowing they will end soon is the beginning of the end for panic attacks.

Thoughts and emotions of the subconscious mind can create a "chemical" imbalance.

If the paradigm of our subconscious mind causes negative thoughts and emotions to arise into the conscious mind, then it causes the release of neurotransmitters and hormones. This constant repetition of thoughts and emotions based in the subconscious paradigm can change the brain chemicals, the brainwaves, and even the physical nature of the brain.

When people talk about a family history of depression and anxiety, I often consider two things. One is the actual genetics, and the other is a family belief system that was fed into the subconscious mind during the early years of the child's life.

If the mother was anxious, the child will often be anxious because it picked up those fears from the mother. If there are a few generations of angry fathers, which may be a reaction to their own anxiety, the child will become anxious because of the anger, and anxious because she can subconsciously feel the father's anxiety. If the family has a history of placing high expectations on their child, the child may feel anxiety because she believes she cannot live up to those expectations, that she is not good enough for her parents, and therefore will never be good enough for anyone.

Consider your own past history.

Consider your childhood and the beliefs of your family, and how they acted and reacted that may have fed into your subconscious belief system. Make a list of thoughts, emotions, actions and reactions that come into your mind that may be incongruent with your conscious belief system. See if any of the experiences of your life may have created these beliefs that are limiting you.

As you come to a conscious recognition of how those beliefs were formed and what they are, you can better work through them and make conscious choices to deal with them and change them.

Remember, it took either constant repetition of beliefs or a major conflict or trauma to create your subconscious paradigm. It will take constant repetition of positive self-talk to change your mind. It is hard work, but you are capable of doing that work. It takes time, but you have your entire life. Take heart, the work is worth it!

The Eight Rules of the Subconscious Mind.

There are very important rules that we learn for hypnosis to be able to affect the subconscious mind, which holds your paradigm of life. These rules will be repeated individually at the end of several of the following chapters to remind you what it takes to change the mind.

1. *What is expected tends to be realized.*

2. *Imagination is more powerful than knowledge.*

3. *Once an idea has been accepted by the subconscious mind, it remains until it is replaced by another idea. The longer the idea remains, the more opposition there is to replacing it with a new idea.*

4. *Each suggested new idea that is accepted creates less opposition to successive new suggestions.*

5. *Opposing ideas cannot be held at one and the same time.*

6. *Every thought or idea causes a physical reaction, or a chemical response.*

7. *An emotionally induced symptom tends to cause organic change if persisted in long enough.*

8. *The greater the conscious effort, the less the subconscious mind can respond. (i.e.—The more you consciously fight depression and anxiety, the harder it is for the subconscious mind to let go and change.)*

Chapter 5

Physical Causes of Depression and Anxiety

Physical causes of depression symptoms.

*J*udy, at age fifty-eight, has been feeling bone tired. She has also been feeling more depressed lately, finding less joy in things she used to enjoy and difficulty motivating herself to do her daily chores. She is having a hard time getting anything accomplished. She feels like her brain is in a fog, and she is having memory problems. She notices her hair is thinning and, even though she is tired, she has difficulty sleeping. She has also been more irritable with her family, which distresses her and causes her to feel guilty. She feels down most of the time.

If Judy had gone to see her doctor with these symptoms, he may have simply stated that she was depressed and put her on an anti-depressant. These certainly are symptoms of depression. However, it is important to recognize there are many physical problems which can mimic the symptoms of depression and should be tested for. Just as depression and anxiety can cause physical symptoms, physical problems can cause depression and anxiety.

Low thyroid.

Judy could have low levels of thyroid hormone. The thyroid hormone regulates the metabolism of the body, and can cause the symptoms Judy is experiencing. If a patient of mine has a Thyroid Stimulating Hormone (TSH) level higher than 2.0 and has symptoms like Judy's, I will put them on a trial of thyroid to see if it improves their symptoms. If it is between 1.5 and 2.0 I will check their iodine levels and start them on a thyroid support supplement with iodine in it. I always recheck their thyroid levels after six weeks to make sure they are getting enough or not getting too much. Levels of thyroid hormone that are too high can cause anxiety, palpitations and fatigue and, over time, osteoporosis.

Hormonal imbalance.

Judy could have a hormonal imbalance. At fifty-eight, she is probably post-menopausal. Many women have no major problems as they go through menopause, but others seem to really be affected by the reduction in estrogen, progesterone, and at times testosterone, pregnenolone and DHEA, especially if they have a lot of stress in their lives. Depression, fatigue, sleeplessness, and irritability are common symptoms, whether the woman has hot flashes or not. Sometimes herbal and natural remedies resolve the symptoms, but sometimes actual hormone replacement therapy is needed to stop the depression. I usually recommend bio-identical hormones when this is necessary, making sure to use bio-identical progesterone along with estrogen to protect the body from the proliferative affects of estrogen, and rechecking levels to make sure they are balanced. Studies show that for a post-menopausal woman using bio-identical hormones, estradiol blood levels around 40–60 pg/ml and progesterone levels between 10–20 ng/ml seem to be the most balanced and protective. (21) DHEA, pregnenolone and testosterone may also be supplemented if the levels are low, and assist a woman in feeling better.

Women who are not menopausal can still have hormonal problems which can add to anxiety and depression. Progesterone is the precursor of cortisol, the body's hormone that deals with stress. When a woman is dealing with a lot of stress it often causes the hormone levels to change, as most of the progesterone is being used to make cortisol.

There is often an estrogen/progesterone imbalance that can cause Premenstrual Syndrome (PMS), endometriosis, fibroids and other problems, such as irregular or no periods, which can be caused by physical and/or emotional stress.

Medication.

Judy may be taking a medication that could be causing depression. Some of the medications that can cause depression include:

- Accutane

- epilepsy drugs

- birth control pills, shots, implants and IUD with hormone in it

- benzodiazepines, like Xanax, used for anxiety and sometimes sleep

- beta-blockers, used for high blood pressure, other heart problems, tremor and migraines

- bromocriptine (Parlodel) used for Parkinson's disease

- calcium channel blockers, used for high blood pressure, heart failure and other heart problems

- hormone replacement therapy or birth control—though often HRT resolves depression, in a few women it can cause or add to depression and/or anxiety. Often the birth control injections or the IUD with hormones can increase symptoms of depression.

- fluoroquinone antibiotics such as Cipro, Floxin, Levaquin (they can also cause tendon problems)

- opioids, used for severe acute and chronic pain

- statins, used to treat high cholesterol, or as a prevention for heart disease

- Zovirax, used for shingles and herpes

- Interferon alpha, used for Hepatitis B and C, and for some cancers

- Alcohol, marijuana, and other drugs, especially if there is addiction involved

Chronic illness.

It is hard, sometimes, to tell if the depression is caused by a medication or by the illness that the medication is treating. Many chronic illnesses, such as Parkinson's disease, diabetes, fibromyalgia syndrome, autoimmune diseases and even heart disease, can cause or add to depression. The only way to tell for sure if it is the medication is to go off for one to two weeks and see if the depression improves. Make sure and do this under your doctor's supervision.

Adrenal insufficiency, or adrenal "fatigue."

Another physical problem that Judy may be dealing with is mild adrenal insufficiency. The adrenal glands are small triangular shaped glands that sit on top of the kidneys. They produce hormones and neurotransmitters. One of their main functions is to deal with the affects of stress on the body. When there is excessive stress, physical and/or emotional, the adrenal glands can become overwhelmed, causing fatigue and possibly depression and anxiety. Adrenal imbalances can also affect the immune system, blood sugar and insulin, hormone levels, thyroid, increased inflammation and allergies, etc. When the adrenal glands are going into failure, a person has a disease called Addison's disease, which is much more serious. Most doctors are not familiar with the signs of mild adrenal insufficiency, but are more familiar with Addison's. If a person has Judy's symptoms I will usually do a cortisol saliva level, with samples taken four specific times during the day, as the levels change throughout the day.

Depression and anxiety can also cause adrenal insufficiency.

Long-term anxiety and depression can also cause adrenal / cortisol / adrenaline imbalances. Sometimes it's hard to tell which came first, the depression and anxiety or the adrenal imbalance. The problem becomes a vicious cycle, with each problem affecting the other. All the problems affecting the adrenals, and all the problems affected by the adrenals, may need to be addressed in order to completely heal.

Physical causes of anxiety symptoms.

Audrey is twenty-six years old, with two children. She started having anxiety after the birth of her first child. Some days she is better than others. She is tired during the day but can't sleep at night. She has had a few panic attacks.

If Audrey went to the doctor, he would probably put her on an anti-depressant that also deals with anxiety, or an anti-anxiety medication. But there are some physical issues which must be looked at.

A caution to those suffering from anxiety.

Giving this list of physical symptoms to someone with anxiety is like feeding fuel to a fire. The anxious person will begin to believe that she has one or more of these problems and it becomes difficult to convince her otherwise. The physical symptoms of anxiety (chest pain, stomach pain, palpitations, tremor, numbness, muscle pain, back pain, headaches, hyperventilation, dizziness, etc.) can mimic many serious diseases, and large amounts of health care dollars are spent daily to rule out those diseases in people that really simply have anxiety with no other physical illness other than the brain not functioning correctly. If you go to your doctor, or end up in the emergency room, and are told that no physical problem shows up, then consider the possibility that you may be suffering with anxiety, and not another physical problem.

Postpartum depression or other hormonal imbalances.

The first thing to consider is postpartum depression (PPD). Most physicians don't consider PPD when a woman is anxious, but the problems related to PPD can translate into anxiety as well as depression. As I stated in Marie Osmond's book *Behind the Smile: My Journey Out of Postpartum Depression*, of which I was co-author, much of PPD is caused by hormonal imbalances. Audrey should be checked for this problem.

Caffeine.

Often when women have a new baby and don't get enough sleep, they may resort to using caffeine to stay alert and reduce their fatigue. However, caffeine is notorious for causing anxiety because it increases the release of adrenaline. In the long run it makes the fatigue worse, because it increases the stress on the body. It also causes sleeplessness, even if the caffeine is used more in the morning. I would encourage any woman with anxiety or insomnia that is using caffeine to wean herself off slowly, and see how much difference that makes for the anxiety, and for the inability to sleep at night.

Low blood sugar.

Another problem Audrey may be dealing with is blood glucose imbalances, especially low blood sugar. Low blood sugar causes a release of adrenaline, which can cause the feeling of anxiety. The symptoms of low blood sugar may be as simple as fatigue and sleepiness, but may increase to a shaky feeling inside, tremors, headache, inability to focus or concentrate (brain fog), forgetting words, mood swings, and of course anxiety. Often when the diet is changed and supplements are given to help balance the blood sugar, the anxiety will reduce or even be resolved. Low blood sugar also increases cravings for food and addictions. Balancing blood glucose can assist a person to feel less anxiety, less headaches, more energy and less cravings, think more clearly and have more self-control.

Hyperthyroid.

After the birth of a baby the thyroid is in a state of flux, and it may go too low or too high. Low thyroid is more related to depression, and high thyroid can cause anxiety. Audrey's thyroid levels should be checked.

Other physical illnesses.

Other health problems that can cause or are related to anxiety include a tumor called a pheochromocytoma, mitral valve prolapse, congenital heart problems, congestive heart failure, heart arrhythmias (though anxiety itself can also cause heart arrhythmias), chest pain (though anxiety can also cause chest pain), asthma and other lung disorders (asthma is also worse with anxiety, and anxiety can cause hyperventilation, which means to breathe too rapidly), migraines, temporal lobe epilepsy, head injury, etc. Anxiety is also part of other mental disorders such as bipolar mania, post-traumatic stress disorder and schizophrenia.

Medications.

Medications which can add to or cause anxiety include:

- Some asthma medications

- Amphetamines for weight loss

- ADHD medications—some people become anxious on ADHD medications, but many with anxiety will improve if their anxiety is related to the problems caused by ADHD

- Drug withdrawal, such as from pain pills, medications for anxiety and depression, or from alcohol or other drugs

- Caffeine, alcohol, nicotine, marijuana, meth, other amphetamines, etc.

Excessive stress.

The most common cause of anxiety is excessive stress, which increases adrenaline release and causes the symptoms of anxiety. If there is a constant level of adrenaline in the body, it is easier to experience panic attacks, which are the result of a sudden release of adrenaline, putting you into the fight or flight mode, making you feel like your life is in danger or something is terribly wrong. Remember that a panic attack is simply a release of chemicals in the body, and is not dangerous, even though it feels awful. No one has died from a panic attack, so keep telling yourself that!

As a woman thinketh, so is she.

Most of my patients suffering from depression and/or anxiety may have some of the problems above that add to and make the depression and anxiety worse, but there are still usually belief systems and thought patterns that have helped to create the chemical imbalances and brain changes. These thought patterns and beliefs need to be dealt with for the depression or anxiety to truly be healed. The holistic medical viewpoint is to treat body, mind and spirit. When each physical problem, mental issue, and false spiritual belief is dealt with, I have seen the greatest healing take place.

✳ *Sixth rule of the mind: Every thought or idea causes a physical reaction.* ✳

✳ *Seventh rule of the mind: An emotionally induced symptom tends to cause organic change if persisted in long enough.* ✳

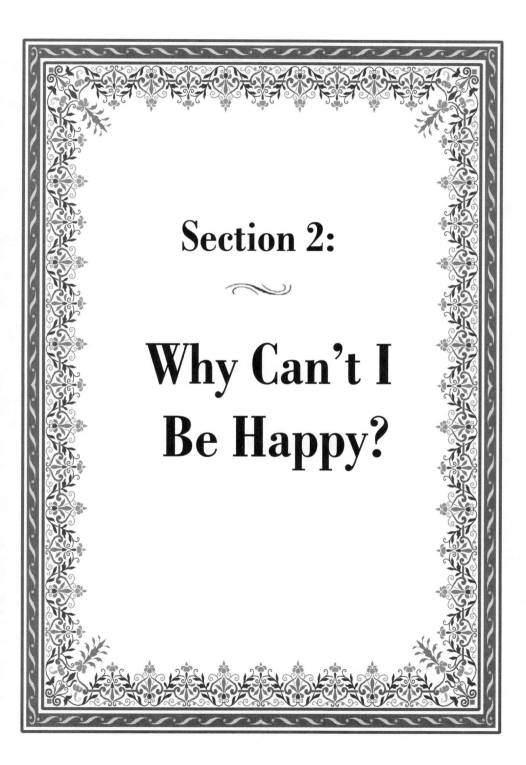

Section 2:

Why Can't I
Be Happy?

Chapter 6

Who Can Find a Virtuous Woman?

Mary woke up to the baby's cries. She looked at the clock. "Oh, dear," she thought, "I was going to get up an hour ago and go jogging. I wish I could have a little more discipline like Sally, who jogs every morning, even taking her baby with her in that jazzy racing stroller." She sighed and got up to feed the baby, while her husband Ron dressed, grabbed himself a bowl of cereal and ran out the door to work.

Soon the entire household was awake. 8-year-old Alice was dawdling, playing with her toy ponies rather than getting ready for school, while 6-year-old Ryan was dressed and ready but in the same clothes he had worn yesterday. She put the baby down, who promptly started crying, to help Ryan change. Ryan clearly wanted to keep his favorite shirt on and loudly protested. 3-year-old Tom had climbed on the counter and was rummaging through the cupboards, trying to feed himself with graham crackers as he was "reawy reawy hungwy, Mommy!"

Mary, after asking Alice to get dressed five times, lost her temper and yelled at her. Alice still didn't have her shoes on when it was time for the bus to come, so Mary gave her some fruit snacks for breakfast and put her shoes in her hands and sent her out the door. Alice started crying. She didn't want to have the kids tease her because she didn't have her shoes on. Giving in, Mary yelled at her to get in the car and put on her shoes, and she gathered up the other kids in various stages of dress, put them in their car seats and took Alice and Ryan to school, complaining to them the entire way about how inconsiderate they were of her.

On the drive back, Mary felt terrible and started crying. She knew she had lost her temper and treated the kids poorly. "Why can't I be more like Alissa, who seems to have eternal patience with her children? I've seen them act horribly and she never loses her temper. What's wrong with me?"

She started feeling resentment for her husband. "I wish Ron would treat me like Brother Thomas treats his wife. He is always helping with the kids and makes sure she has some time to herself every day. Ron leaves everything up to me unless I nag him. I hate being a nag! Why doesn't he just want to help me?"

"I know what was wrong with me this morning. I didn't take time for scripture reading and personal prayer. I really should get the kids up earlier so we can all do it as a family. That's what the Jones' do. Every morning. With eight kids! I don't know how she does it. Her husband must cooperate more. Ron could care less if we do any of that. I wish he would take up being the spiritual leader in the home."

After arriving home, Mary completed dressing Tom and the baby, and made sure Tom had enough to eat. He was a picky eater but he would get cranky if he didn't get enough to eat, so she often gave into his demands for foods that weren't very good for him. "Cheri is amazing. She only has healthy things in her house, cooks everything from scratch, and her kids eat vegetables! How does she do it? Why can't I make my kids eat like that?"

The phone started ringing. Mary saw that it was Marcella. "Oh, no! We're supposed to go visiting teaching today! Darn it, I forgot. I'm so stupid. I never remember anything." She answered the phone and asked Marcella to give her an extra ten minutes, as she was running behind. And by the way, would she teach the lesson? Mary couldn't find her Ensign.

"Marcella is so organized and keeps her house so clean. She would never forget an appointment like I just did. I'm embarrassed to have her pick me up with my house looking like it does. I'd better hurry so I can meet her outside. I hope the kids behave today. I really need to take time to find a babysitter when we do this. That's what my visiting teacher does."

Mary's day continued as it had begun, with Mary feeling like she was running a marathon but always behind her own schedule, and especially behind everyone else. In every situation she compared herself to someone else, always coming up short. Mary felt depressed. She couldn't seem to get it together. She cried several times during the day, and found herself upset at the kids and her husband frequently.

After the impossible task of getting the kids into bed, Mary was exhausted. She couldn't remember the last time she had had any real fun. But when she thought about it, she couldn't think of anything that sounded fun. Everything was drudgery.

Ron was in the other room watching TV. She got ready for bed and climbed in, determined to read her scriptures before she went to bed. Surely that would make her feel better. Mary opened the Bible and started reading the assignment for Sunday School. It was Proverbs 31. "Who could find a virtuous woman, for her price is far above rubies?" Mary started crying. She was not a virtuous woman, and she knew she would find an excuse to not be in Sunday School this week, because this was one of those lessons that would make her feel more like a failure.

The goals of the LDS woman may be unrealistic.

Did anything about Mary's experience sound familiar to you? Have you ever felt frustrated with yourself or guilty that you aren't doing things the way you should? How often do you compare yourself to others and seem to come up short? How often do you wish you could be more like someone else, because who you are certainly isn't who you should be? How often do you feel guilty at church because you aren't doing all of the things they are preaching about?

The LDS woman's list of "shoulds."

As LDS women, we are given a heavy responsibility. We should be clean and virtuous and thin and educated before marriage, attract the perfect returned missionary, be married in the temple, and create a beautiful, well-decorated, always spotless and well running household with delicious and healthy meals, with homemade bread with wheat from our own food storage.

We should remain thin and good looking after marriage as well, but still have lots of babies, and be wonderful, patient, loving wives and mothers who never complain. We are supposed to be modest but sexy, clean and virtuous but wonderful in bed. We should have make-up on and dinner on the table when our husbands get home, and have an educational or spiritual discussion with the family at the dinner table. We are supposed to be supporting wives, allowing our husbands to be the head of the household, never complain when they are gone for work or church work or time out with the boys, and we communicate so effectively that there are never arguments between us.

We should never raise our voice, no matter what time of the month it is, and no matter how sick or tired we may be. In fact, we are supposed to live the Word of Wisdom so well that we never get sick or tired. We should be able to run and exercise daily and not be weary.

We are supposed to be so beautiful and loving that our husbands will never be attracted to pornography or to another woman, because certainly it would mean we were too fat or too ugly or had too small breasts or weren't good enough for him if he did. We should inspire our husbands to be better in their work and in the church and to be Bishops. Because behind every great priesthood leader is a great woman. And therefore if our husband never becomes a great priesthood leader, that means we never were a great woman.

We should raise our children to be happy, to never fight, and to be modest but well-dressed presidents of their Young Men's and Young Women's classes and presidents of their school governments. Our children are supposed to get good grades and play instruments and sports and be a perfect child who is accepted to BYU, and they will never use tobacco or alcohol or drugs or have any form of premarital sex. Because if they do, we will have an empty chair as we gather our families in the hereafter, and that is every LDS mothers' nightmare, that there will be an empty chair.

We should give service to the ladies we visiting teach, the families our husbands home teach, every new neighbor and every new mother and sick person in the ward, and cook and serve at every funeral. We are supposed to friendship and convert all the non-members we know, and even the ones we don't know when they are sitting next to us on airplanes. We should hold positions in PTA and other community organizations, making sure our community is safe and enriching for our children. We should volunteer in school, in the soup kitchen, at the jail, at the women's shelter, and give until it hurts to fast offerings and the humanitarian fund.

We are supposed to go to every single meeting and accept and hold any position we are asked to at church, and to fulfill our callings better than the last person did, with lots of visual aids and handouts and more meetings. Besides our callings, which may be several, we are supposed to substitute for anyone that asks. And we should even give that extra service because the one who signed up for it got sick too.

We should go to the temple at least once a month if not every week, and do all of our genealogy (whoops, family history—it is important to keep up with all of the name changes in the church) or we will never be saviors on Mount Zion and we will have no one to greet us when we go to the other side to tell us how much they appreciate all the work we did for them.

We are supposed to be faithful daughters of aged parents, caring for their needs and going to their home frequently or even taking them into our homes to care for them so they won't have to go to a nursing home.

Of course we need to go to every single wedding reception to stand in line and make sure and be seen by the parents of the bride and groom, because if we don't they won't come to our children's wedding receptions.

And nowadays, we should be breadwinners along with our husbands, because we are never supposed to go into debt, and who can get along with one income and still pay our tithing in this economy? But we should find a way to work so that we are not really leaving our children, because we should stay home with our children. And we are supposed to be happy in our work and fulfill some wonderful life-changing purpose with it and STILL do everything else we are supposed to.

What do we really expect of ourselves?

Hopefully, this tongue-in-cheek example assists us in seeing that we cannot be all things to all people; however, isn't this often what we expect of ourselves? Don't we, as LDS women, secretly wish that we could be all of these things? We aspire to be the best, to raise the bar, to lengthen our stride, to go the extra mile, to increase our capacities.

We might laugh to think that we *should* expect all of these things of ourselves, and yet since we really do expect these things of ourselves, it is no wonder we become depressed and anxious.

Elder Dieter F. Uchtdorf said,

> *How do we become true disciples of Christ? The Savior Himself provided the answer with this profound declaration: 'If ye love me, keep my commandments.' This is the essence of what it means to be a true disciple: those who receive Christ Jesus walk with him.*
>
> *But this may present a problem for some because there are so many 'shoulds' and 'should nots' that merely keeping track of them can be a challenge. Sometimes, well-meaning amplifications of divine principles—many coming from uninspired sources—complicate matters further, diluting the purity of divine truth with man-made addenda. One person's good idea—something that may work for him or her—takes root and becomes an expectation. And gradually, eternal principles can get lost within the labyrinth of 'good ideas.'*
>
> *This was one of the Savior's criticisms of the religious 'experts' of His day, whom He chastised for attending to the hundreds of minor details of the law while neglecting the weightier matters.* (22)

There is often a difference between doctrine and cultural beliefs.

There is a difference between doctrinal law and cultural beliefs that have been created over the years. For example, the Word of Wisdom is a commandment to be lived by members of the church. But there is nothing in the law or the doctrine that states that all women should grind their own wheat and make their own bread, that they should buy only organic food or become a vegetarian. An individual sister may decide to do this because of health concerns in her family, but another woman doesn't have to feel guilty because she is unable to do the same. It is important for us to recognize the difference between "the minor details of the law and the weightier matters," or the difference between the doctrine of the gospel of Jesus Christ that lifts us and the limiting cultural beliefs that can weigh us down.

Are we commanded to do it all?

No wonder we are depressed. No wonder we feel like failures. Our ego mind (the mind of the natural man) lies to us, over and over, assuming that all of the recommendations given by others, and the gifts we see in others, are things that are commanded for *us* to do, and we expect ourselves to be able to do what no one can do. Yes, each woman does one or more of these things. A few blessed women do a lot of these things, but NO ONE does them all. It is physically impossible to do all of these things all at one time in this mortal earth of time and space where we are given weaknesses for our learning, and where opposition reigns. You may notice that Mary, in the story at the beginning of this chapter, did not have just one person to compare her inadequacies to. She had to go through her list of friends and acquaintances and picked the gifts of each individual that compared to her weakness.

> *A good woman knows that she does not have enough time, energy, or opportunity to take care of all of the people or do all of the worthy things her heart yearns to do. Life is not calm for most women, and each day seems to require the accomplishment of a million things, most of which are important...But with personal revelation, she can prioritize correctly and navigate this life confidently (Julie B. Beck).* (23)

We are not required to do it all at once.

All of these things we desire to do are good. I remember one evening around Christmas when I was in medical school, trying to figure out how to fit it all in. I had a test the next morning to study for, a school program for one of my kids to go to, a struggling teen-age daughter that needed some time and attention, and my husband's office Christmas party, all on the same evening. It was impossible to do all of those important things. It was difficult to even try to do more than one of them. I can't even remember what I did, but I did learn some very important lessons from having to make those decisions.

Ask, "What is for the highest good right now?"

I learned to look at each activity and set priorities as to which activity is most important in the present moment. I learned that by asking the Lord, I can discover what is for the highest good to accomplish in that moment, and what I can let go of. Then I have to trust that God will take care of the rest, that whatever effect on my family or schooling or work that comes from me *not* getting something done will end up for the best. When I ask, and do what I feel the Lord desires me to do in the moment, I trust that all is in divine order.

Depression and anxiety make the choices more difficult.

This is not easy. There are so many good things calling for us to do. If we are depressed or anxious or sick everything becomes even harder. We seem unable to do *anything*! Usually that is not true, but it seems true. Even stuck in bed, we can love our family, and what else is more important than that? It may be that what is for the highest good in these situations is to spend the time and energy it takes to be able to heal. Then we get to trust that all is in divine order and God will work with what we can't do.

Create your own list of "shoulds."

Write a list of all of the things you expect you should be able to do or to be if you were "better." Write down the ways of being you always wished you were and the things you criticize yourself about because you don't do. Look at the list carefully, and then laugh at it. Your list will show you how your ego mind is expecting the impossible of yourself. Then look at the list and listen to your heart as to which activities are for the highest good to be involved in right now. God doesn't expect all things at all times from you, and the Spirit can whisper those things that are not important to deal with right now. Cross them off of the list and see what is left. Then follow the advice below.

Do all things with diligence, in wisdom and order.

> *And see that all these things are done in wisdom and order; for it is not requisite that a [woman] should run faster than [she] has strength. And again, it is expedient that [she] should be diligent that thereby [she] might win the prize; therefore, all things must be done in order (Mosiah 4:27).*

All the Lord requires of us is to be diligent and to do things in order. Some synonyms of diligent are steady effort, persistent, steadily persevering. That means continuing to do what you CAN do, and not giving up. You can be the turtle and still win the race!

Doing things in order is a true blessing. When our focus is on raising little children, we may not have time to give a lot of outside service. When we must work, our focus when we get home may be more on our family time than on our family history. When we are physically or emotionally ill, our greatest service may be in learning and doing what is necessary to be able to heal. There is a time and a season for everything. However, there are some things we may never get to in this life because our focus has been called elsewhere, or the challenges we have been given have kept us from having strength to run in that direction. It is important to determine between ourselves and the Lord what is for the highest good in our own personal lives, and let go of comparing ourselves to others.

Do not run faster than you have strength.

> *And do not run faster or labor more than you have strength and means provided to enable you to [do your work]; but be diligent to the end (D&C 10:4).*

The Lord doesn't require that we do more than we are able to do, than we have the strength or means to do. Do we believe that? Do we believe that it is ok to let go of many of the things that we always felt were important but could never quite do? Do we believe that the Lord is pleased with what we CAN do? Do we focus on our successes, our gifts, what we ARE able to do rather than what we don't get done?

Our mortal bodies are limited in their strength and abilities.

Our bodies at this time are mortal. They have limits. Many of my sickest patients are women who WERE doing almost everything on that list, but, as they were striving, they became sick and couldn't do any of those things any more.

As we checked hormone and cortisol and thyroid and blood sugar levels, as we assessed the immune system, etc., we found that they had run faster than they were able, and their bodies just couldn't keep up.

The women were doing what they believed, based on what they had been taught. No one teaches that illness may be the consequence. We are taught to DO to reach the celestial kingdom. And, as women, we take that teaching in a different way than men do, because our brains are different. We feel guilty if we don't DO. So we DO until our bodies and minds are exhausted and sick.

Often depression, anxiety, chronic fatigue and fibromyalgia and many other chronic illnesses are simply manifestations of adrenal insufficiency. Our adrenal glands, which deal with the stresses the body has been given, become worn out with our doing and our worries.

Guilt vs. Divine Remorse.

We often feel guilty because we can't DO what we believe we should. The feelings of guilt deplete our faith and wear down our bodies. There is a difference between guilt and divine remorse. Guilt causes the self-critic within our ego minds (the mind of the natural man) to bring us down, make us feel bad about ourselves, cause us to beat ourselves up, and erode our faith in ourselves, in others and in God.

The general belief is often: "If I don't feel guilty I won't make myself do better." The truth is, guilt keeps us from moving forward. It keeps us stuck. Guilt is a form of judgment against ourselves. *"Judge not, that ye be not judged."* Might that mean not even to judge ourselves? Because when we judge ourselves harshly, we tend to also judge others harshly.

Divine remorse causes us to take accountability for our part in what didn't work. It allows the self-counselor within to ask, "How can I do it different next time?" Divine remorse allows us to feel the love of God and the atonement of Christ lifting and assisting, and it spurs us to move forward and keep at it until we can do it better. There is proper apology and taking accountability to those we have hurt. However, there is no self-judgment or self-criticism, but an understanding that we are all learning and doing our best with the weaknesses and circumstances we have been given.

The majority of people do their best with the weaknesses they have been given.

If you really, really dig deep down into your heart, you will see that you have always done your best with the knowledge and ability that you had at the time. You will see that if you had been able to do it better, to do it differently, to change your behavior, to do it more lovingly at the time, to "figure it out," you would have. That is the true desire of your heart. We are judged by the desires of our hearts, after all we can do.

All the Lord asks of us is to do our best, to run our race steadily, to not give up, but not to run it faster than we are able to in that moment. The atonement of Jesus Christ will make up the difference for what you are unable to do. The Lord is pleased with your desires and your efforts. Can you be? Because, in truth, it is not what we DO that makes us a virtuous woman, in spite what it says in Proverbs, or in spite of what we hear from other church members. A virtuous woman is one who is doing her best to learn how to be like God—to be Love. As long as we are striving and not giving up, we are successful.

The LDS people are a DO-ing people.

Our Works are very important to us. Our good works define us as a people. We know that service is the action that defines love. We want to show our love through our works.

Faith, if it have not works, is dead (James 2:17).

But sometimes we as a people forget the love part of service. Sometimes the works become burdensome, and sometimes we even resent them. Sometimes we do them just because we should. Our works become simply works, without love or faith.

Our works alone do not save us.

I believe that sometimes we forget the greatest truth of the gospel: *good works are a natural result of faith and love.* The opposite phrase to the scripture above is also true: works without faith is dead. When we have faith and love for the Lord, the works come automatically. Our works come from our faith, but our works alone do not save us. It is faith in our Lord and Savior, Jesus Christ, which saves us; faith that His atoning sacrifice can truly cleanse us from everything we do that is unlike love, anything that is unlike God.

> *...be thou partaker of the afflictions of the gospel according to the power of God; Who hath saved us, and called us with an holy calling, not according to our works, but according to his own purpose and grace, which was given us in Christ Jesus before the world began (2 Timothy 1:8–9).*

> *Since man had fallen he could not merit anything of himself; but the sufferings and death of Christ atone for their sins through faith and repentance (Alma 22:14).*

Only through the atoning power of Jesus Christ can we be saved.

None of us can get to the celestial kingdom on works alone, because our works are not perfect. Only through the Grace of the atonement of Jesus Christ can we find that perfection that allows us to be a celestial soul. The celestial kingdom is not made up of people who were perfect on this earth. It is made up of people who have been perfected through the atonement of Jesus Christ.

> *These are they who are just men made perfect through Jesus the mediator of the new covenant, who wrought out this perfect atonement through the shedding of his own blood (D&C 76:69).*

Focus on learning to become more filled with love and faith rather than on doing works. The works will come naturally with the love and faith.

Doing good works is a natural result of love, faith, trust and hope. Love, faith, trust and hope are often what women struggle with when they are experiencing depression and anxiety. So rather than focus on what we must DO to improve our lives, we will focus on our feelings, both positive and negative. Our goal is to increase those feelings of love and faith, so that the good works come easily and naturally, with the inner knowledge of what action is for the highest good in each situation.

✻ *First rule of the Mind: What is expected tends to be realized.* ✻

If we expect the worst, that is all we will see. If we expect the best, that is what we will experience.

✻ *Second rule of the Mind: Imagination is more powerful than knowledge.* ✻

When we believe in our minds and imaginations that we are worthless if we don't do certain things, it is difficult to believe anything to the contrary, even when the facts are right in front of our faces.

✻ *Fourth rule of the Mind: Each suggestion that is accepted creates less opposition to successive suggestions.* ✻

Work on changing one belief at a time. It will get easier over time.

Chapter 7

Unfulfilled Expectations

When I was a teenager I believed it all. I had wonderful lessons in Mutual (yes, I'm old, I went to Mutual or MIA instead of Young Women) about the joys of getting married in the temple and the happy Mormon home where the wife supported and uplifted and took care of her husband and, because she was so supportive and loving, the husband loved and took care of her like a princess (remember, my childhood was in the fifties and early sixties, when "Leave It To Beaver" was considered the norm). I was the only Mormon in my high school except for my little brother and two friends, one that had converted through my invitation, and the other converted by her invitation. There were no LDS boys to date, so my mother relented and let us date non-Mormons.

There was one young man I dated and fell in love with. He was strong in his own religion and loved God. He was moral and upright. He treated me well. But he wasn't a Mormon. I wanted to be married in the temple. I believed that getting married in the temple was what successful marriages were made of. He listened to the missionaries but wasn't interested. He was happy with his own beliefs. When he went to college (he was a year ahead of me in school), I missed him so much that I had to make a decision. Either I was to dedicate my life to him and accept him as he was, or I needed to break up with him. I spent a lot of time in prayer, and decided to break up with him, the hardest decision I had ever made in my young life. I was devastated and heart-broken for a long time. But I knew that God wanted me to marry in the temple. And I felt that I wouldn't have a truly happy marriage without that.

Eventually my heart healed. I went to BYU and dated a lot, had other boyfriends, and eventually married a wonderful returned missionary in the Manti temple. But it wasn't long before I realized that temple marriages can be just as hard as "for time" marriages. My expectation that a temple marriage would guarantee a happy marriage was dashed. I did not fulfill his expectations of what a wife should be, and he did not fulfill my expectations of what a husband should be. Neither one of us could fill all of the other's needs, and both of us, young and inexperienced, believed that we should.

My expectation that my returned-missionary-knight-in-shining-armor would help me live happily ever after was unfulfilled. Yes, there were many, many good times, and I still cherish those years, but it was a very difficult marriage that many years later ended in an unwanted divorce.

We create many expectations of what life and events should be like.

I still believe in temple marriage, but I had set myself up with a false expectation: that a temple marriage equaled a happy marriage. That was "magical thinking." A happy marriage doesn't just happen, in or out of the temple. It takes a lot of work and communication and compromise and forgiveness to create a happy marriage.

In our youth we often create many expectations of our future lives. Most of them do not come true in the way we expect them to. We also have daily expectations of ourselves, of others, and of planned experiences that often don't live up to our image of how they should be. *And one of the greatest sources of unhappiness is unfulfilled expectations, or desiring that which we do not have.*

I had many expectations.

I expected a happy marriage. I expected myself to act in certain ways and do certain things that I wasn't able to fulfill. I expected that my husband would act in certain ways and do certain things that he was unable to fulfill. I expected happy children that I would be able to teach the gospel to and they would obey. Proverbs 22:6 says *"Train up a child in the way he should go, and when he is old, he will not depart from it."* Just like I believed I was going to be one of those "price above rubies" virtuous women Proverbs talked about, I believed that my children would not depart from my teachings. Yes, I knew that there would be problems, but I believed that through love and prayer and my virtuous womanhood those problems would easily be worked out.

I expected my own family to be like the family I grew up in.

I grew up in a simpler time, and those expectations were built on the way it was in my family, with my parents and brothers and sisters. We had our problems, but we lived the gospel and went to church and my parents loved each other in spite of their differences and they both held every position in the church they could and we all did fun things together and enjoyed life together and loved each other through all of our problems. The boys were all Eagle Scouts and all went on missions. We all went to BYU and we all got married in the temple and that's how I expected my life and my marriage and my children to be.

Others may have unhappy childhoods, and expect that when they are out on their own and with their own families, things will be different.

My expectations didn't happen. Marriage was hard, some of my children were difficult to handle from birth, the world changed, temptations changed, and life was not simple. And I believed it was my fault. Except for the part that I believed was my husband's fault. (I have since learned that the more I blame myself the more I blame others for my problems. Because I blamed myself it was very easy to blame my husband as well.) I worked and worked to make everyone happy, and when they weren't, I blamed myself. I worked to keep everyone going to church and doing what was "right," and when it didn't work, I blamed myself. The more things went wrong, the less I liked myself, and the less I liked my husband. I was sinking further and further into depression, believing that I was a horrible wife and a horrible mother, believing that I was a failure, because nothing was turning out like it should have. And I felt that the fact that I wasn't happy was partly the fault of my husband, who, I believed at the time, didn't fill my needs and give me the love I expected and deserved. Except that I didn't really feel that I deserved it.

Our expectations are often based on false beliefs.

I was young and my expectations were based on false beliefs. As my expectations were shattered, one by one, my false beliefs came to only one conclusion: I was a bad person. I was being punished for my many mistakes, past and present. God couldn't bless me with a happy marriage because I had done things I shouldn't have. And I kept losing my temper and yelling at my kids. And I couldn't keep my house clean the way my husband wanted it. And I couldn't get my six little children do their chores without getting angry. Etc., etc., etc.

How I began to let go of expectations of how I "should" be.

One day, when things were particularly bad and I was falling apart inside, my visiting teacher came by and, because of her wonderful female brain being able to read my emotions and feel the Spirit telling her I needed help, offered to watch my kids so I could have some time alone to figure things out. I spent the day crying, thinking, in prayer and scripture reading. Eventually I came across a scripture that I had read many times before, a scripture that had actually made me feel more inadequate in the past:

> *And if men come unto me I will show unto them their weakness. I give unto men weakness that they may be humble; and my grace is sufficient for all men that humble themselves before me; for if they humble themselves before me, and have faith in me, then will I make weak things become strong unto them (Ether 12:27).*

This scripture had often depressed me in the past, because, no matter how hard I tried to improve, my weaknesses did not become strengths, but continued on and on. Every year I wrote a long list of resolutions on New Year's Day, and every year that list looked the same as the year previous. I seemed to be a failure. I couldn't overcome my weaknesses.

God gave me my weaknesses for a purpose.

But this time I saw it differently. The second statement jumped out at me: "*I give unto men weakness...*" All of a sudden the Spirit opened my eyes. If God gave me my weakness then certainly he must not be disappointed in me because of them. If God gave me my weakness it must be for a purpose. If God gave me my weakness to be humble, or teachable, then my weaknesses must be for my learning, and to help me depend on and trust in Him.

God's grace is sufficient for all of our weaknesses.

Then I read the next phrase, *"and my grace is sufficient for all men that humble themselves before me..."* If the Lord's grace was sufficient for Alma the Elder, who had been a priest of Noah and committed many atrocities, and then repented and became a great prophet, then His grace is sufficient for me. If the Lord's grace was sufficient for Alma the Younger, who committed great sins and influenced many to leave the church, and yet who repented and became a great missionary and prophet, then His grace must be sufficient for me.

Our weaknesses become strong through the atonement of Christ.

For if they humble themselves before me, and have faith in me, then will I make weak things become strong unto them.

The Spirit spoke to my heart with great strength, as I realized that this one sentence was the crowning principle of the Gospel of Jesus Christ. It is not always from my own efforts that weakness becomes strength. Often I cannot do it myself. But if I come to Christ in humility, with a knowledge that I can't do it by myself, if I come to Christ having faith that His atoning love can do it for me, then through the Atonement of Christ my weakness can become strong in that moment. Every time I repent with a sincere heart my weakness has been made strong for that moment. My weakness becomes perfected in Christ, through the repentance and atoning process.

Oh, sweet, the joy this sentence gives: I know that my Redeemer lives!

My life has not turned out like I expected. My everyday life, the things I do and experience, are very different than what I had earlier expected my life to be like. Because of my own weakness, the weakness of my ex-husband, the weakness of my children, and the weakness of others around me many of my expectations from life have remained unfulfilled.

My weaknesses have taught me to be more loving and forgiving, to be more like God.

However, I no longer choose to feel depressed, worried, or unhappy about the way life has turned out, because I can see the amazing things I have learned over the years! I have realized that learning how to better love as God loves, and learning to know and depend on Christ, have made my life richer and better than what I had expected as a young woman. It doesn't matter if things didn't turn out the way I had expected. I recognize that, because of my weaknesses, and because of the weaknesses of those around me, I am learning and my life is turning out the way that is for my highest good.

I've come to acquire a testimony about adversity; its absolute necessity, its potential to help us grow, and, most of all, its ability to draw us closer to our Heavenly Father. I have a different understanding of adversity now, viewed not with despair or anguish or regret but with confidence that my loving Heavenly Father is earnestly trying to allow me to learn something very important—so important that he is actually willing to let me suffer in order to learn the lesson. Rex Lee, after being diagnosed with cancer. (24)

How to Deal with Unfulfilled Expectations

Every day we create expectations of how things should be, how we will act, how others should act, how the day will go, how the trip will go, what we are going to accomplish, what others are going to accomplish, etc. And every day one or two or all of those expectations will be unfulfilled. How do we deal with the disappointments day after day without becoming anxious that things won't turn out, without resenting whomever is "at fault," without having obsessive thoughts about how things could have been better, and without becoming depressed?

Here are a few simple hints to change how we look at our day, our job, our marriage, our vacations, our children, or anything that we have expectations of. Remember, simple doesn't mean that it won't be hard, because our patterns and habits of thinking and believing can be quite deep, and changing them takes time. But just changing our PERCEPTION and our ATTITUDE can allow these "simple" changes to come easier.

1. *Let go of expectations.* This seems contrary to our every belief. We *should* be able to expect certain things from our parents, our spouse, our children, our co-workers, and even from life. We believe that we should *especially* be able to expect certain things from ourselves. But the truth is, often our expectations are unrealistic to our own true capacity because of our weaknesses, and the capacity of those around us who have been given weaknesses of their own to deal with. Unrealistic expectations bring us, and them, stress and pain. Let's go further so that you can see what this means.

2. *Feelings are more important that doings.* Generally, when we expect something to happen a certain way, what we are really looking for is the good feelings that we believe will come to us and our loved ones if things happen the way we expect them to. However, it is possible to receive the same feelings without the event happening the way we expect it to. And having the event happen the way we expect it to doesn't guarantee that we will feel those feelings.

For example, if Joey is expecting a pony for Christmas, but he gets a puppy instead, he can obtain the same feelings he was seeking from the pony, and probably more, from developing a relationship with that puppy. However, if he holds onto the belief that the only way he can be happy is by getting a pony, then he will be sad and angry and upset that his expectations weren't fulfilled. If he lets go of the expectation that happiness comes only from a pony, and seeks the *feeling* of happiness instead, he can be happy and fulfilled with the puppy.

3. *It doesn't have to look a certain way.* Again, we can achieve the same feeling we are seeking even if things don't turn out the way we expect them to, if we choose not to hold on to that expectation as the only way we can achieve that feeling.

If I am planning a Relief Society lesson, I may have all of these ideas for visual aids to make the lesson better. However, a crisis comes up in my family and I don't have time to make those visual aids. If I hold onto the belief and expectation that the only way my lesson will be any good is to have those visual aids, I will feel major anxiety. If I choose to believe that the Lord will help me with the lesson by touching the hearts of the sisters whether I have visual aids or not, I can be at peace. My lesson doesn't *have* to look a certain way to be successful and achieve the same results.

When Keith Hamilton, a black convert to the church, was a missionary in Puerto Rico in the early 1980's, he was sent to the island nation of Barbados, which was predominantly black. The authorities there would not let him enter with a work visa as they had the other white elders, and only granted him a 90-day tourist visa with strict instructions not to proselytize or he would be deported. Rather than feel like this time was a failure and give up because he couldn't do what most missionaries do, he chose to trust in the Lord to get the work done. By working with the members instead of searching out investigators, it became one of the most successful times of his mission. It doesn't have to look a certain way. (25)

4. *Be flexible with your plans.* It is good to make plans and organize what is coming. But when the schedule is broken because of unexpected events and needs, can you still be happy at the end of the day when all of those plans weren't completed? Allowing ourselves to be flexible rather than rigid with what we expect to happen will reduce a lot of anxiety.

Consider when you plan a vacation. You have in your plan a certain number of hours for travel to get to your destination, and you plan certain activities that you feel will bring happiness to your family. However, while driving along your husband sees something that he wants to stop and do. If you stop and do this, you may not have time to do one of the other activities that you had so carefully planned ahead for. Your anxiety goes up and you become irritable or even angry. Your expectations for this trip are not being met. You and your spouse argue over his insensitivity and your stubbornness. It is not a happy trip.

However, if you are flexible in your thoughts while making the plans, and open to the possibility that there might be something better that may come up, then you won't have such strong emotions attached to your expectations. With the ability to be flexible, you don't need to feel anxious if there is a possibility of change. Without that anxiety, which usually turns to irritability or anger, you and your husband can calmly discuss the possibilities, and maybe even with the input of the children decide together which activity would be the most fun for everyone.

Remember, the *feeling* is more important than the *doing*. Even if you don't get to all of the activities that you had planned, your family can still have fun and be happy spending the time together, which is the real goal of the vacation to begin with. It doesn't have to look a certain way to achieve the result you desire!

5. *Let go of everything needing to be perfect.* It won't be. Why should we expect perfection when nothing is perfect? Why do we fill ourselves with anxiety trying to make this or that perfect when there will always be little or big things that will keep it from being perfect? If we expect the unexpected, if we expect that not everything will go exactly as planned, if we let go of worrying about what others will think, if we are able to laugh when "Murphy's Law" goes into effect, then we will feel less anxiety, stress, and sadness.

6. *Ask "What is the worst thing that will happen if things don't go as I expect them to?"* Because of that over-active part of our brain that is causing anxiety and depression, elevated reactions to unfulfilled expectations are common. When things don't go as we expect them to, that part of our brain expects the worst, and we react to that expectation that the worst will happen. But the truth is, usually the worst *doesn't* happen. We over-react to the situation with worry, anxiety, irritability or sadness because of what our brain is telling us.

If you take a moment to ask yourself, "What is the worst thing that will happen?" you will usually see that it is very unlikely that the worst will happen, and you will be able to see that your fears and worries are most likely unfounded. The anxiety or depression is causing you to see the situation unrealistically. Ask, "Am I over-reacting?"

7. *Ask "Am I truly doing what is for the highest good or am I really seeking for approval?"* We have such a strong need for love and approval that many of our expectations are that others will love us and treat us the way we expect to be loved and treated. So we plan our lives according to that expectation. "If I do that, then he will love me." "If I act this way, then she will love me." "If I am good enough, then they will approve of me." "If I look good enough, then they will like me." "If I do something nice for him, he will do something nice for me that will make me feel loved."

We spend our whole lives trying to get others to love us the way we believe we should be loved. We constantly worry if others think well of us or not, or if they like us. But our expectations of being loved in that way will usually be unfulfilled. The hard truth is that we can rarely receive the love we are looking for from others. They are in the process of seeking love from others as much as we are. They usually cannot give us love in the way that we need it. A future chapter will be dedicated to this subject.

So when something isn't going the way you expect it to, ask if you are doing it to seek approval, to impress someone, or to be loved? Let go of that expectation. There are better ways to feel love. The highest way is by giving it to ourselves and others. We can rarely get pure love from someone else, we can only get love by giving it to ourselves and others without expectation of anything in return. We cannot expect them to give it back to us. The feeling of love will naturally come when we are truly giving it without expectation.

8. *Be open to all of the possibilities.* When Jesus was born, the Jews were expecting a Messiah. But their expectation was that the

Messiah would become their political king and save them from their national enemies. Because they refused to give up their expectations, to be open to other possibilities, the great majority of the Jews missed the greater blessing, of allowing them to be saved from the enemy within, the enemy of their own weaknesses, through the atonement of Jesus Christ.

When we hold onto specific expectations, it is like putting blinders on. We see only one thing, and are closed to all of the other possibilities. In doing so, we may miss out in being able to see the greater blessing that we are being given.

Keep the forgotten tenth commandment, "Thou shalt not covet."

Let go of expectations. The greatest source of pain is comparing what is with what isn't. When we want something we don't have, we are breaking the tenth commandment, "Thou shalt not covet." When we want what we don't have, when we want our husband or children to be more like some other husband or child, when we want a difficult experience to go away and are jealous of others who don't have that experience, when we covet the life of someone who is living without depression or anxiety or pain or chronic illness, when we want someone to treat us differently, when we want to be something we are not, we are coveting.

To me, the often forgotten tenth commandment is one of the most important commandments. Coveting, or wanting what we don't have, is the source of most of the emotional pain in the world. It is the root cause of people breaking many of the other commandments. It is the source of broken homes, violence in the community and war in the world. It stems from fear and a lack of trust in the Lord. It keeps us in depression and negativity.

Love what is! Let go of expectations. Accept and love and find joy in people and events as they are rather than how you believe they should be. *Trust in the Lord, that all these things shall be for your good.*

✷ *Third Rule of the Subconscious Mind: Once an idea has been accepted by the subconscious mind, it remains until it is replaced by another idea. The longer the idea remains, the more opposition there is to replacing it with a new idea.* ✷

Replace your expectations of specific things happening with another idea—that you can find joy no matter what the situation, no matter how it looks, no matter what plan fell through.

Chapter 8

Why Do I Have So Many Weaknesses?

We are experts at beating ourselves up.

Most of us have inside our minds an overactive self-critic which uses a beat-up stick on us. We go around all day criticizing ourselves and beating ourselves up. We look in the mirror and beat ourselves up over a pimple or a wrinkle or an extra bulge around our middle. We do something "bad" and beat ourselves up. We do something "good" but it's not good enough and we beat ourselves up. We talk to someone and beat ourselves up because we could have said it better. We find ways every day, all day, to beat ourselves up.

Our ego mind, or the mind of the natural man, has somehow convinced us that beating ourselves up is good. If we don't beat ourselves up we might be worse. We believe that beating ourselves up, allowing the self-critic in our brains to have full access to our thoughts, keeps our behaviors in check. Our ego minds tell us that we would be much worse if we didn't frequently tell ourselves how awful we were.

Constant self-criticism causes emotional and physical illnesses.

The truth is that the beat-up stick really beats us up. It gives us depression, anxiety, headaches, stomach aches, chest pain, sore backs, fatigue and chronic illness. The beat-up stick increases our stress and wears out our bodies. We might as well hand someone a bat and say "Beat away." That is what we are doing to ourselves.

We believe we must keep criticizing ourselves to improve ourselves.

But how do we overcome our weaknesses, or at least keep them in check, if we are not always criticizing ourselves when those weaknesses show their ugly heads in our lives? We tend to believe it is important to keep after ourselves for what we do wrong so we don't do it again. But the truth is, the more we beat ourselves up, the harder it is to change.

Why did God give us weaknesses?

First of all, it is important for us to understand why we have been given weaknesses. This brings us back into the pre-existence.

When we lived with our Heavenly Parents, we lived in a state of light and love.

When we lived with our Heavenly Father and Mother, we were consistently and constantly surrounded by love and light and good. We were in the presence of God, and *"no unclean thing can dwell with God"* *(1 Nephi 10:21)*. We saw that Father and Mother were gods because one hundred percent of the time they chose that which was love and light and good. If they chose anything different, they would no longer be gods. We had dwelt our entire spiritual lives in that atmosphere. We knew nothing different.

We wanted to become like our Heavenly Parents, but we didn't have bodies or experience.

We wanted to continue to grow up to be like Mother and Father. We are their children, in effect, baby gods. Just like colts are baby horses and tadpoles are baby frogs, we were different from Mother and Father but had everything necessary to become like them; except for bodies and experience. We knew love and light and good, but we knew nothing different. We had the capacity to choose love and light and good, but not the experience to do so. Just as if we lived in a green room our entire lives, and then had to choose between blue and green, we could make the choice, but we wouldn't know what we were doing because we had never experienced the color blue before.

The Plan of Happiness requires opposition.

So Father presented to us the Plan of Happiness: to create a place where we could experience the opposite of what He is—the opposite of Love in all of its forms: fear, hate, anger, pain, illness, sadness, anxiety, weakness, betrayal, and even murder. None of this was in existence where God dwells, and the one being that created opposition there in heaven could not dwell in God's presence. He was cast out with his followers to give us that opposition here on earth.

> *For it must needs be, that there is an opposition in all things. If not so... righteousness could not be brought to pass... wherefore there would have been no purpose in the end of [the earth's] creation... (2 Nephi 2:11–12).*

We willingly chose to follow this plan.

We shouted for joy at this news! This didn't exactly sound like a happy place, but we knew it truly was the plan that would bring us happiness. Now we could experience what the gods knew: the difference between good and evil, light and dark, love and fear. Because of this knowledge we could continue on our growth and progression; because of this new experience we were now facing we knew that in the future we could become gods ourselves.

When we came to this earth we were given weaknesses.

So we came to this mortal earth and were given mortal bodies. Our bodies were given weaknesses: congenital defects, physical and mental illnesses, obesity or ugliness, noses and thighs that are too big, acne, difficult hair, etc. Not everyone received the same physical weaknesses, but everyone received them, and in the end, every body reaches the ultimate weakness, the ultimate opposition, which is death.

Our minds were also given weaknesses: worry, anxiety, negative thoughts, tendencies towards addictive and negative behaviors, anger, fear, depression, negative personality traits, etc. Again, not everyone was given the same weaknesses, but everyone received them.

And we were given to families and put in environments that had weaknesses: poverty, hunger, physical, emotional and sexual abuse, criticism, fears, and every form of lack of love. With these weaknesses we couldn't remember what real love was. Love became conditional, a power tool to get people to behave. And yet because we are all children of Love, we spend our entire existence seeking for it.

Our weaknesses give us the experience of opposition that we may learn how to choose, and because of our weaknesses we are preprogrammed to fall.

We came to this earth to learn how to choose. The complexity of these choices is brand new to us. In our entire eternal existence we have never before made the difficult choices that we must make here on earth. Because of our own weakness and the weakness of those around us, we are pre-programmed to fall. In making choices, with the veil of eternity closed, and with the weakness of our mind and body, we are destined to fall.

Like little children learning to walk, we fall down again and again during our learning process.

And like we do with little children who fall down when they are learning to walk, God gets out the beat-up stick and says, "Bad, bad children!" Of course He doesn't. Just like we do with our own little children, when we fall He is there to lift us up, to hold us and comfort us, and to encourage us to walk again. "You can do it! Come on! Get up again! Walk again!"

The Gospel of Jesus Christ is the Good News.

The good news is that we knew all of this before we came. God knew we would fall, and we knew we would fall. But because no unclean thing can dwell in His presence, He provided a way for us to stand up again after we fell. Each time we fall, He lifts us back up through the Atonement of Jesus Christ. Jesus offered Himself at that Grand Counsel to do what the Father asked. He, a God Himself, chose one hundred percent of the time that which was light and love and good, even when he was a mortal man upon this mortal earth. To satisfy justice He offered His life as payment for our sins, which are the choices that we make that cause us to fall. His divine Love fulfilled what the Father had asked. His Love fulfills our divine mission.

> *...they...transgressed the first commandments as to things which were temporal, and becoming as Gods, knowing good from evil, placing themselves in a state to act... (Alma 12:31).*

> *For God doth know that in the day ye eat thereof, then your eyes shall be opened, and ye shall be as gods, knowing good and evil (Moses 4:11).*

> *And Eve, his wife, heard all these things and was glad, saying: Were it not for our transgression we never should have known seed, and never should have known good and evil, and the joy of our redemption, and the eternal life which God giveth unto all the obedient (Moses 5:11).*

It is Love that gave us weaknesses.

Our weakness provides the knowledge of the opposite of Love. Our weaknesses teach us, and provide us with the opportunity to become like Mother and Father, knowing good from evil, light from dark, love from fear.

> *Love is what inspired our Heavenly Father to create our spirits; it is what led our Savior to the Garden of Gethsemane to make Himself a ransom for our sins. Love is the grand motive of the plan of salvation; it is the source of happiness, the ever-renewing spring of healing, the precious fountain of hope (Dieter F. Uchtdorf).* (25)

It is Love that lifts us after we fall. It is Love that cleanses us. It is Love that allows us to heal. It is Love that encourages us to keep going, to move forward, to do it again and again, no matter how often we fall, until we learn what Love truly is.

Fear doesn't help us overcome our weaknesses.

There is so much fear among members of the church that if they don't overcome their weaknesses on this earth that they will never get to the celestial kingdom. From that fear they constantly berate themselves and others for not having overcome those weaknesses already. It is very important to have a desire and to do our best to improve ourselves continuously. But it is also important to love ourselves as God loves us, and to depend on the atonement of Christ through repentance while we are in the process of learning how to improve, which takes a lifetime.

The Celestial Kingdom is made up of those perfected in Christ.

Remember, the celestial kingdom is not made up of those who have lived perfect lives on earth, because none of us do. It is made up of those who are perfected in Christ, through His atonement. That doesn't mean that we can willfully sin and be just fine, but it does mean that if the true desire of our hearts is to be like Him, but we come up short, His Love will make up the difference for us.

> *For all have sinned, and come short of the glory of God; Being justified freely by his grace through the redemption that is in Christ Jesus (Romans 3:23–24).*

Create a self-inventory of weaknesses and growth from each weakness.

Write a list of your weaknesses. It should be easy to do, as people with anxiety and depression, and even most people without anxiety and depression, give constant focus to their weaknesses. When you complete your list, consider each weakness. Write beside it how that weakness has helped you or is helping you grow.

For example, one of my weaknesses has been the inability to keep a constantly clean and organized house. For a long time this caused me to feel very inadequate as a wife, a mother and an LDS woman, where I learned that cleanliness is next to godliness. I was embarrassed to have people come to my house, and though many never judged me because of it, I do know that I have been judged by others because of this weakness.

As I started learning that my weaknesses had purpose, and were for my good, and were part of the opposition that I was to experience on this earth, I began to repent of my angry and despairing thoughts towards myself. Rather than focus on what I was unable to do, I started focusing on what I could do, and learned to love myself more just the way I was.

My husband loved to invite people over for meals and socializing. Although I enjoyed the company of friends, it was a huge stress for me to try to clean the house with six little kids so that I wouldn't be embarrassed when the company came. I finally began to learn to let go of what others thought of me. I began to do what I could, and let go of what didn't get done. I would reason with myself, "If they don't like my house the way it is they don't have to come. If they choose to judge me because of my house it is their problem, not mine. I know I am doing my best." When I learned to do this, I really enjoyed my friends so much more. And surprise! They kept coming, even when my house was far from perfectly clean!

Love is the greatest thing we can learn from our weaknesses.

Though he were a Son, yet learned he obedience by the things which he suffered;

And being made perfect, he became the author of eternal salvation unto all them that obey him (Hebrews 5:8–9).

We, in similitude of Christ, learn obedience to Him by our suffering, caused by our weaknesses and the weaknesses of others. Obedience to Christ is simple: love the Lord with all our hearts, and love our neighbors as ourselves.

The most important thing I have learned from my weaknesses is love. I have learned better how to love myself in spite of my weaknesses, and therefore love others better in spite of their weaknesses. I have learned to feel the love of the Savior as I plead for forgiveness. And when I feel that love for myself and for others, I am filled with the Love of God, and am blessed to partake from the Fruit of the Tree of Life. What joy that is! I am so grateful for my weaknesses!

> *Every compliment, criticism, promotion, setback, good vibe, cough or really long line you have to wait in is a gift that was meticulously designed to make possible your becoming more than who you were, and ultimately, happier than ever before, as we dance into forever (Mike Dooley). (26)*

* Fifth Rule of the Subconscious Mind: Opposing ideas cannot be held at one and the same time. *

You cannot hate your weakness and love yourself at the same time. So just love yourself in spite of your weakness, and even because of your weakness.

Chapter 9

Fear and Love Cannot
Exist Together

Maryanne spends a lot of time worrying. She worries about herself and her health, and about her weaknesses and what she isn't getting done, the mistakes she has made in the past and that she's not good enough and what others are thinking about her and saying about her.

Maryanne worries about her children, about their health, about when they're not obedient, about their safety, about their friends and what they're learning from them and if they are going to get into trouble with them, or if their friends are going to make fun of them and hurt their feelings, about what they are learning in school, about what they aren't learning in school, about their homework and are they doing well enough in school, about what the teachers think of them, about what the teachers think of her, about what her children think of her, about if she is ruining their lives, about is she disciplining them too much, or not enough, is she too controlling, or too lenient, about are they going to get into drugs, are they going to have sex out of marriage, or with one son she knows is drinking, about what he is doing when not at home, about his eternal welfare, about what others think of their family with kids like that, etc.

Maryanne worries about her husband. He travels a lot for his job and she imagines him getting into a plane crash or a car crash or getting sick and not coming home. She has even imagined his funeral and has cried thinking about it. She worries about what he thinks about her, that maybe she's not pretty enough and not a good enough wife and he will find someone better on his travels. And though she has no reason not to trust him, she can't help but worry that maybe he would be unfaithful to her. She feels guilty for thinking those thoughts, but they come anyway.

Maryanne worries about money. Her husband makes enough but they do have a tight budget, and sometimes she can't get things she wants or things the kids want. She worries that the kids will feel less than their friends if they can't have the same things. She worries about the poor economy and how it will affect her husband's job. She wonders if she should get a job and lessen the load on her husband and get some money into savings and pay off some of the bills. She worries about what would happen if her husband were killed on his travels. She worries that she wouldn't be able to handle the money or pay the bills or do the taxes. Then she would have to go to work, and what would she be able to do, and how would she take care of the kids?

Maryanne worries about her mother. Her father passed away several years ago. Her brother has moved in with her mother after his divorce and she believes he is taking advantage of her mother in her old age. She goes over to her mother's house at least once a week to help, as her mother's health is poor, and it seems that her brother is doing very little. Her mother is hard to deal with, complains a lot, and at times says hurtful things. Maryanne often dreads going, and is a little afraid of her mother. But she also worries that after all of her hard work in caring for her mother, that her brother will use up her mother's money.

Maryanne is miserable. She is anxious and depressed. She lives her life in a state of fear, her mind never stopping with constant worries about her mistakes of the past, and that the worst will happen in the future concerning whatever she is thinking about in the moment.

All human actions are motivated at their deepest level either by fear or by love.

Fear and love are at the core of the opposition God created on this earth plane. Love is more than an emotion or feeling. Love is power that gives action to all around it. Love is the power of life.

God is Love, or charity, pure, powerful and wise unconditional love that creates all things, and we wanted to become like God. But we had to experience the opposite of what God is so that we would have the knowledge of what love truly is. The opposite of true, unconditional love is fear. Every negative emotion is rooted in fear. The greatest block to growth in life is fear.

> *For God hath not given us the spirit of fear; but of power, and of love, and of a sound mind (2 Timothy 1:7).*

Don't feel guilty about having anxiety.

Remember that anxiety is caused by physical changes in the physical brain, and until you learn techniques to deal with it and begin to change the brain, you can't help the thoughts and feelings that continually come up.

So as guilt feelings arise because you have a lot of fear, let them go, and tell yourself that you are not bad, these worries are simply the obsessive thinking of anxiety, that you are ok, and you are learning. The workbook has techniques to stop those obsessive worry thoughts. The following is simply to assist you in gaining knowledge to be able to make the change, and not to make you feel guilty.

Where our fears come from.

If you could remember who you truly are, a remarkable, splendid woman of light, and if you could remember why you are here, and the choices you made before you came here, you would not fear. However, the veil has been drawn and you do not remember who you really are. Because of the fall, you have suffered spiritual death, or separation from God. This has separated you from the pervasive and perfect love you had always been surrounded with before coming here. You have learned fear, which is Satan's greatest deception.

We generally learn fear and false beliefs from experiences related to our parents.

You learned in this mortal existence that you are much less than magnificent. You have generally learned this from the people that love you the most, your mother and father, from teachers, siblings and friends. Even the best parents, in their zeal to make sure that their children live happy lives and are safe, teach their children that they are not good enough, without knowing that they do so, and having no desire to do so.

Even the best parent becomes fearful as a little child runs towards the street, and may yell out of that fear to get the child to stop. But the little child, in their innocent mind, may not understand that the yelling is to keep her safe. She may perceive the yelling to mean that she is bad.

Parents' desires to teach their children may be interpreted by the child differently.

Because of your parents' belief that they must teach you to be perfect, they may have told you things that you did wrong, that you were not enough of this or were too much of that. They may have said these things in words and through punishment, or they may have said it through their teachings of what a good person should be, a good member of the church should be, what a good member of the family should be.

Though your parents are doing what they think is best for you, these teachings and expectations may cause you to feel that you don't measure up, because you keep making mistakes and can't do it all right. It is usually your parents who have taught you that love is conditional. You may have felt their conditions many times. You know they love you, but if you break their rules they may get angry and punish you or withdraw from you. They said they loved you, but it didn't feel like love. Even as an adult you may possibly feel or imagine their disappointment or anger or withdrawal of love when you don't do things the way they expect you to.

What we experience from our parents often shapes our belief about God.

It is from these childhood experiences that you drew your own definition of love. It is from these experiences that you created your beliefs about God's love. You may believe that God is a loving God, but if you break His commandments, He will withdraw from you and stop loving you and punish you and banish you to a lower kingdom where you cannot find joy or love. Or you may see God as a worried parent, worried that you will make wrong choices and not come back to Him, and disappointed with every wrong choice you make.

We have forgotten what heavenly love, or charity, really is.

You have forgotten the experience of powerful and wise loving without condition. You do not remember the experience of the love of

God. And so you compare God's love to the love you have experienced in the world.

This fear-based love is not only what you receive, it is also what you give to others, knowing nothing different than what you have received. And even while you withhold and retreat and set your conditions, something inside tells you that this cannot be what love really is.

You feel unhappy and uncomfortable with the way you are treated and the way you are treating others, but it is what you have been taught and you know no other way. To do it differently makes you too vulnerable and might allow you to be hurt. But you are hurting anyway.

Our deepest fear is the loss of love.

Every person on the planet is, in their own way, seeking for the love they lost when they were born onto this planet. This seeking actually introduces fear into their lives. Every thought, word or action is based in love or in fear. Love and fear are at the root of every other emotion. And what is the deepest fear? That we will lose love. That we will not be loved. That we will be separated from love. That we will suffer, which does not feel like love.

The world has a warped view of what love really is.

Many think that if they have enough power, or wealth, or beauty, or fame, or health, they will be happy and loved. Their view of love is based in false beliefs. All of our worries about ourselves and others and finances and war and the world and even our fears of death are based, deep down, in the fear that we will lose love. But the truth really is that we are always surrounded in love. We have just forgotten how to connect with it.

What is God's love like?

Because of many scriptures, especially in the Old Testament, it seems like God's love is conditional. It appears that He is a punishing and vengeful God. Elder Jeffrey R. Holland gave a beautiful talk on this in the October 2003 general conference entitled "The Grandeur of God."

> *...some in the contemporary world suffer from a distressing misconception of Him.... there is a tendency to feel distant from the Father, even estranged from Him....many moderns say they might feel comfortable in the arms of Jesus, but they are uneasy contemplating the stern encounter of God. Through a misreading (and surely, in some cases, a mistranslation) of the Bible, these see God the Father and Jesus Christ His Son as operating very differently....*

"He that hath seen me hath seen the Father" (John 14:9).

Elder Holland goes on to teach that one very important role that Jesus took on as He came to this earth was to show us what God the Father is truly like.

> *After generations of prophets had tried to teach the family of man the will and the way of the Father, usually with little success, God in His ultimate effort to have us know Him, sent to earth His Only Begotten and perfect Son, created in His very likeness and image, to live and serve among mortals in the everyday rigors of life.*

Jesus came as a representative of and in the likeness of Elohim, to show us what the Father was really like.

> *To come to earth with such a responsibility, to stand in place of Elohim—speaking as He would speak, judging and serving, loving*

*and warning, forbearing and forgiving as He would do— this is a
duty of such staggering proportions that you and I cannot
comprehend such a thing. But... Jesus could comprehend it and He
did it. Then, when the praise and honor began to come, He humbly
directed all adulation to the Father.*

*'My Father doeth the works,' he said in earnest. 'The Son can
do nothing of himself, but what he seeth the Father do: for what
things soever [the Father] doeth, these also doeth the Son likewise.'
On another occasion He said: 'I speak that which I have seen with
my Father.' 'I do nothing of myself; but as my Father hath taught
me.' 'I came down from heaven, not to do mine own will, but the
will of him that sent me.'*

If we want to have greater knowledge of what Heavenly Father is like, study the life, works and words of Jesus.

*... Jesus...came to improve man's view of God and to plead
with them to love their Heavenly Father as He has always and will
always love them. The plan of God, the power of God, the holiness
of God...they had occasion to understand. But the love of God, the
profound depth of His devotion to His children, they still did not
fully know—until Christ came.*

Jesus showed us through His own words and actions that the Father is loving, serving, merciful and forgiving; not condemning us, but sacrificing His Son to save us all.

*So feeding the hungry, healing the sick, rebuking hypocrisy,
pleading for faith—this was Christ showing us the way of the
Father, He who is 'merciful and gracious, slow to anger, long-*

suffering and full of goodness.' In His life and especially in His death, Christ was declaring, 'This is God's compassion I am showing you, as well as that of my own.' In the perfect Son's manifestation of the perfect Father's care, in Their mutual suffering and shared sorrow for the sins and heartaches of the rest of us, we see ultimate meaning in the declaration: **'For God so loved the world, that he gave his only begotten Son, that whosoever believeth in him should not perish, but have everlasting life. For God sent not his Son into the world to condemn the world; but that the world through him might be saved'** *(Jeffrey R. Holland).*

The opposite of love and eternal life (life with and as God) is fear and damnation.

The greatest block to our growth in life is fear. Fear is a wall that dams, or damns, our progression. It cuts short our attempts at working through problems. It limits our enjoyment of life and keeps us from the purpose of our life, to have joy. But experiencing fear is what allows us to strive to change until we feel love, peace and joy; until we learn to become more like God.

If we came to earth to learn to be more like God, and God is love, then we came to earth to learn how to love with charity, the pure love of Christ.

Every weakness and opposition teaches us what love isn't. The sufferings and travails of the world cause us to seek for something better. We feel like we don't belong here. We feel homesick for a place that is different than this world. But when we have experienced the pain that comes with fear, the opposite of love, eventually we remember the teachings and the example of Christ, and doors begin to open so that we can begin to learn what true, pure, powerful and wise love really is.

As we learn how to better love, we are given the spiritual gift of charity. We may be imperfect in this feeling, this new way of being, but the glimpses of love, peace and joy that come from true charity lift us enough to keep us striving for more.

This is the beginning of partaking of the fruit of the Tree of Life, which is the Love of God.

God's love is powerful.

God's love is not weak-willed. It is a power unto itself. The power of love is greater than the power of fear and darkness. The power of love is the power that generates life. Fear and darkness are generators of death. All fear and darkness can be overcome by the power of love.

God's love is wise.

Our Father knows there is a consequence for every action, whether our own actions or the actions of others. God, in His eternal wisdom, allows us to receive and live with those consequences.

God's loving and wise Plan of Happiness allows us to go through unhappiness, fear, emotional and physical pain and suffering, abuse, betrayal, anger, death and all kinds of sin so that we can experience the opposite of what He is, so that we can have greater knowledge and become more like Him by knowing the opposites.

Our Heavenly Father allows us to experience all that we came here to experience. He does not take away from us our learning experiences that we desired to have while we are in this mortal plane of time and space. He allows these things because, in His infinite wisdom, He knows the long-term results of allowing us to experience these things.

God's love is merciful.

Our Father, knowing what we would be experiencing on this earth, knowing that we all would "fall" from the state we were in before we came to earth, knowing that we would all sin because of the weaknesses we have been given, knowing that the consequence of those sins would keep us from His presence, sent His Only Begotten Son not to condemn us for our sins, but to save us from them. His mercy keeps us from the eternal consequence of sin, as we truly repent.

God's love is unconditional.

Because God knows the purpose for sin on this earth, He always loves us, even while allowing us to live the consequences of those sins. There is nothing we can do or not do to change His perfect, powerful and wise eternal love for us. We may not always feel that love because of our own state, but His love is always there. He loves us even when we sin, for we all sin, and He loves us all. Our Father is no respecter of persons. He loves us each fully and perfectly, no matter what we do.

However, in His wisdom, He will not take away from us the difficult things that we choose to experience in this mortal life. He will not take away from us the consequences of our thoughts and actions. He always, in every moment, provides the opportunity for us to partake of the Atonement of Christ through repentance. But no matter what, He loves us.

As I stated in chapter 1, but it bears repeating: at the end of our mortal lives, as we pass through the veil, we are not going to be asked, "How many people hurt you? How were you mistreated? How often did you teach a lesson to others by getting back at them? How important was your job? How thin and pretty were you? How successful were your children?"

Rather, we will be asked, "How much did you love? How did you show compassion? Were you able to love your enemies? Did you treat others the way you wanted to be treated, no matter what they did to you? Smile at others? Say a kind word? Lift another? Forgive another?"

The more we can let go of fear and be able to love, and the more we can inspire others to do the same, the more the world will change.

✳ *Fifth Rule of the Mind: Opposing ideas cannot be held at one and the same time.* ✳

Fear and love cannot exist together. Healing comes from releasing fear and embracing love.

Chapter 10

False Beliefs About Love and Fear

Author's note: This chapter is longer than many of the others because it is so important. Do not feel that you have to read the entire chapter in one sitting. It may work better for you to take one or two concepts at a time and ponder about how they may relate to your life. Read the chapter in the way that works best for you.

All healing is a release from fear, which allows for perfect love.

The power of love is healing to both body and mind. Loving ourselves, loving God, loving our families and loving our fellow men is the greatest source of healing.

However, because we grow up with an imperfect view of love, we develop false beliefs about what love really is. Much of what we believe is love actually stems from fear. The brain, especially the subconscious mind, cannot hold two opposing thoughts or feelings at the same time.

It cannot hold love and fear at the same time. So when we are seeking for love and striving to love, and yet we are full of worries and fears, we usually don't get what we are seeking for.

The following are *13 common false beliefs* we often hold about love:

Feeling worthy of love.

1. *I am not good enough to be loved, or, I don't deserve to be loved.*

We are imperfect humans living in a mortal body with an imperfect mind. We all give and receive imperfect love. None of us is "worthy" of love. But love has nothing to do with "being worthy," or "being good enough." This belief is based in fear because of experiences we have had of being rejected by imperfect people. We believe that rejection is proof that we are unlovable.

The truth is: we are all loved by God. Do you love your children and others even when they make mistakes? So does God, but more perfectly. His love is already perfect. Because of the state of our minds we may not be able to feel God's love. We may feel abandoned; we may be very depressed or anxious and so we can feel very little; we may feel that He cannot love us and so we are unable to feel that love. But the truth is that there is nothing we can do, either good or bad, that can increase or decrease God's love for us, whether we can feel that love or not.

The truth is: so can others love you. You are loved and you can be loved, no matter what you have done in the past, no matter how imperfect you are today. Love has nothing to do with how "good" we are. In fact, one of my favorite scriptures is *"And above all things have fervent charity among yourselves: **for charity shall cover the multitude of sins"** (1 Peter 4:8). This scripture is very comforting to me, especially when I make mistakes with my children or grandchildren. At least they know I love them, and that makes all the difference.

Loving self is selfish.

2. *Loving myself is really being selfish. I should love others more.*

Often the scripture, *"He that findeth his life shall lose it and he that loseth his life for my sake shall find it"* (Matthew 10:39) is quoted as proof that this is true. However, this scripture has nothing to do with love for ourselves, but with having enough faith in Christ to give our lives to Him and His will.

The truth is: this belief is often based in the fear of what others will think of us if we take time for ourselves, especially when they want us to do something for them. We fear that if we don't give to them at our own expense they won't love us.

The truth is: when we truly love ourselves, we feel the love of God, and we love God who created us, and we naturally love others and serve them. We cannot give what we do not have. We must love ourselves to be able to love and serve others. We cannot love others with true charity until we can love ourselves with true charity.

The truth is: loving others does not mean we allow ourselves to be a martyr to their wants and needs. And loving ourselves *does not* mean that we do *not* choose to give of ourselves to someone else because we love them. We love ourselves equally to how we love others, and we follow the Spirit and do what is for the highest good in the moment, whether it is to take care of ourselves or to serve someone else.

Fearing God is loving God.

3. *We should fear God. Our fear causes us to be obedient.*

Although the phrase "fear the LORD God" is common in the King James version of the Bible, why should we fear or dread the very Arms that hold us and shelter us, and with every breath, we are lovingly drawn into? The word most often translated in the Old Testament as fear is the Hebrew word *yirah,* which can possibly mean fear, but also means awe, reverence, respect and devotion.

The truth is: fear is the opposite of love, faith and trust. We are commanded to love God with all of our heart, might, mind and strength. We are commanded to trust in the Lord with all our heart. If we replace the word "fear" in the scriptures when it relates to God with the words revere, or praise, or have awe for, or give devotion to, many of these scriptures make more sense and allow us to better feel the merciful love of God.

Worry is loving.

4. *When I worry about loved ones, I am showing my love for them. My worry spurs me to action to make sure and take care of them and keep them safe.*

All of us have worried about children, spouses, parents or other loved ones. We have worried about their safety and well being, and we believe that we do this because we love them.

The truth is: worry is a sum of thoughts and feelings based in fear. It creates the chemicals of stress and anxiety in our brains and our bodies. Worry is not based in love. It is based in lack of faith and trust. Worry sets off the negative thinking cycle which erodes our faith and trust, and with constant repetition can lead to depression and anxiety.

The truth is: when we send love from our hearts and in our imaginations to our loved ones rather than worry and fear, there is a complete change in our feelings and in our perspective. Our loved ones actually respond positively to the change in feelings radiating out from us. And our minds and bodies respond to the positive chemicals with healing effects.

The truth is: when our hearts are filled with love rather than worry for those close to us it is much easier to feel the Spirit. It is much easier to be inspired as to what action is most important to take in their behalf, if any at all.

The truth is: when we are filled with worry and fear we tend to do too much, say too much, and be overprotective, keeping our loved ones from the experiences that lead to growth. Our worry often distances our loved ones from us. Most people don't like others to worry about them.

The truth is: when we send love to those we care about, rather than worry, it is much easier to trust that God is watching over and caring for our loved ones. It is much easier to trust that our loved ones won't go through anything that is not for their best good, even though it may be difficult. It is much easier to see that it is important for those we care about to experience the opposition created for this earth life, and to learn and experience for themselves what they came to this earth to learn.

The truth is: when we radiate love rather than fear, as President David O. McKay stated, we can affect the entire world for good.

Jealousy is loving.

5. *If I am jealous, I am showing how much I love someone.*

When we love someone, the ego mind (or the mind of the natural man), is afraid of losing that person's love. Therefore, whenever there is attention from or towards anyone else by that person, feelings of jealousy arise.

The truth is: jealousy is based in fear that we will lose that person's love. It is not based in love. Jealousy eventually drives our loved one away. Jealousy is based in the need to control and easily turns to abuse. Jealousy is very destructive to a relationship.

The truth is: jealousy is based on the fear that love is scarce, and that love is a competition. Love is ever abundant and does not compete.

The truth is: just because a person pays attention to someone else, it does not mean they do not love you. Just because a person is receiving attention from someone else, it does not mean they do not love you.

The truth is: love multiplies, love accepts, love trusts.

The truth is: we cannot control how another person chooses to feel. We cannot control who they choose to love. If they choose to love someone else more than us, we cannot control that, no matter how upset or jealous we may become.

The truth is: trust is not for the other person, but for us. The other person will make their own choices, which we cannot control, but if we trust the other person, we will in our own hearts feel better and happier, and it becomes easier for love to grow and for the relationship to improve.

The truth is: if the other person has proven that they cannot be trusted many times, we can trust in the Lord that it is still for the highest good, to "love our enemies, and do good to those who despitefully use us." (This does not mean we allow ourselves to be abused, or that we choose to stay with that person.)

The truth is: if the other person chooses to love someone more than us, of course it will hurt. But with time and faith we can simply see that their love is not yet perfect either, and trust that we are still lovable and loved. We can trust in the Lord that He loves us and is supporting us through our trials.

The truth is: if we trust the one we love, if our hearts are filled with true charity for that person, then even if they break that trust, God will hold us through the pain and we will move forward out of the pain faster and with greater ease.

Loving someone means I need to fulfill their needs and expectations of me.

6. *Loving someone means I need to please them and fulfill all their needs and wishes. If I don't please and fulfill the expectations of the one I love, they will not love me.*

Often we go into a marriage with the belief that love consists of fulfilling each other's needs and wants so we will be happy. We seek out ways, little and big, to please them and make them happy. We may write little notes telling of our love. We may spend extra time on a good meal, or wear a sexy negligee just to please them. It feels good to please our husbands and make them happy and help them to feel loved.

However, over time, we find that we cannot please our spouse in every way, that we cannot do everything that he may desire of us. Life intrudes, children come along, we get tired and don't have time or energy to do it all. Or he may desire of me what I can't do because of my weaknesses, or he may even demand that I "run faster than I am able."

We often feel guilty and feel like we are not good wives if we cannot do everything our spouse wants of us. If he needs sex in order to feel loved, I should be able to give him all that he needs, even if I'm tired or not feeling well. However, when I give him sex when I don't want it, I start resenting him, and then I start disliking sex.

I should be able to look thin and pretty for him, but I'm gaining weight and not eating as well as I should because I'm so busy. I should be able to fix good meals and have a clean house like he wants me to. I should be able to assist him with the finances so he is not so stressed. I should be able to stay within his budget, even though it is so tight I can't get the kids what they need. All of these things that he wants of me, I should be able to do, if I love him enough. So why can't I do them? What is wrong with me? When I can't do what he wants me to, I feel inferior and I resent him.

Sometimes we make assumptions about what our husbands want, without really knowing. Our husbands may be happy with us but we are not happy with ourselves. We may be harder on ourselves than they are on us.

Some husbands can be overbearing and demanding. Some husbands believe we should do everything that they want us to, and may complain about our inadequacies and weaknesses. We begin to dislike ourselves and resent them.

The same thing happens with children. We love those little babies and want them to be happy always. We are distressed when they cry and we can't make them happy. As they grow older, sometimes it is too easy to give into their demands because we feel guilty when we say no and they are unhappy. We are their mothers and our job is to please them and make sure they are happy.

The truth is: when we truly love someone, our desire is to serve them, but in this mortal existence it is impossible to be the sole provider for someone else's needs and wants. We do not have the capability to do so.

The truth is: each person is responsible for their own happiness. Happiness does not come from having someone else provide all things for us. True joy comes from within. If we were able to provide for all of someone's wants and needs, they would never need to search to find that love and joy from within. God did not create us to be able to fulfill all things for our loved one. It is important that our loved one discover their own strength within.

The truth is: when we expect that we should be all things for our loved ones, we will always eventually feel inadequate and weak, because we cannot fulfill that expectation. We may be able to do it for a week, or maybe a month, or maybe even a year or more, but eventually we will give out, because in becoming what someone else wants us to be, we cannot be ourselves. We lose ourselves, and our psyche cannot keep up with that.

The truth is: as we learn to draw from that love within ourselves, in spite of our weaknesses, we can be happy and satisfied with what we are able to give others, even though it may not be everything they want, or even everything that we want to give them.

The truth is: if they demand more from us than we can do, it is their problem and not ours.

The truth is: all God requires of us is to do our best with the weaknesses that we have been given. When we have charity towards ourselves and others, we will not expect from ourselves more than what we can truly do.

I am not loved if my needs and expectations are not fulfilled by my loved one.

7. *He must not love me because he didn't fulfill my expectations of how he should love me.*

We often believe that the ideal vision of a loving relationship is that we both fulfill each other's needs and wants. If I need lots of affection and words of love, he should be able to give me affection and words of love. If I tell him so over and over, why can't he just hug me more, or tell me he loves me? He must not love me.

If I'm exhausted caring for kids and house at the end of the day, he should be able to take over and give me time to be alone. Even when I tell him I feel loved when he helps me, he comes home and turns on the TV until dinner is ready. I have to nag to get him to help me, and then I don't feel loved.

At the beginning of my marriage I was sure that my husband didn't love me because he didn't fulfill my dreams and expectations of how a husband should love and treat a wife. This false belief, which I held onto for a long time, had a very negative effect on my marriage.

The truth is: the brains of men are different than the brains of women, and they love differently express love differently from women.

The truth is: our husbands cannot read our minds. Because they don't understand our minds they don't know what we want. It is important from the very beginning of a relationship to express those actions and ways of being that help us feel loved.

The truth is: even if our husbands know the things that make us feel loved, they may not really be able to fulfill our desires because of their own beliefs and past experiences and weaknesses. They can only do their best with the weaknesses they have been given.

The truth is: none of us can love perfectly. We may be able to love our husbands in the way that we desire to be loved, but we usually don't have the ability to give love to our husbands in all the ways that they desire to be loved. It goes both ways.

The truth is: if we demand more from our husbands than they can give, it is our problem and not theirs.

The truth is: by being grateful for any and every evidence of love that you are given, you will begin to feel loved anyway. Express your desires but let go of expectations. Focus on the positive, on what you get, rather than what you aren't getting, and slowly but surely, it will be easier for your husband to treat you the way you desire.

And the truth is, interestingly, that we often stop desiring the things we used to desire when we choose to feel loved with what is actually given to us by their best ability.

The truth is: this is true for any relationship, not just for husbands and wives.

Withholding our love is a good teacher.

8. *If I withhold my love (don't talk or interact) when I believe someone does something wrong, they will change and be better.*

It is so easy to use our love as a weapon. We have all had it happen to us, when someone has withdrawn their love for us by giving us the "silent treatment," or blasting forth angry words, when we displease them. As children we often become "pleasers" because we fear that love will be withdrawn from us if we don't please everyone.

The truth is: this need to please causes anxiety and depression because it is impossible to please anyone all of the time. How often have you felt, "I can never please him/her? Whatever I do, it's wrong."

The truth is: when love is withdrawn to "teach a lesson" the only lesson learned is "I am not loved because I am not good enough."

The truth is: when love is withdrawn, it is not truly love. It is fear and lack of faith, and a form of force and manipulation to get someone else to behave as we want them to. This is not how God loves us. This is not charity.

The truth is: letting go of condemnation and showing forth an increase of love is a greater teacher, as Jesus taught. *"God sent not his Son into the world to condemn the world, but to save the world* *from sin." John 3:17 "Neither do I condemn thee. Go thy way and sin no more." John 8:11*

I love my children by forcing them to obey. If I don't then they won't make it to the Celestial Kingdom.

9. *When I force my children to obey, to go to church, to do what is right, I am loving them by teaching them what is right. If I show them love and affection they will be rewarded for their bad behavior.*

This is a concept that is very difficult for all of us. We are taught to bring up a child in the way he should go, and he will not stray from it. We fear that we will be bad parents if our children fail and do wrong things. We fear for our children's eternal welfare if they make wrong choices. We want to ensure, especially when they are young, that they make the right choices so they will learn to be happy. So we use force in the form of harsh, angry punishment, guilt, manipulation, and physical force to make sure they make the right choices.

The truth is: the only lesson force teaches is "I am not loved because I am not good enough." This often leads to rebellion against what we are forcing them to do.

The truth is: force leads either to the child having anxiety that they are not good enough to make their own choices, which causes them to be afraid of making decisions, or it leads to rebellion against all of the parent's rules.

The truth is: force is Satan's plan, not God's plan.

The truth is: we all have to make mistakes and suffer the consequences of those mistakes in order to learn what we came here to learn on this earth. Providing consequences in love is not force. It allows the child to make a choice.

The truth is: being the true example, and inspiring others through words and actions by following the guidance of the Spirit, is God's way.

The truth is: using natural consequences with an increase in love rather than punishment with anger is God's way.

Concerning this last truth, often when dealing with our childrens' misbehaviors we think of the scripture, *"Reproving betimes with sharpness, when moved upon by the Holy Ghost; and then showing forth afterwards an increase of love toward him whom thou hast reproved, lest he esteem thee to be his enemy"* (D&C 121:43).

I often used that excuse in my own mind when I would get upset at my children and yell at them and punish them harshly. I would later go and tell them I was upset because of whatever wrong they had done but I really loved them.

The truth is: that form of treatment did not teach them what I wanted them to learn. It taught them to feel angry at my anger, to feel that life is unfair, to not trust themselves, to feel that they were inadequate, and to rebel against me. These were not the lessons I wanted them to learn.

The truth is: when I truly examined those times, I had not been moved upon by the Holy Ghost. When I started making the choice to stop, pray and ask before I disciplined, I was never told to yell or punish physically or harshly. There were times when I was given the inspiration to be blunt and forthright in my words, but never to be angry or yelling. In fact, surprisingly, many times I was told to do nothing, that the problem was more my problem, my needs, and my fears than theirs.

The truth is: remember the words of the verses previous to the above scripture:

> *No power or influence can or ought to be maintained by virtue of the priesthood [or motherhood and wifehood], only by persuasion, by long-suffering, by gentleness and meekness, and by love unfeigned;*
>
> *By kindness, and pure knowledge, which shall greatly enlarge the soul without hypocrisy, and without guile (D&C 121:41–42).*

The truth is: this is God's way. We are not required to "punish" our children, but we *are* asked to love them and to teach them, and to use the inspiration of Holy Spirit in our dealings with them.

The truth is: discipline is usually not needed immediately, except to keep a child out of imminent danger. We can always stop, pray and ask for inspiration before we deal with something we believe is a problem for our child.

The truth is: love and affection are the greatest teachers. If we show love and affection consistently through good behavior and bad, the child will feel loved and have a more natural desire to do what is right as they mature.

President Joseph F. Smith gave counsel on this topic: *"Fathers [and mothers], if you wish your children to be taught in the principles of the gospel, if you wish them to love the truth and understand it, if you wish them to be obedient to and united with you, love them! And prove to them that you do love them, by your every word or act to them. For your own sake, for the love that should exist between you and your [children]—however wayward they might be…. When you speak or talk to them, do it not in anger; do it not harshly, in a condemning spirit. Speak to them kindly: get down and weep with them if necessary, and get them to shed tears with you if possible. Soften their hearts; get them to feel tenderly towards you. Use no lash and no violence, but… approach them with reason, with persuasion and love unfeigned."* (27)

The truth is: often misbehavior is a cry for attention, even negative attention. Attention is a form of being loved. A child who is given lots of unconditional love, affection and attention will usually exhibit less misbehaviors.

The truth is: rather than telling a child they are right or wrong, good or bad, ask questions such as "Did that work for you? Did that work for the other person? How did it make you feel? How do you think the other person feels? What could you have done differently? What would you like to do next time?"

Through loving questions, the child can learn to form their own beliefs rather than simply be told. The child will behave better if these concepts are created in their own mind and heart rather than just following the parent's belief.

Pointing out faults in others is an act of loving them.

10. *When we criticize our spouse, child or loved one, we are loving them because we are teaching them what is wrong with them so that they can change and be happier.*

It is hard to understand how we can teach anyone without criticism. Often the words "constructive criticism" are used. I have used criticism often in the past. It was how I was raised and I knew nothing else. But over time it became abundantly clear to me that *criticism didn't teach and it didn't change hearts.*

The truth is: criticism comes from fear. Telling someone what they have done something "wrong" is a form of judgment. Judgment never feels good or feels loving to the receiver, even if the judgment is true.

The truth is: the only thing that criticism teaches is "I am not loved because I am not good enough." It also breeds self-doubt, and resentment towards the criticizer.

The truth is: "constructive criticism" is still criticism and judgment. It simply allows us to justify to ourselves that the criticism is necessary.

The truth is: that which we focus on increases. If we focus on the negative aspects of someone else it will NOT go away. The other person generally cannot change simply because we criticize them. And the anxiety and bad feelings caused by being criticized and judged make it harder for that person to change.

The truth is: focusing on the positive and the successes allow a person to move towards change. By praising and loving and thinking about and focusing on what a person does that is working for you, the things that they do that make you feel loved, that make you feel good, the result is that the person feels better about themselves and it becomes easier for them over time to naturally do more and more of the good.

The truth is: we are each given our own weaknesses for our learning and often, as strong as our desire is, we cannot always change when we want to. Give your loved one the benefit of the doubt. Choose to believe that they desire to change and they are working on it but they are unable to. This is usually true. Even someone who acts like they don't want to change and doesn't seem to be working on it, usually has given up because they believe they can't change.

The truth is: we often have different opinions on the correct way to believe and to act. If the other person believes something different than we do, criticism will change nothing, but it will drive them away.

The truth is: if we marry someone thinking he will change, we will be disappointed. The only thing we can do is learn to love what is or leave. But often, if we truly love what is and give up the need for the other person to change, change happens over time and with patience.

The truth is: love, affection and praise allows a person to change much more easily than criticism.

The truth is: if you spend a month and completely ignore the negative behavior of your spouse or child or the person you are having difficulty with, and truly search for the positive in them, watch for their successes, seek for what is good about them, and discover what you are grateful for about them, and if you comment on those things, express love and gratitude and give up every criticism, you will be amazed at the change in your relationship with them. Even if they have been unable to change, your relationship with them will improve and you will feel more love for them, which is what Christ asked of us.

The truth is: if there is something very important to talk to a loved one about, something that is truly causing you distress, questions about their feelings and expressing your own feelings lovingly will encourage communication. Criticism, accusations and judgment will stop communication, put up walls and cause defensiveness. And during this conversation let go of the expectation that the other person can change for you. They may want to but at this point they may be unable to. But loving communication can often reduce negative feelings, whether anyone is able to change or not.

The truth is: if someone becomes defensive when you are talking to them, they are feeling criticized whether you meant to or not. Stop and review what you said that caused them to feel criticized or judged.

The truth is: there are times when we are truly moved upon by the Holy Spirit to be blunt, honest and forthright when someone is oblivious to the problems they are creating. When this is done they may become defensive, but if it is done in love and with the power of the Holy Spirit, it will most likely touch their hearts and cause them to ponder later on when they have calmed down.

It is impossible to love those who judge us or hurt our feelings.

11. I cannot love so and so because they hurt my feelings, judged me, or criticized me.

The opposite of criticizing others is also true. When we are criticized and judged by someone else, we feel unloved. The hardest people to love and keep from judging are those who have criticized and judged us.

The truth is: when Christ told us to love our enemies, and do good to those who despitefully use us, it was not for the other person, it was for us.

The truth is: no one can offend us or hurt our feelings unless we choose to be offended and have our feelings hurt.

The truth is: if we choose to be offended and hurt by others' words or actions, we allow them to have power over us.

The truth is: when we choose to be offended and hurt by others we are usually hurting ourselves more than them.

Elder David A. Bednar taught: "*When we believe or say we have been offended, we usually mean we feel insulted, mistreated, snubbed, or disrespected. And certainly clumsy, embarrassing, unprincipled, and mean-spirited things do occur in our interactions with other people that would allow us to take offense. However, it ultimately is impossible for another person to offend you or to offend me. Indeed, believing that another person offended us is fundamentally false. To be offended is a choice we make; it is not a condition inflicted or imposed upon us by someone or something else.*

"*In the grand division of all of God's creations, there are things to act and things to be acted upon (see 2 Ne. 2:13–14). As sons and daughters of our Heavenly Father, we have been blessed with the gift of moral agency, the capacity for independent action and choice. Endowed with agency, you and I are agents, and we primarily are to act and not just be acted upon. To believe that someone or something can make us feel offended, angry, hurt, or bitter diminishes our moral agency and transforms us into objects to be acted upon. As agents, however, you and I have the power to act and to choose how we will respond to an offensive or hurtful situation."* (28)

The truth is: though some people choose to deliberately hurt and offend, most often when we have our feelings hurt it is by the words or actions of someone that has no idea what they have done and they had no intention of ever causing problems for you.

The truth is: most people believe they are helping when they criticize. They are NOT helping, but they believe they are, and believe it is loving to point out what is wrong with you so you can change. They even truly believe you should be grateful for their advice!

The truth is: things look very different when we see it from a different angle, don't they?

The truth is: becoming defensive and upset during a conversation in which we feel criticized never moves the conversation forward towards a positive end. We do not have to defend ourselves or make others understand. It usually makes things worse when we do so.

The truth is: the best response to advice given by another that feels critical or judgmental is, "Thank you for your advice. I will think about it." Then let go of the negative feelings that have come and let go of the "advice," unless you know that what they say is true and you choose to work on it. If it doesn't fit, trust that they were well-meaning and not trying to cause pain, and let it go.

The truth is: when we can love "our enemy," pray for them and let go of judgment towards them, we can let go of the pain and find joy in ourselves, rather than live with hurt feelings and bitterness. Jesus is always right!

I can only be happy if I feel loved by someone else.

12. *I cannot be happy until I find the perfect soul mate, the love of my life. If so and so would love me, then I will be happy.*

The truth is: when our happiness depends on someone else, we will always, eventually, end up disappointed and unhappy.

The truth is: even if we find our "soul mate," they will not be perfect and fulfill all of our wants and needs. No one can do that. We can only do it ourselves.

The truth is: happiness comes from within, not from someone else. Of course our joy is multiplied when we have outward evidence that we are loved, but we will never be happy until we can feel that love for ourselves, feel love from within, and find joy in our lives no matter if we are with someone or alone. Until then, even if we are loved, we will not feel happy.

I am loving myself by defending myself when I have been wrongly accused.

13. *When my husband or someone criticizes me I must stand up and defend myself so they won't believe I am bad.*

The truth is: the other person will never really understand you. Don't keep trying to get them to do so. Defending yourself so that they will understand rarely works. It usually brings conflict.

The truth is: conflict is an expression of fear. When you are in conflict you must somehow have chosen not to love, or the fear could not have arisen.

The truth is: it is more important to correct our own fear than the other person's, which we have no control over.

The truth is: when we feel the need to defend ourselves, the way to get out of the conflict is not to defend ourselves against others, but to look at ourselves and why this fear came up. Recognize that this is not love but fear. Fear arises from lack of love.

The truth is: the way out of fear is to seek for perfect love, which is found in the Atonement. Ask for forgiveness for your fear that led to conflict. Forgive the other person that triggered your fear. Express your love to the other person. Trust that God's love will heal you both, even when you don't completely understand each other.

Changing ourselves and our beliefs is not easy.

If we have been living our lives by many of the beliefs above, and others that were not mentioned that are based in fear rather than love, we may find a desire to change. However, usually changing habits, ways of being, thought processes and beliefs takes time. It is hard to come up with alternative ways of speaking and acting when the old ways are all we know.

Be patient with yourself. Take one belief at a time, the one that is most important to you. Write down what doesn't work for you. Write down other ways that might work better. Discuss this with your spouse or a trusted family member or friend. Work on it together. Spend time in prayer; ask for the strength to change, ask for the gift of Charity. Spend time in meditation and contemplation. Visualize yourself the way you desire to be, and feel what it will feel like when it all comes easy to you. And trust that you CAN change!

The Atonement of Christ casts out all fear.

Because the Atonement is the wisest and most powerful act of perfect love, as we truly partake of it through repentance, fear is dispelled and loving peace fills our hearts. The mercy and love of God allows us to trust in the process of this earth life, created through the Plan of Happiness.

Remember that we are not here to change the people around us, but to change the natural man within us. As we do the work to increase love and peace and joy within, it spreads outwards and begins to change our relationships as well. Rather than focusing on what may be causing our pain from without, focus on what is causing pain from within.

Trust in the Lord with all of your heart. Trust in the atoning power of Jesus Christ. Humble yourself and come unto Him, and allow His atoning power to cleanse you and to change you.

The results are worth the time and effort!

Perfect love casteth out fear (1 John 4:18).

MOTHER TERESA'S PRAYER

People are often unreasonable, illogical and self centered;
Forgive them anyway.

If you are kind, people may accuse you of selfish, ulterior motives;
Be kind anyway.

If you are successful, you will win some false friends and some true enemies;
Succeed anyway.

If you are honest and frank, people may cheat you;
Be honest and frank anyway.

What you spend years building, someone could destroy overnight;
Build anyway.

If you find serenity and happiness, they may be jealous;
Be happy anyway.

The good you do today, people will often forget tomorrow;
Do good anyway.

Give the world the best you have, and it may never be enough;
Give the world the best you've got anyway.

You see, in the final analysis, it is between you and your God;
It was never between you and them anyway.

—Kent M. Keith

(Reportedly inscribed on the wall of Mother Teresa's children's home in Calcutta.)

✱ *Third Rule of the Mind: Once an idea has been accepted by the subconscious mind, it remains until it is replaced by another idea. The longer the idea remains the more opposition there is to replacing it with a new idea.* ✱

It may be hard to change from a false belief to the truth when it has been there for years, but the effort is worth it!

✱ *Fourth Rule of the Mind: Each suggestion that is accepted creates less opposition to successive suggestions.* ✱

Just start with one false belief and work on it. Once your mind has changed and accepted the truth, it will be easier to change others.

Chapter 11

I Hate My Body

I went on my first diet when I was twelve years old. My body was going through the changes of puberty, which causes a little fat to be put on creating a woman's curves, but I was used to my young girl body and I thought I was fat. I didn't know the changes were normal. My weight was normal. But I felt really fat.

It was time for my sister's wedding. I had made, with my mother's help, a bridesmaid's dress. I had grown a little since it had been made, and I thought I looked fat in it. A friend told me about a diet she had gone on—eating only orange juice popsicles. I tried it. I lost 5 pounds in three days. My mother didn't discourage me, which made me believe she thought I was fat, too. I don't know that she believed it, but I believed she did. It was the first of many fad diets over the next 40 years. Because ever after that I always felt too fat, except for the short amount of time after I had lost weight on some fad diet.

I tried them all. I lost weight, but eventually gained it all back, over and over. But each time, I would gain even more than I had lost. Until eventually I really was "too fat." As I got older the fad diets stopped working. My body was wiser and told me, "Sorry, I'm not going to let you starve yourself anymore. It's not healthy." But I didn't hear it. All I heard is "You're too fat." And I didn't like myself because of how I looked. I didn't like myself because I seemed to have no self control. And I didn't like myself because no matter how hard I tried, I would hardly lose anything. So I gave up. And I didn't like myself because I gave up.

A negative body image is very common in depression and anxiety.

Almost every woman who comes into my office with depression and anxiety also has a poor body image and dislikes her body. Some of them feel they cannot get over the depression until they can change their body. They believe that the way their body looks is the one of the main causes of their depression, and if they could just lose weight (or gain weight, or have bigger breasts, or smaller breasts, or less wrinkles, or a better looking neck, etc., etc.) then they would be happier.

The perceptions we have about our bodies are usually lies.

This is all a lie. Our body image is all in the perception we have of ourselves and has nothing to do with truth. I've known absolutely beautiful (to the typical American perception), thin women who hate their bodies and are severely depressed and unhealthy, and "chunky" women who see both their inner and their outer beauty, accept themselves and are very happy and healthy. Happiness does not come from having a perfect body. It comes from our own inner perceptions about ourselves. And the good news is, we can change those perceptions.

Our body image has nothing to do with eternity.

As I tell my patients, the number on the scale or the size of our breasts or the amount of cellulite on our thighs has never kept anyone from the celestial kingdom. These are simply part of the mortal weaknesses we have been given to better learn how to love. It is important to let go of the judgment of men and women and ourselves and focus on what is important eternally.

Having different bodies is part of the Plan of Happiness.

We were each created differently. We each have different genes, different looking skin, different hair, different shapes, live in different environments, have different strengths, different weaknesses, and value different things. This diversity is part of the Plan of Happiness. If we were all the same, how could we experience the "opposites" of life?

The weaknesses of our bodies were given to us for a purpose— to learn.

Each of our bodies has been given inherent weaknesses for a purpose. Some of us grow fatter on less food than others. Some of us can't gain enough weight no matter how much we eat. Some of us have bigger breasts and buttocks. Some of us are simply flat everywhere. Some of us have bigger abdomens and no waist, some have thin waists but larger thighs. Some have acne late into life and some have facial hair. Some get wrinkles early and some seem to never age. Some get sick easily and some seem to be healthy. Some have brains that more easily create depression and anxiety, and some have a natural ability to see the bright side.

Because of these weaknesses our bodies can be our greatest teachers. As we learn to deal with the weakness of the body and the body's brain, we learn better how to love ourselves and love God who created us, just the way we are.

Comparing ourselves with others creates pain.

When we compare ourselves to others, we always fall short. That is because we tend to compare our own weaknesses with someone else's strengths. We become unhappy because we judge ourselves in those comparisons, and assume that others are also judging us.

Trying to change because of the world's judgments never works.

No man can serve two masters: for either he will hate the one, and love the other; or else he will hold to the one, and despise the other. Ye cannot serve God and mammon (Matthew 6:24).

Mammon is a Greek word meaning riches. I use the word to mean how others perceive us—as rich, beautiful, successful, powerful, etc.

If what others think of us becomes the master that directs our lives, it becomes impossible to truly serve God, because the judgment of the world will keep us thinking negative thoughts about ourselves, and that is not God's way.

We cannot be in the world, or in other words, strive to abide by the world's standards, and serve God. The world's standards are superficial and know nothing of the heart or the spirit. How the world judges us had nothing to do with who we really are. And when we judge ourselves according to the world, we will always fall short.

The Tenth Commandment—the forgotten commandment—is the greatest source of pain.

I've discussed this before, but it bears repeating. The tenth commandment is one of the most important commandments, and yet it is the most forgotten commandment. "Thou shalt not covet." Or, in other words, thou shalt not want anything others have that you do not have. When we wish our husband was like her husband, or our child was like that child, or our body was like her body, or our skin looked like her skin, or our house was like their house, that we could keep our house as clean as she does, etc., etc., we are breaking the tenth commandment.

Coveting, or comparing what is with what isn't, is the source of most pain. Wanting what we don't have causes us to break the other commandments. It is impossible to truly love God and be unhappy with what He has given us. When we want what we don't have it is harder to love the people that do have it. It is easier to dishonor our parents because they didn't provide it for us. It is easier to judge others. It is easier to lie and steal and commit adultery and even kill. Most commandments are broken because of coveting.

Change comes from self-love, not from self-criticism.

This doesn't mean that we stop striving to change things that aren't working in our lives. This doesn't mean that we let go of seeking for better health and of finding ways to improve ourselves. But these things become much harder to accomplish when we don't love and accept ourselves exactly the way we are in this moment, as God does.

Gratitude is the key.

The secret, as always, is gratitude. When I was struggling with my body image, and desired to change, I started considering all of the ways my body serves me, and began expressing gratitude for all that it did for me. I am grateful that my heart continues to beat faithfully, even after sixty years. I'm grateful I can see, even if I do use glasses to see better. I'm grateful that I can walk and hear and touch and feel. I'm grateful my fingers work so I can write this book. I'm grateful that my body carried and bore me six children. It sacrificed a lot for that, and still carries scars and evidence of that eternal and spiritual work. I'm grateful my body can feel emotions because they give variety to my life.

Not everyone is able to see or use their fingers or walk or bear children. But each person has something that they can be grateful for about their bodies.

I also started expressing gratitude to each part of my body when I was in the bathtub or shower, while I was washing it.

"Thank you, legs, for supporting me even when I weigh more than you expected." And I laugh, and my legs laugh back.

"Thank you, neck, for holding up my head all of these years. I know it sometimes feels like a bowling ball and you complain a little, but we're working through that, right?" And we laugh together.

"Thank you, breasts, for providing milk for my little ones and pleasure for my husband. I know you're worn out and are hanging lower each day, but you've served me well." And we laugh together.

"Thank you, belly, for being like a bowlful of jello that my grandchildren like to poke and watch jiggle. Thank you for carrying everything inside of me for so many years. I know the stress of my life has added fat to you, but we're doing our best to deal with that, aren't we?" And we laugh together.

I now weigh 30 pounds less than when at my highest weight. I am still not at my most healthy weight. I am not dieting, but I am striving to eat and live more healthily. I fail at times. But I choose to love myself and my body anyway. I choose to LOVE WHAT IS. When I see the muffin top hanging over my pant waist, I laugh at how I'm trying to squeeze everything in. And I truly do love my body!

Treat your body like a little child.

Self-love, used with wisdom and power, allows change to come much easier than when we hate ourselves and constantly judge and criticize ourselves. It's time to treat our bodies like little children. It is time to love them, compliment them, forgive them for their weaknesses, listen to them, be kind to them, be grateful for them, take care of them, and enjoy them.

This process is very, very healing for our bodies, when they start feeling our love rather than our criticism, judgment and hate. Our bodies can be our greatest teachers, if we choose to listen to their wise messages.

✳ *First Rule of the Mind: What is expected tends to be realized.* ✳

If we expect our bodies to fail us in some way, they probably will. If we expect them to work well for us, they probably will.

✳ *Second Rule of the Mind: Imagination is more powerful than knowledge.* ✳

What we believe about our bodies is often only a perception of our imagination, but that is more powerful than the truth. Work on imagining your body as beautiful, as it truly is.

Chapter 12

Dealing with Tragedy and Trauma

How do we avoid depression and anxiety when life's burdens become too heavy to bear?

here are times when difficult experiences are thrust upon us. There are times when our load seems more difficult to bear than we can handle. There are times when we cannot avoid those burdens, when there is nothing to let go of to make our burden lighter. We may become weak, fatigued, depressed and anxious because of the load.

We may be dealing with extended or severe illness, serious problems with spouse or family, difficult financial issues, or the loss of a loved one. We may be experiencing severe loneliness and lack of support from anyone. We may be experiencing unavoidable oppression by others, poverty and hunger, or the trauma of war. We may be suffering from trauma from childhood such as extended abuse, the trauma of hospitalization, an alcoholic parent, etc. We may be dealing with the consequences of major mistakes we have made in the past, addictions, and even depression and anxiety themselves—and we may not know how to pull ourselves out of the deep hole we seem to be stuck in.

At times, the traumas of life cause us to struggle with our beliefs.

These struggles often cause us to question our faith, to question God, to question all of the good things we have tried to do in our lives. We may pray and yearn with all of our hearts for a way out of our pain, and yet the heavens seem closed. We may feel the loss of our inner compass, the loss of our foundation. We may feel the loss of the Spirit, and feel like we are receiving no answers to our prayers. We may possibly question the church, the divinity of Christ, or even the existence of God. Life can become bleak and dark, seemingly without any light to cling to. It becomes difficult to trust anything or anyone.

"Trust in the Lord with all thine heart...and He will direct thy path" (Proverbs 3:3–5).

And yet this is the time when trust is of utmost importance. The trust that is needed is that light will come out of the darkness. The trust that is needed is that the dawn is close, even though you see no evidence now that anything will ever change in this darkest of nights.

I have been through several of those dark, dark times, when I lost my way for a time because it was too black to see, and the iron rod seemed to lead to nowhere in the mists of that darkness. I believe that most everyone, at some point in their lives, lives through something so dark that they seem to lose themselves.

"Magical thinking" causes unrealistic expectations.

Sometimes as we read the *Book of Mormon* stories telling about cycles of "obedience equals prosperity, peace and joy, and disobedience leads to war with the Lamanites," we come to believe if we do everything "right" that we should be living lives filled with prosperity, peace and joy. Then when horrible things happen in our lives, we lose faith in ourselves, believe we must be doing something wrong, and often lose faith in everything else we have believed in.

Sometimes we indulge in what may be called "magical thinking." These thoughts go along the lines of "If I am as hard working and as kind and beautiful as Cinderella I will marry the prince and live happily ever after." "If I am good enough, nothing bad will happen to me." "If I have Family Home Evening every week then my children will all stay close to the Church." "If I serve every time I am asked, then I will be blessed and my husband will gain a testimony." "If I accept every calling, then I will be loved and respected." "If I read the scriptures every day I will be able to overcome this addiction." "If I lose enough weight I will then be able to love myself." "If I serve a mission God will remove my same sex attraction."

This doesn't mean that striving to be good, having Family Home Evening, giving service, accepting callings, reading scriptures, losing weight, and serving a mission are without merit, because they all bring blessings of one kind or another, for others and for ourselves. However, when we put specific expectations of specific detailed blessings from God on the acts that we do, it is like putting an ultimatum on God. "If I do this, I expect You to do this."

But our ways are not His ways, and our thoughts are not His thoughts. He knows us better than we know ourselves. He knows our life plan, which because of the veil we have forgotten. If we allow ourselves to depend on "magical thinking," we will often find ourselves disappointed. The blessings may not come as we expect them to.

Faith building stories by others can be devastating to us if we don't have the same experience.

The disappointment becomes even stronger because this "magical thinking" is perpetuated through testimonies of faithful individuals who did something good and another good thing happened. We've all heard the wonderful and faith-promoting stories of tithing paid and subsequent financial blessings, or of receiving healing blessings and miraculous healing took place. I have many faith-building testimonies of my own that are very special to me. Those experiences are very real and build our trust in the Lord.

But what happens when tithing is faithfully paid for years and there is financial ruin? What happens when Priesthood blessings promise complete healing and there is no healing? What if Patriarchal Blessings don't seem to "come true"?

Often, what results is self-doubt and a loss of faith, because the "magical thinking" didn't produce results. We may think any of these things: "If it happened to them and it didn't happen to me, there must be something wrong with me." "I have destroyed my life through wrong choices, so I don't get the promised blessings." "I must not be faithful enough." "Maybe God doesn't love me." "Maybe He doesn't know I exist." "I am God's greatest mistake." "Maybe there is no God and these are just foolish imaginations." The thoughts can go in any direction.

Let go of expectations.

This doesn't mean that when we receive a revelation to obey a certain law and then we will be blessed that it is false. Often, when I have been in financial straits, when I have asked, I have been told to pay my tithing and I'll be taken care of. What I have learned, however, is not to expect what being "taken care of" specifically means. There are times when I paid my tithing and miracles happened and my bills were paid. There were other times when I couldn't pay all of my bills when I paid my tithing. But, over time, I was always supported and pulled through the various financial crises that have arisen in my life, and I have been blessed in many ways other than financial. But if I had been holding onto the magical thinking that I would always be able to pay my bills if I paid my tithing, I would never have seen the greater blessings. Remember to let go of expectations and be open to all of the possibilities so that the greater blessing can come.

"The rain falls on the just and the unjust" (Matthew 5:45).

Being a Mormon does not shield us from the tragedies of life. Being Mormon does not hold a special magical power that keeps the horrors of life at bay. Terrible things happen to Mormons and non-Mormons alike, to the "obedient" and the "sinner" (though, again, we are all "sinners"). Coming from a strong Mormon family does not protect us from bad things happening: illness, accidents, death, financial ruin, war, abuse, divorce, adultery and even incest. We all have strengths and talents, and we all have weaknesses: Mormon, Fundamental Christian, Catholic, Buddhist, Muslim, and atheist alike. We as a people are generally a good people, however, we are all prey to temptation. The arrows of temptation always seem to be able to find the weak spots and the holes in our armor.

No one is immune to the great problems of life.

There may be some who think that General Authorities rarely experience pain, suffering, or distress. If only that were true. While every man and woman on this stand today has experienced an abundant measure of joy, each also has drunk deeply from the cup of disappointment, sorrow, and loss. The Lord in His wisdom does not shield anyone from grief or sadness. Elder Joseph B. Wirthlin

Every family has its problems.

Every family has at least one "ghost" in their closet. We just don't hear about them, often even among family members, because of many reasons. We may be trying to protect a family member from pain and embarrassment. We may be protecting ourselves or the family name, because of fear of what everyone else will think. We may be frightened to tell, because of threats, or fears that no one will believe us. We may be afraid that if we talk about it, no one will consider us a good Mormon anymore. There are many reasons why no one talks, but that leaves the person dealing with the pain of the trauma feeling very alone; feeling like they are the only one in the ward with this kind of pain.

We can lift each other in times of trauma, but we each suffer our own pain alone.

It is good to be able to talk through our pain with others, and it would be nice to feel enough acceptance and lack of judgment from those around us to be able to be completely honest with others, so that we can lift each other up. This is truly the ideal world, but in this mortal world of weaknesses, things don't often happen that way. We are often alone in our pain.

I had an experience that was devastating to me when I was about 34. The Bishop told me not to talk about it with anyone else. Even now I don't feel free to discuss it because it would cause negative judgment against someone else, and I no longer choose to judge that person. My heart at that time was full of such acute pain that I didn't know how to handle it.

At the same time, in my ward, another sister lost her baby to meningitis. The entire ward gathered around her during her time of grief. I was actually envious of this poor grieving mother because we had both lost something precious and she had the "whole world" grieving with her while I had to suffer alone.

I can see now that we all suffer alone. Our pain is our pain and no one else's. Others may feel pain for us, but that is actually their pain. That mother suffered alone in her heart just as intensely as I suffered alone in mine. No one can take that pain away. We get to learn to work through it ourselves, whether anyone else knows about it or not. It really does serve to have others around us that we can talk to, as women often feel a need to talk to be able to work through their pain. However, whether we have someone to talk to about it or not, we are the ones who have to work through our pain.

In dealing with trauma, we must go through the grieving process.

No matter what has happened to us, we are dealing with grief. We have lost something dear to us. It is obvious that if someone dies, or leaves us, that we will grieve our loss. However, there are many other kinds of loss. A child who has been abused, or a young woman who has been raped, has lost her innocence, her feeling of safety, and possibly her virginity. A woman who has grown up with an alcoholic parent, or a sick or emotionally ill parent, may have had to take over care of the younger children and lost her childhood.

A woman who becomes chronically ill has lost her health and her ability to do what she wants to do for her family. A mother who finds out her child has been abused feels the loss of her sense of being a "good" mother—she could not protect her child as all mothers should. She feels the loss of her child's innocence, and the loss of a normal childhood for that young one.

A family going through financial problems may be grieving the loss of their home or previous financial status. Someone who suffers with depression and anxiety has lost who they are. "I don't feel like myself," I often hear patients say. All of these are losses, and all of us feel grief at these losses.

Grief is actually a healing process. Allowing ourselves to grieve is the way we heal from loss.

We are often afraid of grieving, because the feelings seem so painful, but grieving is actually the way that we heal from trauma. Grief is the emotional suffering we feel after a loss of some kind. The grieving process consists of working through those emotions. During grief, it is common to have many conflicting feelings. Sorrow, anger, loneliness, sadness, shame, anxiety, and guilt often accompany serious losses. Having so many strong feelings can be very stressful.

Because we don't know how to deal with the strong feelings, we often avoid or ignore the feelings of the grieving process.

At another time of trauma in my life I was fortunate enough to be able to take a break from my work to deal with the grief. I was told by someone that the best thing for me to do to deal with the grief was to "get right back into your work and lose yourself in it." That is a very traditional viewpoint, because it does help a person avoid and possibly suppress the grief, but it usually doesn't help the person to work through the painful emotions. The pain and emotions of a severe loss will always be with us unless we feel them and work through them rather than suppress and avoid them.

When people, in their desire to help, suggest "looking on the bright side," or other ways of cutting off difficult feelings, the grieving person may feel pressure to hide or deny these emotions. Yet denying or suppressing the feelings, and failing to work through the grief, is harder on the body and mind than it is to go through them.

Many major illnesses, both physical and mental, come after a traumatic event or a severe loss. It takes longer for healing of mind and body to take place if the feelings are ignored or avoided. If the grieving has been suppressed and not processed, we can hold onto the pain for years, and actually develop physical illnesses from the suppressed grief.

The five stages of grief are:

1. ***Denial.*** "This can't be happening to me." There is no crying, no accepting or even acknowledging the loss. There may be a feeling of numbness, of no feelings whatsoever. This may last a few moments or quite a while. A person who has "disassociated" from their trauma is partially stuck in this state, because they often cannot even remember all or parts of the trauma, and so it is as if it didn't really happen.

2. ***Anger.*** "Why Me?" Anger is very normal to the grieving process; anger and blame towards someone else, anger at the person who died or left, anger at ourselves, anger at the world, displaced anger towards other loved ones, anger at God. Some people suppress this anger because it feels "wrong." Anger is only a problem if we use it to hurt another person. We must acknowledge and work through the anger within us or it will become stuck inside our subconscious mind and burst out at times towards other people when the pressure is too great.

    Some people use their anger for good, by changing conditions or creating organizations to reduce the chances of this trauma happening to others, or to help others who are suffering from the same trauma. This is good if the person doesn't use this to avoid feeling the anger or the pain, but as a way to work through it.

3. ***Bargaining.*** This is part of the "magical thinking." "If I change, will you stay?" "God, if I fast and pray enough, if I promise to do this or that, will you keep her from dying?" This step may take place before the loss, or during the drama of the loss. This may consist of attempting to make deals with the spouse who is leaving, or attempting to make deals with God to stop or change the loss. Begging, wishing, praying for the person to come back, or for God to make the pain stop, or for someone to make things all right, or for someone to take care of us.

4. ***Depression.*** "I can't survive this pain." This is one of the hardest stages to deal with, and the one that many people try to avoid and suppress because the feelings are so strong and difficult. The emotions consist of overwhelming feelings of hopelessness, frustration, bitterness, self pity, mourning the loss of person and/or the hopes, dreams and plans for the future. Often there is a feeling of lack of control, or feeling of numbness. There is a lack of motivation, and a loss of any enjoyment in life. Perhaps the person might feel suicidal.

A person may become stuck in this phase of grieving because they naturally avoid the painful feelings. The ways of avoiding this kind of pain are many and varied. Avoidance may come through constantly working or putting all energy into caring for the rest of the family. It may come from spending all of one's time in church work or spiritual quests. It may be through addictions, such as pain or anxiety pills or other drugs, pornography, food, or even exercise such as long distance running. It may be through escaping reality through psychosis. It may be through TV or video games, or spending every free moment on a hobby. Many of these activities are not inherently "bad," but when an activity is used to keep from having to be alone with our thoughts and feelings, when it is mood altering, it is avoidance.

Many feel that avoiding, such as throwing yourself into your work, is the best way to deal with a loss. You are doing something productive, what is wrong with that? Nothing is "wrong" with any of it. But suppressed emotions are always there. We can't run away from them. And if we don't feel them and deal with them now, they will affect our minds and our bodies in more difficult ways in the future.

Many feel that they have accepted the loss, that it hasn't affected them that much, or that they have gotten over it, because they have suppressed the feelings enough that they don't feel anything. This can only work for so long, however. Symptoms of mental or physical problems arise later, often years later, and it is difficult at that later time to see that the symptoms are related to the loss from some traumatic event years earlier.

5. *Acceptance.* "My loss is no longer painful." Acceptance is a process, and comes in steps. There are certain aspects of a loss that we can accept right away, and others that may take years to completely come to peace about. Because that is what acceptance is: finding peace from the good that can come out of the pain of loss, finding comfort and healing, being able to truly forgive and feel forgiven, and finally being able to let go of the pain. We come to accept this loss as part of the process of life,

and know that all is in divine order. We come to the knowledge that God is a loving God, and that He is not punishing us, but is with us to comfort us, lift us, carry our burdens and take away our pain, when we are finally able to let it go. There does come a time, if we have allowed ourselves to grieve, when we can think of the loss and not feel pain from it.

Each of the Steps of Grieving has an important purpose.

In my personal experience, I have found that if I skip feeling and working through any of these steps, those emotions will come back to haunt me later. For example, soon after my divorce, after much prayer and seeking, I decided to go on a mission, which ended up being a wonderful healing experience for me.

However, while I was in the MTC, I had a dream which woke me and caused me to be filled with anger. The rage was overwhelming. I knew that I could not be an effective missionary being filled with that kind of anger, and prayed all day for the anger to be lifted. I awoke the next morning with the anger gone, and for the most part didn't have to deal with it on my mission.

On my return home, I had taken in a young man as kind of a foster son. I soon found myself frequently exploding at him. I couldn't understand why I would be that way, because my nature is not generally angry. But I couldn't control it. I spent quite a bit of time in prayer, asking where this anger was coming from. The words came to my mind: "Remember when you asked for the anger to be lifted? Well, now is the time to feel it."

I realized I still had to go through the anger part of grieving. The Lord had lifted it for the duration of the mission, but He knew the importance of experiencing it. So He let it return. Once I knew what it was, I could see how some of the actions of this young man triggered memories of my ex-husband from the past, bringing up the anger.

Seeing this, I no longer needed to be angry at him. I allowed myself time to purposely feel anger towards my ex-husband, myself, and sometimes even God, until it finally passed. Then I was eventually able to let the pain go and forgive myself and him. I was finally able to enter the acceptance stage.

The next chapter will assist you in learning how to work through your own grieving process.

* *Eighth Rule of the Mind: The greater the conscious effort, the less the subconscious response.* *

The more effort you exert in fighting the grief, in trying to suppress it or will it away, the less the subconscious mind will be able to work through it. The more you accept the feelings and allow them to be and allow yourself to feel them, the better ability the subconscious mind has to heal them.

Chapter 13

The Only Way Around Grief Is to Go Through It

How do we deal with truly painful and overwhelming feelings of loss and grief? How do we keep from getting lost in them? How do we allow grief to heal us rather than tear us apart?

There are many ways of working through grief, and sometimes each person has to find their own way. However, some of the steps below may assist you with your own process of healing from trauma.

1. *Remember who you REALLY are.*

   We sing from the time we are in Nursery "I Am a Child of God." We are taught this from childhood for a reason. Knowing who we really are is the most influential lesson we can learn in this life. It changes our perspective towards everything.

We know intellectually that we are children of God, but so often it is hard to really connect with who this true offspring of God is, or even recognize that we are something way beyond this mortal, weak shadow of our true selves.

We can understand and appreciate the condescension of God, when Jesus Christ, a God Himself, became a mortal man, choosing not only to die but to descend below all things to redeem us.

But we often forget the condescension of man. We each are glorious spirits, true offspring of a Heavenly Father and a Heavenly Mother. We are eternal beings who also chose to become weak, mortal beings for this grand experience called earth life. With the veil drawn, all we know is this weak being we are right now. But this weak being is just a small piece of the magnificence of who we truly are.

"'I am a child of God' is not an idle or meaningless statement. You were there 'when the morning stars sang together, and all the sons [and daughters] of God shouted for joy' (Job 38:7). You brought some of that inheritance with you when you came "trailing clouds of glory ... from God who is our home" (William Wordsworth). ...You were among those who chose to follow the plan of Him who became our Redeemer rather than the plan of him who became our adversary. Great and marvelous is your place in the plan of God our Eternal Father" (Gordon B. Hinkley). (29)

As I have said before, but choose to repeat, we are baby gods. Just as a colt is a baby horse, and a tadpole is a baby frog, we may seem different from our Heavenly Parents but we have every capacity to become what They are, and that truly is Their greatest desire for us. We are Light. We have darkened ourselves to become mortal and to be able to experience the opposite of what God is, and the opposite of what we really are.

Often our weaknesses are the opposite of our true gifts. Consider that in your own life—do you see this principle? We truly are experiencing the opposite of who we really are, the glorious spirit offspring of God.

If you are struggling with seeing yourself in this light, I encourage you to read my book *Healing from the Heart: the Inherent Power to Heal from Within*. Chapter one, along with the guided imagery CD, will assist you in finding that incredible You that you are.

When you can truly grasp the concept of your own magnificence, it gives a different perspective on the traumas of life. It is easier to get out of the drama and to see the bigger picture. The pain is still there, but it becomes easier to see the pain for what it is—an experience that is for our learning on this earth.

When we truly know that we are precious daughters of Heavenly Parents who love us with a perfect love, we can better trust that all is in divine order. We can trust that *"all these things shall give thee experience, and shall be for thy good"* (D&C 122:7).

2. *Accept the feelings as a normal and natural part of grieving.*

   Often we believe that if we are feeling negative emotions for a long time something must be wrong, or that we are wrong. The emotions of grieving are a normal and natural part of mortality. Accept them as such. Know that it takes time for the grieving process, and some of the emotions may come in and out for months, or sometimes even years. It can take up to five years to work through the emotions of losing a spouse. All of this is normal.

3. *Take time to feel the emotions.*

   There is often a fear that if we allow ourselves to feel, we will get lost in the difficult emotions. However, the truth is that it is much easier to get lost in those hard feelings if we try to suppress them rather than if we deliberately allow ourselves to feel them.

   I encourage my patients to actually set aside time every day or every few days to just feel. Find a private place and set the timer for 15 minutes. Allow yourself to feel whatever emotion has been coming up—sadness, anger, betrayal, loneliness, unloved, etc. If it comes up and you are able to, cry, yell into your pillow, beat your fists on the bed, or anything else that allows your body to be involved in feeling as well. Then, when the timer goes off, you can stop, or you may choose to continue until the feelings are spent. Then move on to the next step.

   There were times in my grieving when I couldn't seem to feel anything, when I was numb. During those times I would watch a sad movie to deliberately cry, or listen to an angry song that fit my feelings at the time, just to get myself to feel something. I knew it was important to feel to work through my grief.

4. ***Follow the times of feeling negative emotions with something that lifts your heart.***

When depression hits it seems like there is nothing enjoyable to life anymore. However, it is important to continue to do things that used to make you feel good, especially after allowing yourself to feel the difficult emotions. After the difficult emotions have been spent for that moment, it is important to fill up with light the places in your mind and heart where the darkness was, or the darkness will just return again to fill you up.

> *When an unclean spirit is gone out of a man, he walked through dry places, seeking rest, and findeth none.*
>
> *Then he saith, I will return into my house from whence I came out, and when he is come, he findeth it empty...*
>
> *Then goeth he, and taketh with himself seven other spirits more wicked than himself, and they enter in and dwell there... (Matthew 12:43–45).*

It is important that we don't just leave ourselves empty after we have felt and released the dark emotions. It is important to fill up those dark places with things and feelings of light so that when the darkness returns it cannot return to the same state it was before.

Make a list of things that lift your spirit and are enjoyable, or things that used to do so, if you currently cannot find anything enjoyable. I encourage you to make a list, because some things work for some times but usually not all times. Reading the scriptures at times lifted me, and at other times I couldn't focus on them. There were even other times when all I could see was negative in them.

Some of the things from my list that I would do after I had released difficult emotions:

- Watch a funny or romantic movie
- Call and talk to loved ones and friends
- Read a good, uplifting novel
- Crochet—or some other way to create
- Go for a walk and look for the beauty around me
- Go for a drive or a hike in nature
- Find a stream or lake or ocean to put my feet in
- Watch a silly TV show
- Write my thoughts and feelings in my journal
- Spend time with my grandchildren
- Take a hot, relaxing bubble bath
- Listen to music that uplifts me, or that I can sing along to
- Turn on the music and dance
- Play the piano or the violin
- Read the scriptures

- Pray a prayer of love and gratitude

- Exercise

- Do an anonymous act of service for a loved one

- Do an act of service for someone I don't know

- Write a gratitude list

When I was on my mission as the Area Medical Advisor for the South America South Area, the first Mother's Day after the divorce arrived. I didn't have a companion at that time and I awoke early feeling very lonely and sorry for myself. It was my first time alone on Mother's Day in 34 years.

So I allowed myself to have a pity party for a short time. I felt the loneliness and cried at my losses and the changes my life had taken and the unfulfilled expectations.

Then I tried reading the scriptures, but all I could find were messages of how much of a failure I was. When we are in that frame of mind, it is easy to lose the uplifting spirit that the scriptures can hold.

So I pulled out a notebook and started writing a gratitude list. I wrote all of the big and obvious things down, but I wasn't feeling better yet. Then I wrote about the little things, like hot water for my shower, which a lot of people in the slums of Argentina didn't have, and a comfortable bed, and sunsets, and glasses so I could see, which many couldn't afford. I started writing down individual missionaries that I was working with, and how they blessed me. Then I started listing the "negative" things that had happened to me and how I had become a better person because of them. I continued on and on for over an hour, my list numbering over 200, until I finally was feeling the gratitude I was writing about. In fact, I felt very good, and really enjoyed my Mother's Day.

5. *Repeat this process—feel the dark emotions and then fill yourself with light—again and again.*

For serious losses, one time of feeling is not going to complete the process. There are many different things that will come up, and many times the same thing will come again and again. It is not that we are just repeating the same old thing all over again. Usually we are dealing with a different aspect of the same thing, though the feelings may be the same.

Don't get discouraged. I know that I had to deal with difficult emotions for up to five years after my divorce, though with time those feelings came less and less often. But when they did come I knew that it was important to allow them, to feel them so they could let go, and then to do something that uplifted me and filled me with good feelings.

6. *Take time to be outward focused; give service from the space of love.*

Often with severe depression or anxiety, we don't feel well enough to do much of anything. In fact, it is often a source of pain that we cannot serve in the way we would wish to. However, there are many ways to serve, if we are open to all of the possibilities.

Start with your family. Even if you are having a hard time getting out of bed, you can write a short note of love and appreciation to a family member. Now that everyone has cell phones, you can communicate a kind thought or word by phone or text, even if they are in the next room. Don't expect anything in return from them. Just do it because you love them.

If you are able to function, consider doing an anonymous act of service for a neighbor, or even sign up for some volunteer work. Being outward focused allows us to increase the feel-good chemicals in our brains, if we are acting simply from a space of love and not from a sense of obligation, and not from a space of "should" or "have to," or with an expectation that we will receive gratitude or respect or favors in return.

Give for no reason. Give because you love. Give wisely. Give anonymously.

Unless you are doing an anonymous act, always ask if you can assist the person before you give. Ask how you can assist them.

There is always a way to give, no matter what circumstance you are in. Ask in prayer and the Lord will show you how.

Chapter 14

Victim vs. Victorious

All of us could be considered victims.

When bad things happen to us we become a "victim." We are a victim of abuse, a victim of a natural disaster, a victim of an illness, a victim of a crime, a victim of fraud, a victim of an accident, a victim of someone else's behavior.

Being a victim implies that we have no choice in what happens to us. It breeds fear because if something bad happens without our choice, through no cause of our own, then it could happen again. The experience which causes one to become a victim may become the focus of obsessive thoughts and negative feelings. The future becomes foreboding, and anxiety takes hold. Being a victim increases the risk of anxiety and depression.

We cannot always avoid the bad things that happen to us.

In some situations it really does seem as if storms are raging and waves are crashing over us without any control of our own. We may feel that we are drowning in an ocean without a life raft and with no ability to save ourselves.

Natural disasters happen without our choice. Abuse happens without our choice. Other people's actions can cause major problems for us without our choice.

Considering ourselves a victim stops our progression.

There are times when things happen to us that are out of our control. But becoming a "victim" of that experience only keeps us from moving forward. The highest good is to learn how to float over the waves rather than let them crash on us. The highest good is to see that God will provide a rescue ship for us, but in the meantime we may need to learn how to swim. When we see that we can be in charge of our own lives and how we choose to perceive things no matter what happens to us, we cease to be a victim and become victorious.

The Law of the Harvest teaches us how to change.

The Law of the Harvest states that what we sow, we reap. What seeds we plant, and what soil they fall on, determines the harvest that we receive. The Law of the Harvest is true in our own lives. What we think, how we feel, how we act at one point in time yields results immediately or later in our lives.

What we put out eventually comes back to us. If we spend a lot of time in anger, our harvest will be more things to be angry about. If we think constant negative thoughts, depression results. If we are constantly full of fear and worry, we become anxious. If we love without expectation, we feel loved, no matter what the people around us are doing. If we feel like a victim, we may continue to be victimized. If we choose to let go of pain and forgive, we receive peace.

Susan was a victim of her husband's behavior.

Susan was a widow, dealing with depression. I thought, when she first came to see me, that maybe she was struggling over dealing with the loss of her husband, but she responded, "My life without him is so much better than my life was with him." I asked her to explain.

Susan felt the pressure of living in the "high society" of community and church leadership. Her husband was a successful businessman that ran in the "high society" circles. He had been called to multiple leadership positions.

Susan's husband loved to play golf, and would often go off with his buddies to play. In their early marriage he would often leave her to care for their young children alone while he played, which she resented.

As they grew older and he was in leadership positions, he would often invite people over for dinner parties. He would be gone all day while she prepared the meal, cleaned the house, dealt with the kids, and got the party ready. After the party he and his friends would leave to go off to some activity, leaving her to clean everything up by herself.

On top of that, her husband had been what she considered a horrible speaker. She was embarrassed when he spoke, so she started writing all of his talks. He would go off with his friends while she would write his talks. She was full of resentment towards him for playing while she worked for him, and that resentment did not stop after he died.

There were many other things her husband did that brought distress to Susan. She felt like a victim to her husband's behavior. She felt like she had no choice but to do the dinners and write his talks when all he would do is go off and leave her to play with his buddies.

I asked her why she gave the dinner parties if he refused to help. She stated that she wanted to give the guests a good time, and she really did enjoy having them over. She just resented the fact that he wouldn't help.

I asked her why she wrote the talks if he was never there to help her. She answered that she didn't want to be embarrassed when he gave a poor talk.

We are always "at choice."

I pointed out that during these times she was always "at choice," able to make a different choice. She could have not had the parties, but she chose to have them anyway because she enjoyed them—and she would be embarrassed if she didn't have a wonderful party. She could have stopped writing his talks, but it was more important to her not to be embarrassed because he gave a poor talk.

It was very important for her to see that she chose to do those things. She was never forced to do those things, even though she believed at the time that she had no choice. He wanted her to do those things, but she finally agreed that he never forced her to do them.

He did not help her, and it probably would have been better if he had, but she had no choice over that. Her feelings are not unusual and may have been justified. However, resenting her husband for things that she was choosing to do only made her unhappy. He was off having fun and she was choosing to be unhappy.

If she had chosen not to do those things for him, if she had chosen to do something fun instead of working while he was gone, he may possibly have seen what a problem they were for her; he may then have had reason to give some of his time and attention to assisting her. Or he may not have, and was fine living with the consequences.

If she had chosen to do those things for him, but had viewed them as giving service to him simply because she loved him, or saw that she was doing them because she enjoyed giving the parties and liked people to feel her husband was a good speaker, she may have been much happier. But she will never know, because she always did them while full of resentment, blaming her husband for her unhappy life.

Susan was sowing the seeds of resentment and blame. She received the harvest of an unhappy marriage and depression.

The mind of the "natural man" (woman) blames others for her unhappiness.

It would be easy to say that this was all her husband's fault. It was true that he did things that weren't best for their relationship. It would have been better if he had been there for her more, and showed her that he cared for her more, and sacrificed for her as she was for him. But he didn't, and she chose to stay with him. She allowed his behavior to determine her happiness or lack thereof.

Luckily, Susan was able to see that she could have done things differently. She did the best she knew how to do at the time, but she can now see that it is possible if she had made different choices, and if she had chosen to view these experiences differently at the time, she wouldn't have had to be unhappy her entire married life. She can now see that she chose to be a victim. Learning how she could have created different results in the past is now helping her deal with problems in her current relationships.

This isn't about blame. Susan isn't to blame for her choices. She didn't have enough knowledge or ability at the time to make different choices. It wouldn't have served Susan if she started beating herself up for her choices of the past. But looking back and seeing that she had the possibility of making different choices in the past allows her to move forward into greater joy now.

The mind of the natural man chooses to be a victim to other's behaviors.

I have found both in my own life and in the lives of many of my patients that we wives tend to feel victimized by our spouse's or our children's behavior. Depression is worsened because our spouse or child doesn't do the things we feel they should to make us happy, or they do things which we don't want them to, which makes us unhappy. We tend to have an irresistible urge to focus on how our spouse or child should be changing to increase our personal happiness.

We cannot make another person change. We can only, with much effort, change ourselves.

But the truth is, *we can never change someone else*. It is hard enough to change ourselves. We seem to believe that if a person loved us enough, they would change for us. But no one can change for another person, only for themselves, as they begin to see that their behavior is not working for them because of the results that it causes.

We can't change anyone but ourselves. If our spouse isn't doing what we want, we can express to him what we do want, but we can't expect him to change. It may be good to lovingly communicate our feelings, and he may be able to change because he now knows what we want, but possibly his weaknesses may keep him from changing at this time. All *we* can do is change our perspective about it. All we can do is begin to plant different seeds.

True happiness is not created by our circumstances, but by our own choices.

True happiness doesn't come from outside circumstances or from other people. I have seen people in other countries in abject poverty, and they are happy. I have seen people with horrible deformities, and they are happy. I have seen people go through incredible tragedies, and they are happy.

Happiness doesn't come from what happens to us or how people treat us. It comes from within. Of course life is easier when the people around us are loving and helpful. Of course it is easier to feel good when life is easy and abundant and people are kind. But that isn't the experience most of us have in mortality. We are here to experience the opposite of what God is; the opposite of love, and our weaknesses and the weaknesses of the people around us will cause life to be harder than we would like it.

True happiness comes because we choose to be happy no matter what happens around us—because we learn how to love ourselves and others without expectation. True happiness comes when we plant seeds of positive and optimistic thoughts, feelings of love without expectation, and actions of service from the space of love.

Happy thoughts and feelings often don't come automatically. Negative, fearful, angry, and irritated thoughts and feelings may come more naturally, because we are in mortality experiencing the natural man. But when the negative thoughts and feelings come we can either hook into them and stay stuck in negativity, or we can do the work of changing them.

The mind of the natural man sows seeds of anger, resentment and fear.

The natural man, or the ego mind, wants to be angry and get even, and say it's not fair. The natural mind thinks angry, judgmental and depressed thoughts. The natural man blames others and feels like a victim to other's behaviors.

The spiritual mind desires to communicate with love, inspire change with love, and accept with love what cannot be changed. The spiritual mind gives others the benefit of the doubt, and doesn't take things personally. The spiritual mind looks at herself honestly when someone else complains, changes what can be changed, and lets go of what cannot be changed or what she hasn't yet learned how to change.

Madeline learned that changing the seeds she plants results in a better harvest.

Madeline also was dealing with constant negative feelings about her husband. She felt that he treated her poorly, had no respect for her, and got angry too easily. She was also depressed and chronically ill. Her negative feelings about her husband had affected her body and her mind.

I told Madeline that if she wanted to feel better and begin to heal, she would either need to accept her husband and love him as he is, or leave him.

"You mean I have a choice?" she asked. "We've been married in the temple. I didn't think I could leave."

"We always have a choice," I answered. "A temple marriage does not always mean eternal marriage unless we create an eternal marriage. If you truly hate him as much as you state, is that truly an eternal marriage?"

Madeline left my office excited at the prospect of having a choice. She promised to go home and pray about what was for the highest good.

When Madeline returned, she was still excited. She felt that her answer was that she was to stay with her husband, and knew if that was what God wanted her to do, that she could learn to be happy in her marriage.

We worked on triggers from her childhood that caused her to be hurt by things her husband did and said. We worked on her ability to see his actions and reactions from a different perspective. We worked on her ability to not take it personally when he was angry or disrespectful, as this was his problem, and not hers. We worked on her true desire to be the best wife she could be. We worked on assisting her to let go of being a victim to her husband's behavior and simply build her own life of happiness. We did not work on changing her husband, because we have no ability to change anyone else's behavior.

However, after a couple of months, Madeline came in quite amazed. She told me that her husband was starting to treat her better. Because she was learning to love and respect herself, and because she didn't respond with anger to his "emotional abuse," his reactions to her started changing. She was planting different seeds and getting a different harvest.

No major miracle happened, he didn't change his core personality, there were still things he did which bothered her, but she was learning how to be happy in spite of it all, and there were positive changes all around.

"Reframing" an experience can allow a victim to become victorious.

Betty, at the age of nine, was walking home from school when a man grabbed her, pulled her into the bushes, threw her on the ground, and raped her. She did not tell her parents, because she felt they wouldn't believe her and would blame her. She held this secret in her heart, becoming a victim, and it ate at her. She became depressed and anxious, and eventually was diagnosed with bipolar disease. This event became hidden in the back of her mind, and as an adult she did not really recognize that it may have been the cause of her emotional issues.

As long as Betty believed she was a victim, she remained in the frame of mind that she would always be victimized. In her mind, she became victimized by her family, friends, husband, and her own illness. She believed she had no choice in living her life, but was a victim to how people treated her and to her own depression and anxiety, and to the diagnosis of bipolar disease.

This was not her fault. It was the belief that was created in her mind when she was forcibly raped as a child. However, as adult, Betty learned how to remember the emotions of that horrible incident, let them go, and move forward.

We did a technique with Betty that allowed her to go back in her imagination and reframe what happened. Even though as a nine-year-old she didn't know how to get out of what happened to her, as an adult she recognized that if she had been able to scream and kick, she was close enough to houses and people that it might have frightened the man into leaving. We don't actually know what would have happened if she had done that, but in her imagination, becoming that little girl once again, she kicked and screamed, and the man ran away. She felt more powerful, and she no longer felt like a victim. That little girl stuck inside of her subconscious mind felt more powerful.

The imagination is very powerful. The brain cannot tell the difference between imagining something with feeling and actually doing it. This technique of reframing a past experience, under professional guidance, can change the emotional attachment to that experience, and remove the feeling of being a victim.

Now Betty has learned that she is always "at choice." She has learned the Law of the Harvest: that what she sows, she shall reap. She has learned that if she doesn't like her current harvest, she can look at what seeds she was planting in the past that created that harvest. And she can learn to change what seeds she chooses to plant, and what type of soil she uses to plant them in (see *Healing from the Heart*, chapter 2).

Betty could not have prevented the horrible abuse that happened to her. In no way was that abuse her fault. But she can choose to see that, if she had known, she may have done it differently. Most children submit to abuse out of fear of what will happen if they say no. Of course, as a young child, that belief is normal and natural. That little child didn't know that she had any choice at the time, and it was not her fault that she didn't make that choice. She is not at fault for what happened to her in any way.

But just knowing, as an adult, that she could have made a different choice is one the ways that may allow her to pull out of being a victim, because now that "little girl Betty" inside knows that she doesn't have to submit to that again. By imagining herself as a little child kicking and screaming, and imagining that the man gives up and lets her go, that little child within can feel more powerful. It changes the mind pattern that was created because of the abuse. It allows her to stop being a victim and to be "at choice."

Because Betty was able to let go of being a victim of the past, she began to learn that she was not a victim of how the people around her acted. She did not need to react to their words or behavior, but could choose her own actions from the space of love. How different are her experiences with her family and friends now! She has learned how to plant different seeds to be able to receive a better harvest.

There are truly times when we are not "at choice" with what happens to us, but we are "at choice" as to how we perceive it and what we choose to do about it.

Even if Betty had kicked and screamed, she may have been raped anyway. She would have had no choice in the matter. When people are bigger and stronger and have physical power over us, we have no choice. These things are horrible, and not to be taken lightly. However, Betty has chosen to look at that time in her life from a different perspective, and has grown from it.

When there is a natural disaster, there are many things we can choose to do to strive to keep ourselves and our families safe. If a tornado is coming, we can seek shelter in a basement or an inner closet. If a tsunami is coming we can seek higher ground. Often we are given spiritual promptings that something is wrong and we can listen to those promptings.

However, we may still have harm come to us, to our loved ones, and to our property. My family lost our house to a fire. We have no choice in what happens to us in those situations. These are horrible things and we will naturally feel grief and pain. However, we can feel the grief and work through it and come out stronger rather than staying stuck in the grief. We can choose to view it as a very difficult but growing part of life rather than something that ruined us forever.

When we can let go of being a victim, of being a doormat, of being a martyr, we will no longer allow ourselves to be abused and used. When we let go of the belief that whatever happened to us has ruined our lives and we can never be the same again, we can begin to grow and move forward. Anger and depression are natural parts of grieving, but when we learn to work through and let go of the pain and anger, we can choose to plant different seeds and receive a harvest of joy.

✳ *First rule of the subconscious mind: What is expected tends to be realized.* ✳

If we see ourselves as a victim of one thing, often we see ourselves as victims of many things, such as victims to the behavior of others, and we tend to be victimized again and again.

If we can work through and let go of being a victim, or if something bad happens to us we don't view ourselves as a victim but view the experience as something to learn and grow from, we stop being victimized.

Section 3:

Healing
with the
Master Healer

Chapter 15

Healing through the Gospel of Jesus Christ

God and Jesus know our pain, our suffering, and our afflictions.

And he shall go forth, suffering pains and afflictions and temptations of every kind; and this that the word might be fulfilled which saith he will take upon him the pains and the sicknesses of his people.

And he will take upon him death, that he may loose the bands of death which bind his people; and he will take upon him their infirmities, that his bowels may be filled with mercy, according to the flesh, that he may know according to the flesh how to succor his people according to their infirmities (Alma 7:11–12).

Jesus declared that He is the Healer.

In the synagogue, Jesus announced who He was by reading aloud this prophecy of Isaiah: *'He hath anointed me to preach the gospel to the poor; he hath sent me to heal the brokenhearted, to preach deliverance to the captives, and recovering of sight to the blind, to set at liberty them that are bruised...'* (Luke 4:18).

Jesus healed all who came to Him.

When Jesus appeared in the New World, He asked all to come forward who were lame or blind or had other physical ailments.

> *"Bring them hither and I will heal them" (3 Nephi 17:7). Jesus "did heal them every one" (v. 9).*

All healing comes through the Atonement of Jesus Christ.

> *The Savior teaches that we will have tribulation in the world, but we should 'be of good cheer' because He has 'overcome the world' (John 16:33). His Atonement reaches and is powerful enough not only to pay the price for sin but also to heal every mortal affliction....*
>
> *He knows of our anguish, and He is there for us. Like the good Samaritan in His parable, when He finds us wounded at the wayside, He binds up our wounds and cares for us (see Luke 10:34). Brothers and sisters, the healing power of His Atonement is for you, for us, for all (Dallin H. Oaks).* (31)

Then why I am not yet healed?

For all the pleading in your prayers, for all of the healing blessings you have been given, for all the times your name has been put in the temple, why are you not yet healed? If Christ healed "every one," then what happened to you?

If the atonement gives you the power to heal from your infirmities, from your depression, from your anxiety, from the scars of abuse, from the pain of divorce, from the grief of the loss of a parent or spouse or child, from the fears and worries about loved ones who are seriously struggling, then how do you access that power?

What does the Gospel of Jesus Christ really consist of?

When you hear that healing comes through living the Gospel of Jesus Christ, what comes to mind? What does living the Gospel mean to you? Do you picture going to church every Sunday, paying your tithing faithfully, living the Word of Wisdom, accepting and fulfilling callings in the Church? Do you picture reading the scriptures daily, having Family Home Evening, family prayer daily, and personal prayer at least twice a day?

All of these are very important ways to assist us in better living the Gospel, but they are not the basic Gospel of Jesus Christ. These things are given to us by inspiration and revelation to help us grow closer to God and learn more of Him. They provide ways for us to be blessed, and they assist in increasing our faith, but they are not the basic Gospel of Jesus Christ. The Gospel of Jesus Christ, as presented by Him to the New World after His death and resurrection, is very simple.

Jesus Christ declared Himself as the God and Savior of the world, establishing the Nephite's faith in Him.

When Jesus descended from Heaven after his resurrection and appeared to the Nephites and Lamanites, He introduced Himself as Jesus Christ, the Savior of the world, saying, *"I have drunk out of that bitter cup which the Father hath given me, and have glorified the Father in taking upon me the sins of the world, in the which I have suffered the will of the Father in all things from the beginning"* (3 Nephi 11:11).

He then took the time to have each individual present come and feel the wound in his side and feel the prints in his hands and feet, *"that ye may know that I am the God of Israel and the God of the whole earth, and have been slain for the sins of the world"* (3 Nephi 11:14).

By doing this, Jesus increased their faith in Him and in His role as their God and their Savior. He introduced the first principle of the gospel, **"Faith in the Lord Jesus Christ."**

Jesus taught them to repent and gave authority to baptize.

Jesus then called forth Nephi and others, and gave them power to baptize. He taught them exactly what baptism consisted of, saying, *"On this wise shall ye baptize; and there shall be no disputations among you.*

> *Verily I say unto you, that whoso repenteth of his sins through your words, and desireth to be baptized in my name, on this wise shall ye baptize them—Behold, ye shall go down and stand in the water, and in my name shall ye baptize them (3 Nephi 11:22–23).*

He then taught them the words to say and the manner by which they should be baptized. By doing this, Jesus taught the second and third principles of the gospel, **"Repentance"** and **"Baptism by immersion for the remission of sins."**

Jesus doesn't want us to argue over the points and interpretation of His doctrine, but to do away with contention and arguing.

Jesus then made a point to declare that it is important NOT to argue over doctrine. This was the third thing He did after appearing to the people, so it must have been very important to him. Through this He taught another point of His doctrine, to **"love one another."**

> *And there shall be no disputations among you, as there have hitherto been; neither shall there be disputations among you concerning the points of my doctrine, as there have hitherto been.*
>
> *For verily, verily I say unto you, he that hath the spirit of contention is not of me....*
>
> *Behold, this is not my doctrine, to stir up the hearts of men with anger, one against another; but this is my doctrine, that such things should be done away (3 Nephi 11:28–30).*

"I will declare unto you my doctrine."

Jesus then taught them what His doctrine is.

> *And this is my doctrine...that the Father commandeth all men, everywhere, to **repent** and **believe in me**.*
>
> *And whoso believeth in me, and is **baptized**, the same shall be saved; and they are they who shall inherit the kingdom of God (3 Nephi 11:32–33).*

Again, Jesus teaches **faith** in Him, **repentance**, and **baptism**. He continues:

*Verily, verily I say unto you, that this is my doctrine, and I bear record of it from the Father; and whoso **believeth in me** believeth in the Father also; and unto him will the Father bear record of me, for **he will visit him with fire and with the Holy Ghost** (3 Nephi 11:35).*

Thus He taught the fourth principle of the Gospel, **"receiving the gift of the Holy Ghost."**

He then repeats His doctrine several times:

*And again, I say unto you, ye must **repent**, and **become as a little child**, and **be baptized** in my name, or ye can in nowise receive these things.*

He adds **"become as a little child"** to his doctrine, and repeats it again.

*And again I say unto you, ye must **repent**, and **be baptized** in my name, and **become as a little child**, or ye can in nowise inherit the kingdom of God (3 Nephi 11:37–38).*

Jesus then declares that this is the simplicity of His doctrine, and we should not add or take away from these simple principles.

Verily, verily, I say unto you, that this is my doctrine, and whoso buildeth upon this buildeth upon my rock, and the gates of hell shall not prevail against them.

And whoso shall declare more or less than this, and establish it for my doctrine, the same cometh of evil, and is not built upon my rock but he buildeth upon a sandy foundation... (3 Nephi 11:39–40).

The Gospel of Jesus Christ is simple.

We believe that the first principles and ordinances of the Gospel are: first, **Faith in the Lord Jesus Christ**; *second,* **Repentance**; *third,* **Baptism** *by immersion for the remission of sins; fourth, Laying on of hands for the* **gift of the Holy Ghost** *(Joseph Smith, Fourth Article of Faith).*

These principles and ordinances are the things, along with "**become as a little child,**" and "do away with disputations among you" (or in other words, "**love one another,**") that Jesus declared to be His doctrine. These six things are the principles and doctrine of the Gospel of Jesus Christ. Everything else is given to us to assist us in living these six important principles.

But how does the Gospel of Jesus Christ allow us to heal?

The next chapters will look at each principle individually, and how we may use them in our healing process.

✳ Sixth Law of the Subconscious Mind: Every thought or idea causes a physical reaction, or a chemical response. ✳

By substituting our negative thoughts with thoughts concerning faith, repentance, baptism and the sacrament, becoming as a little child, and loving one another, our bodies and minds will respond with healing.

Chapter 16

Healing through Faith in the Lord Jesus Christ

What is faith in the Lord Jesus Christ, the first principle of the Gospel?

Faith is talked about constantly in the Church, but it sometimes seems to be such a nebulous concept that it is difficult to grasp what "having faith" really entails. We have the oft quoted scripture below, but what does it mean?

> *And now, I, Moroni, would speak somewhat concerning these things; I would show unto the world that faith is things which are hoped for and not seen; wherefore, dispute not because ye see not, for ye receive no witness until after the trial of your faith (Ether 12:6).*

Faith requires hope and action.

I would like to add to that definition of faith: **"things which are hoped for and not seen,"** *but are acted upon as if they are true.*

The following is what constitutes faith in the Lord Jesus Christ: the great majority of us have never seen Jesus, but we have hope that He lived, suffered and died for us as our Savior, that we may be free of the effects of our mistakes. We have hope that those we hurt will also be free from the effects of our mistakes as well, in the end.

By living our lives as if this is true, by doing our best to trust in Him and His plan for us, by repenting and trusting that our sins are forgiven, by doing our best to learn how to love one another, we are exhibiting faith in Christ.

> *The fundamental principles of our religion are the testimony of the Apostles and Prophets, concerning Jesus Christ, that He died, was buried, and rose again the third day, and ascended into heaven; and all other things which pertain to our religion are only appendages to it (Joseph Smith). (32)*

Hoping that this is true is not enough. **When we truly act on that hope** by repenting and striving to love ourselves and others more, as Jesus does, **it becomes faith**. Through that faith we will find that our burdens become easier to bear and the stresses of our lives seem lighter.

Our hearts, minds and bodies are affected by the guilt and pain we hold related to our weaknesses and mistakes. We are also affected by the weaknesses and mistakes of others.

We often hold great anxiety and guilt over our own past mistakes. We may have fear about making decisions because we might make the wrong decision. We feel pain from what others have done which has affected us negatively.

We often fear for our loved ones, sometimes to the point of over-controlling, because of fear that they might have to experience pain from their own or other's mistakes. All of this has a profound effect on the feelings of our hearts, the thoughts of our minds, and the health of our bodies.

Physical and emotional illness often comes because of the chemicals that come from long-term stress having a negative effect on our bodies and minds. Some of the greatest stress that Mormon women deal with is the guilt from their own weaknesses and mistakes.

Dealing with weaknesses on this earth is part of the Plan of Happiness.

As God is Love, and the opposite of love is fear, we want to let go of fear and learn true charity, the pure love of Christ. If our souls only knew love and peace, and never knew pain and heartache, we would not be able to gain insight or truly appreciate the value of these positive feelings. *A soul grows to become like God by working to overcome all negative emotions connected to fear.*

Without weaknesses we would not experience the negative emotions and fear that allow us to grow. Our weaknesses are part of the purpose of this earth life, to experience the opposite of what God is, so that we can learn to become more like Him. God gave us our weaknesses for a purpose, so feeling guilty over them is not god-like. Feeling godly remorse is important, as will be seen as we discuss repentance in the next chapter, but that is different from guilt.

Jesus Christ is the reason we don't have to feel guilty, and the way to let go of pain.

Because we came to this earth with weaknesses to experience the "opposites," we were preprogrammed to fall, to make mistakes. That is why God sent His only begotten Son, not to condemn the world, but to save the world from sin. He doesn't condemn us, so there is no need to condemn ourselves.

Jesus, through His atoning sacrifice, provides the way for us to learn from our mistakes and the mistakes of those around us, and *yet be able to be perfect, through repentance*, so that we can again return to the presence of our Heavenly Parents. Because of His atoning sacrifice, we can choose to let go of the pain of mistakes from the past, either our own or those of others that caused us pain.

Being able to let go of our mistakes and our pain through the Atonement is "The Good News."

The word *gospel* means *good news.* This is the good news that we cannot see but we hope for: that Jesus Christ can actually "save" us from our mistakes and our pain, and from our negative and fearful thoughts and actions. This is the primary focus of our faith—that we can actually hope that we, each one of us personally and individually, can be made perfect through the Atonement of Jesus Christ, in each moment that we truly repent.

Having hope that the Lord Jesus Christ has that power to cleanse us allows us to use that power in every moment we realize we have made a mistake. **Living our lives based in that hope**, remembering and using that power through daily repentance with an increase in love for ourselves and others, **is faith.**

The Atonement of Jesus Christ also cleanses the effect our sins have on others.

Whenever we make a mistake, it has an effect not only on ourselves but on others. Everything we do, positive or negative, spreads out like ripples in a pond and has an effect on our fellow beings. We may strive to make things right again, but sometimes we don't have the power to take back the effects of something we said or did.

As mothers, we make many mistakes which affect our children. We may do our best, but our mortal weaknesses and our lack of knowledge will cause us to make mistakes. We are imperfect mothers. Our children will always be affected by our mistakes. This is part of the plan. But we often feel pain and guilt for what we have done that has caused pain in our children, our spouse, our parents and siblings and others, and we usually cannot resolve that pain for them.

The Good News is that the Atonement not only cleanses us from our sins, it also cleanses the results our sins create for others. They will not be held accountable for the effect of our sins, but only on the free choices they made themselves on how to deal with the problems in their lives. We can find peace as we have faith in the Lord Jesus Christ, that in the end all will be made right with those we have affected through our mistakes. We cannot see this, but we can hope that it is true, and living our lives from that hope becomes faith.

It is physically impossible to do all of the good things that we would like to do, or that others would like us to do.

Our lives are often so full of good things that are important to do that we cannot do them all with the time we have been given. I had the opportunity of being the sole caretaker for four of my grandchildren for nine months. One day I came home from work quite late and relieved the nanny, and my two-year-old granddaughter was vomiting. As I was trying to take care of her, my other grandchildren naturally wanted my time and attention. There was no physical way I could give each of them all that they needed.

Often when I am with a patient they have needs which take longer than expected, and yet the next patient on the schedule needs to be seen on time in order to make another appointment. There is no physical way possible for me to fulfill both of their needs.

I may discover that a friend could use my help, but I have visiting teaching scheduled. I may have planned to read my scriptures but a child starts crying. I may desire to exercise but then I would be late for work. If I get up earlier I won't get enough sleep. I may start to make a good breakfast for myself to keep myself healthy but I get a phone call from someone needing to talk. I may plan to clean my house but my daughter may need someone to babysit for her.

Asking, "What is for the highest good in this moment?" assists us in making difficult choices.

I have found in these situations that I cannot get everything done, that I cannot please everyone, that I cannot give as much as I would like to, that I must make choices and leave something out. In these situations I ask *"What is for the highest good in this moment?"* I listen and feel for the answer in my heart. I then do my best to choose to do that thing which is most important to do in the moment.

At times the highest good in that moment may be to sacrifice my needs to serve someone else. At other times the highest good may be to care of myself so that I have more energy and ability to serve others in the future.

The Atonement of Jesus Christ makes up the difference for what we cannot do ourselves.

In each situation, I then choose to trust that Jesus can make up the difference for what I cannot do. If, after asking, "What is the highest good in this moment?" I choose to take care of my sick granddaughter, I have to trust that the other children will be okay without my attention.

If I choose to spend the time with one patient, I have to trust that the other patient will be able to deal with their own situation without me. If I choose to serve a friend, I have to trust that the person I am supposed to visit teach will be served in some other way, or that I will be able to visit her some other time. If I choose to eat a good breakfast, so that I can keep my blood sugar stable and have better energy, I have to trust that the person on the phone will be taken care of without me.

The Atonement of Jesus Christ allows me to make decisions without fear.

This is the Good News, that through faith in the Lord Jesus Christ, I can do my best and trust that He will make up the difference for what I cannot do. If I make a mistake in my choices, He can also make up the difference for those mistakes, if my heart is truly desiring the highest good. And if I always ask, "What is for the highest good in this moment?" I can trust that if I *do* make a mistake, that the Lord will let me know in some way before I get too far down the wrong path.

This Good News allows me to move forward in making choices, to learn from them, and not to allow fear to keep me from making choices because I might make a mistake. This Good News allows me to say my little mantra, which I use all of the time, *"What gets done gets done, and what doesn't, doesn't, and it will all be good in the end."* By acting on this hope, that the atoning power can make up the difference for my weaknesses, it becomes faith, and the stress and worry in my life is lessened.

Faith is power. All miracles come through acting upon that which we hope for and believe are true, but do not see or know the results. Faith precedes the miracle.

Now faith is the substance of things hoped for, the evidence of things not seen...

*Through faith we understand that **the worlds were framed by the word of God**, so that things which are not seen were made of things which do appear...*

*By faith **Enoch was translated** that he should not see death...*

*By faith **Noah**, being warned of God of things not seen as yet,...**prepared an ark** to the saving of his house;...and became heir of righteousness which is by faith.*

*By faith **Abraham**, when he was called to go out into a place which he should after receive for an inheritance, obeyed; and he **went out, not knowing whither he went**...*

*Through faith also **Sara** herself **received strength to conceive seed**, and was delivered of a child when she was past age, because she judged him faithful who had promised...*

*By faith **Abraham**, when he was tried, **offered up Isaac**: and he that had received the promises offered up his only begotten son,*

Of whom it was said, That in Isaac shall thy seed be called:

Accounting that God was able to raise him up, even from the dead...

*Through faith [Moses] **kept the Passover**, and the sprinkling of blood, lest he that destroyed the firstborn should touch them.*

*By faith they **passed through the Red sea as by dry land**: which the Egyptians assaying to do were drowned.*

*By faith **the walls of Jericho fell down**, after they were compassed about seven days...*

*And what shall I more say? For the time would fail me to tell of **Gideon**, and of **Barak**, and of **Samson**, and of **Jephthae**: of **David** also, and **Samuel**, and of the prophets:*

*Who through faith **subdued kingdoms, wrought righteousness, obtained promises, stopped the mouths of lions,***

Quenched the violence of fire, escaped the edge of the sword, out of weakness were made strong, waxed valiant in fight, turned to flight the armies of the aliens.

Women received their dead raised to life again: and others were tortured, not accepting deliverance; that they might obtain a better resurrection... *(Hebrews 11).*

All of these, from Jesus Christ forming the worlds, to the many miracles and promises obtained through individuals, had the power to fulfill their purposes through faith in God and in Jesus Christ.

Having the hope that God would support them, that His promises to them were true, and that the inspiration and revelations they received were true, even though they couldn't see ahead of time the results, allowed them to act on that which they hoped for, but could not see. It allowed them to have faith. Miracles followed, because God did fulfill His promises and did support them in their desires and good works.

The healing power of Jesus Christ cannot be seen. But we can move forward with faith that He does have that healing power and we can be blessed by it.

We can receive the power to fulfill our purpose through faith.

When I went on my mission as Area Medical Advisor to Argentina my scripture theme was:

> *Trust in the Lord with all thine heart; and lean not unto thine own understanding.*
>
> *In all thy ways acknowledge him, and he shall direct thy paths (Proverbs 3:5–6).*

I went on my mission alone, three months after my divorce. I was given the responsibility for the health of all of the missionaries in Argentina, Paraguay and Uruguay. I had no companion for much of my mission. I didn't know Spanish well, and especially not the Argentine version of Spanish. I had to speak over the phone all day to Mission Presidents and their wives and to the missionaries, over half of which spoke only Spanish. I also had to speak to Argentine doctors.

I had no idea what my duties really were and had to wing it. I didn't know the Argentine health system, or how to deal with the hospitals and doctors there. I had many missionaries visiting me from the Buenos Aires area with medical problems. I had to learn to drive myself on the roads and highways when the Argentines kept no rules and didn't drive in the lanes, which was quite frightening for me.

I had left a family in crisis. Though they were all grown and married, they were each struggling with their parents' divorce in their own way. Their own marriages suffered, one daughter was on IVs with her pregnancy, another son couldn't find a job, and one daughter was suffering from severe depression.

Trust and Hope are the beginning of faith.

My own testimony was weak because of the loss of my own identity from the divorce. But I had again come to know that God lives and Jesus is my Savior. And I had received a witness that I was to go on a mission at that time. I knew that I had to trust and have hope in God and my Savior, that His atoning sacrifice would make up the difference for my weaknesses and my mistakes, for my lack of faith, lack of knowledge of what to do and lack of ability to speak Spanish.

I had to trust and have hope that He would make up the difference to my children and grandchildren when I wasn't available for them, to assist them through their problems, and when I couldn't be there for births and baptisms and all of the other important family events. I had to trust that the angels were with them, whispering to them, guiding them, lifting them better than I could were I there.

True faith causes us to act on that which we do not see or know.

I knew that it was important to act on the hope that this was true in order to receive the power to fulfill my purpose there. I chose to pick up the phone and speak to those on the other end in very broken Spanish, trusting that we would each understand from each other what was important to know. I chose to open my little office and run a practice with minimal equipment, trusting that the missionaries would benefit from my care.

I chose to venture onto the roads, trusting that the Lord would protect me and assist me back into the right direction when I got lost, which was daily (I called it my "daily adventure"). I chose to go out and speak at the zone meetings in my broken, child-like Spanish. My faith in the Lord's power to assist me even in my weaknesses grew with every action. In my own little way, I was Moses putting my staff in the waters, having faith that God would do the rest and part the Red Sea.

Faith precedes the miracles.

And, with time and patience, the miracles came. Missionaries got better. I became comfortable on the roads and lost my fear, and learned my way around large sections of Buenos Aires. I spoke and understood what was necessary to missionaries, Mission Presidents and their wives, doctors, etc. My broken Spanish in zone meetings was effective, as missionaries would open up to me about their physical and emotional problems later. I didn't always understand exactly what the missionaries were saying, but I was given the ability to understand what they needed. I was given inspiration to know when a health concern told over the phone was serious and needed attention, or was something that would take care of itself.

I was very weak, but the Lord made me strong. I was fearful, but the Lord gave me courage. I made mistakes, and the Lord forgave me and lifted me up when I fell down so that I could continue to move forward. The mission didn't always go smoothly; there were many problems as there always are, but the Lord gave me patience and wisdom to work through them or simply let the issues go.

Acting in faith is the power that creates miracles.

To receive those blessings I worked on creating the hope that He would be walking beside me and putting words in my mouth, and act on that hope by moving forward and doing the things I was asked to do, even though I absolutely did not have the capacity to do many of them on my own. By acting without knowing if I could, I was showing my faith, and this faith was a power that brought forth miracles.

I can do all things through Christ which strengtheneth me (Philippians 4:13).

My family survived without me. It was hard for them and for me to be apart, but they grew in their experiences. My experiences with the missionaries assisted me in better understanding and relating to my children. We loved each other even more when I returned, as we set about working to repair our broken family.

Faith brings the miracles. Hope that God's promises are true and acting as if they are true, even through the fear that our own weaknesses may cause us to fail, brings forth faith and miracles.

✱ *Second Rule of the Subconscious Mind: Imagination is more powerful than knowledge.* ✱

Act with faith and imagine that Christ and His angels are standing beside you, walking with you, guiding your words and actions, and taking care of you and others when you and they make mistakes and truly repent.

Chapter 17

How to Grow in Faith

Faith is weakened with depression and anxiety.

epression and anxiety generally cause a weakening of faith. That is because when one is depressed she is usually focusing on her own weaknesses and the weaknesses of others. The overactive deep limbic system and basal ganglia cause "automatic negative thinking," as Dr. Daniel Amen calls it (33). It takes a huge effort to create a positive thought. It is very difficult to have faith in ourselves, in others, and in God when all we can see is the negative.

I can't, but God can. God is bigger than the problem.

We do not have enough faith to overcome these problems by ourselves. If we did, we would be perfect by now. However, The Power higher than us can do for us what we cannot do for ourselves. Those who belong to Alcoholics Anonymous say "Let go and let God."

Faith in Christ allows us to believe that the atonement of Christ, the Love of God, the Light of Christ and the power of the Holy Spirit are more powerful than we are, are more powerful than our pain, our thoughts and feelings and our compulsions. Begin by having a desire to grow that much faith, faith that this power can heal us.

Begin to let go of believing you should be able to control the depression and anxiety, and whatever other problems you have. You cannot. Surrender the depression and anxiety to God. Surrender your lack of faith to God. Give it all to God and allow Him to take over. Do it now. "I cannot control this depression, this anxiety, God. I give it to You, because I believe that Your Power can take this away as I learn. I choose to have patience and believe that You can do this for me."

The things that often build faith may be hard to do when experiencing depression and anxiety.

Faith can be built by **reading the words of Christ and the prophets through the scriptures**, by **attending our meetings**, through **prayer**, by **obedience**, etc.

However, when a woman is dealing with depression and anxiety, she may find that she cannot focus on reading the scriptures. She may feel too unworthy to pray, or feel like she is not heard or her prayers are not answered. She may be unable to deal with large numbers of people and not attend meetings, and often things that are said in meetings may trigger her emotional pain. Often those experiencing depression and anxiety feel distant from God, and the things that normally increase faith may actually increase feelings of inferiority.

Faith comes by focusing on our strengths rather than focusing on our weaknesses.

However, there are still things that can be done to increase faith. By making the huge effort to **focus on our strengths**, faith begins to grow.

By **changing our minds** every time we recognize that we are beating ourselves up about our weaknesses, faith begins to grow. When we can make the supreme effort to **spend some time seeing the evidence of God in our lives**, faith begins to grow. When we can, through great effort, **make a gratitude list** of blessings that we have been given, even the blessings from the trial of depression and anxiety, faith begins to grow.

When we can, for a moment, **have hope that Christ has the power to heal** us, faith begins to grow. When we can **have hope that we are forgiven**, faith begins to grow. When we **have hope that God can give us an increase of love for others** that we are having problems with, faith begins to grow. When we **have a desire to forgive rather than hold pain in**, faith begins to grow. When we can, for a moment, **trust that God is directing our path** even when we can't see it, faith begins to grow.

Each little act of hope and trust, each little negative thought that has been changed into a positive one, each heartfelt kind word we say to ourselves and others, each moment of being forgiven and forgiving others builds our faith.

Each time we have **the courage to look into the mirror and say "I love you,"** even though it is incredibly hard, builds our faith. Each moment we walk outside and see the sunset and say, "**Thank you, God, for allowing me to see this beauty**," builds our faith. Every time we **seek to hear what another's spirit is trying to communicate to us** rather than being offended at what is coming out of their mouth, our faith grows.

Faith grows through gratitude.

When a person is truly feeling gratitude, they cannot stay focused in that part of the brain which causes depression and anxiety.

In every thing give thanks: for this is the will of God in Christ Jesus concerning you (1 Thessalonians 5:18).

I believe that when this scripture mentions "every thing," it includes those things we consider bad and hard as well as those things that bring us pleasure and joy.

If there is purpose to all things, if it is important to experience the "opposites" for us to be able to fulfill our purpose here, then it is possible to see that even the difficult times of our lives may be positive in the long run. "It's all good," a friend of mine keeps telling me, when I start complaining too much, and he is correct. It *is* **all** good. Every thing.

I define faith as the stubborn resolve to see God's goodness in everything that happens to us. (Wallace Goddard).

Start by considering the things that lift you and feel the gratitude for those things. Then consider all of the little details we take for granted in this country: hot water, indoor plumbing, a home, whether a small apartment or large mansion. Continue on in your list.

Then do that which is hard to do. Start expressing gratitude for the depression, the anxiety, the illness, the pain, the divorce, the wayward child, etc. Even if you don't understand the purpose, even if you feel that your life has been ruined, even if you believe your problem is the result of a mistake that you or another has made, make that leap of faith and say the words of gratitude to your Heavenly Father. As we thank the Lord for *every thing* in our life experience, we open the door to blessings.

The promise given to those who give thanks in everything is that their prayers will be answered and their afflictions will work together for their good.

> *Verily I say unto you my friends, fear not, let your hearts be comforted; yea, rejoice evermore, and* **in everything give thanks.**

> *Waiting patiently on the Lord, for your prayers have entered into the ears of the Lord of Sabaoth, and are recorded with this seal and testament—the Lord hath sworn and decreed that they shall be granted.*

> *Therefore, he giveth this promise unto you, with an immutable covenant that they shall be fulfilled; and all things wherewith you have been afflicted shall work together for your good, and to my name's glory, saith the Lord (D&C 98:1–3).*

Everything is in divine order. God can always make lemonade out of lemons! Give thanks for the lemons and the lemonade, and for our Father who puts the sugar in.

Prayer changes the brain for good.

Brain scan studies show that prayer to a loving and merciful God has the effect of stimulating the anterior cingulate, where the balance between thought and feeling is sustained. Prayer stimulates, strengthens and enlarges the anterior cingulate, which in turn lessens the stimulation of the limbic system, which is related to depression and where emotions like anger are processed. This enables empathy and compassion to override the more destructive, less rational reactions of the limbic system. Prayer thus affects physiologic alterations of the brain structure for good.

Studies have shown that those who practice the art of prayer and meditation are characterized by enhanced cognitive abilities and greater empathy and compassion than those who do not meditate or pray. (36)

But most of all, prayer to a loving, compassionate and merciful God increases our faith, because it increases our ability to feel His love.

Pray to be able to feel that love in some small way. Pray that you can trust the love is there. Pray for peace and gratitude in the midst of difficulty. Express that gratitude. And pray that you can have the faith that the atonement of Jesus Christ has the power to completely heal you and the effects of this illness on your family, in this life and the next.

Faith brings healing power.

In medicine, the power of the placebo effect is well known. Generally 30 % of people will improve given a placebo medicine. It is the faith of the person in the doctor or in the treatment that allows for their healing. Tribal cultures throughout the world use this effect. The healing men and women know that if their patients believe in their cure, they will get better. And they do.

It has been shown through studies that, except in very severe depression, anti-depression medications work no better than placebo. People get better because they believe the medicine is making them better. They have faith in the cure, and their bodies and minds respond to that faith.

I love the placebo effect. If faith brings about healing, what a beautiful way to heal! However, when our faith is placed in Jesus Christ, this is NOT placebo. That faith brings forth true, healing power.

All healing comes through the Atonement of Jesus Christ.

Faith in the Lord Jesus Christ is the most powerful healer. All healing comes through the Atonement of Christ. As we build our faith through each small action and each word of gratitude, our faith that Jesus Christ can heal us grows. **Pray for the gift of faith.** That kind of faith is a spiritual gift that we are all entitled to receive.

To be "cured" and to be "healed" are two different things.

I use the words "cure" and "heal" independently. I use the word "cure" to mean that a physical or mental ailment is turned into complete health. I use the word "heal" to mean that we are feeling complete peace in our minds and in our hearts about whatever we are experiencing right now, because we know that whatever we are experiencing in the moment is for our highest good.

However, "cure" often follows "healing." When the body no longer has to experience the stress of the mind fighting against its current situation, it has a greater capacity to repair itself. When the mind has joined with the spirit in faith that all is in divine order, the burden of the illness becomes lighter and the body and mind can become stronger.

We must remember that we will all die from something. That is the definition of mortality. Not every affliction or disease will be cured. However, I believe that everyone can "heal," and that "healing" can lead to "cure" more often than not.

Rather than praying for a cure, **pray for faith and for peace of mind and spirit**, for the ability to allow yourself to feel at peace and be exactly where you are in this moment. This peace will bring healing, and no longer will the disease be a burden. Jesus Christ has the power to heal. Faith in this power is where our hope lies.

The healing power of the atonement of Christ turns our trials into our treasures.

Jean, a good friend of mine, at age 65 started recovering memories of incest committed by her stepfather when she was a child. Though the memories explained a lot of feelings she had experienced throughout her life, they created much suffering, anger, guilt, regret, and shame. She saw how her entire life had been affected by those early experiences, and she saw the many sins she had committed because of them.

Jean prayed daily for relief. She was guided to several emotional healers who assisted her in gaining some relief, but she still regularly descended into despair. She continued to pray, especially asking "Why?"

Jean was blessed to receive a very sacred vision of Christ who spoke to her. This is her account of her vision of Jesus speaking to her:

> *I am sorry that you went through such trouble, but it helped you to need ME so I could heal you.*
>
> *Can you give me all the gore, the filth, the pain, disappointment, corruption, disillusionment, loneliness, the guilt and shame, the horror and terror and all of the consequences of it throughout your life to this point?"*
>
> *I looked down at my hands and they were full of all sorts of stinking, bloody, gory things. I handed all of this to Jesus, who began to glow more brightly.*
>
> *In His hands, all of that gore suddenly was transformed into the purest gold and precious jewels. Smiling, He handed it to me.*
>
> *I was dumbfounded! Could all of that filth really be turned instantly into a treasure that was mine alone?*
>
> *Quickly I set the treasure down and rushed into His arms as we embraced for long moments, His love and light flooding my whole being. He cried with me at the relief and healing power that He*

was sending into my soul. Then He looked deeply into my eyes and said, "It is all right!"

Jesus told me that I could come back to this vision again and again in the future. It would endure for me and the healing would continue on until it was complete.

Then He said, "I am delighted that I can offer you my healing power. It gives me GREAT joy that you can receive this blessing which I can give because of the infinite price I paid for it. I know the effect of my love on those who are meek and humble, of a broken heart and contrite spirit."

It is now crystal clear what a treasure my sufferings are to me. They truly are a pearl of great price that I cannot be grateful enough for. I feel to be the least of the Lord's children, and I know I am truly snatched from the jaws of hell, like Alma the Younger.

Now, even though the memories remain in my mind, the sting and pain is truly gone! Praise the Lord forever and bless His holy name for eternity!

Most of us will not receive such a beautiful vision as Jean did. However, the love of Christ for each of us still bids us to turn over our pain to Him. And just as He did for Jean, He can turn our trials into treasures of light, growth, knowledge and wisdom. Each one of us can receive the same gift Jean did as we act on the faith that Christ can heal us!

Our trials can increase our faith.

My trials and afflictions have tested my faith, and at times my faith has been weak. But as I have put these principles into practice, my faith has grown.

Because of my trials, I now know Jesus Christ. He is my best Friend. He is always there for me. I continually give Him my burdens and He gives me strength to carry them. His love surrounds me and lifts and carries me through the difficult times. He directs my paths and assists me in my work.

I am so very grateful for my Savior, Jesus Christ, who has made it so that I can mess up royally because of my weaknesses, and yet come out on top in the end, through the desires of my heart and through repentance. His grace is sufficient for me, a weak sinner. That is the Good News!!

It hasn't always been this way, for it took a lot of learning on my part, but I am eternally grateful for the suffering I have experienced, because it has truly, over time, and with patience, increased my faith and trust in the Lord Jesus Christ. Because of this faith I have increased in my love of God, my love for myself, and my love for my fellow men.

> *Now no chastening for the present seemeth to be joyous, but grievous: nevertheless afterward it yieldeth the peaceable fruit of righteousness unto them which are exercised thereby (Hebrews 12:11).*

✱ *Sixth Rule of the Subconscious Mind: Opposing ideas cannot be held at one and the same time.* ✱

We cannot have fear and faith at the same time. Work through fear and begin to desire to believe. Give your burden of fear to Christ and let Him carry it. Let His atoning power bring you peace and love.

Chapter 18

Healing through Repentance:
Letting Go of Pain Caused by
Our Weakness

What is sin?

We know that we must repent of our sins in order to partake of the atonement and return to our Heavenly Parents. But what is a sin? The dictionary defines "sin" as:

> *Noun: Deliberate disobedience to the known will of God...*

> *Verb: To violate a religious or moral law...* (37)

I believe a sin is **any way of being, thinking or doing that is unlike our Heavenly Father.** God always follows eternal law. If He didn't, He would no longer be God. So when I think or do something that is unlike God, I am breaking an eternal law. I am sinning.

Because God is Love, in essence, anything that is unlike love is a sin. And because we all have fear and act from fear, we all sin.

I sin when I lie, but I also sin when I think judging or hateful thoughts towards someone rather than love those who despitefully use me. I sin when I cheat someone in business, but I also sin when I think negative thoughts about myself rather than being grateful and acknowledging the gifts I've been given.

I sin when I commit adultery, but I also sin when my thoughts are full of fear rather than faith and trust. I sin when I steal from my employer, but I also sin when I am feeling depressed and anxious. I sin when I covet, or want what I don't have, whether things or relationships. These things come from fear, the opposite of love. And because of this we all sin, every day.

The LDS Church differentiates between the word *sin* and *transgression*. Sin is violating God's law knowingly, while transgression is violating God's law without adequate knowledge. However, even though Adam and Eve committed a transgression, there were still consequences to that act, and they still needed to repent of it. Because of the need for repentance for everything we do that is unlike God, I will use the word *sin* for both definitions to keep things more simple.

What is repentance?

> *The Greek word…denotes a change of mind, i.e. a fresh view about God, about oneself, and about the world. Since we are born into conditions of mortality, repentance comes to mean a turning of the heart and will to God, and a renunciation of sin to which we are naturally inclined. … All accountable persons are stained by sin, and must be cleansed in order to enter the kingdom of heaven. Repentance is not optional for salvation; it is a commandment of God (Bible Dictionary, LDS Scriptures).*

The Hebrew word often used for the translation of repentance means "to return," or "to turn around." Repentance is the process that allows us, when we are facing away from God, from His will, from His love, to turn around, to return to Him and face Him, and receive of His loving grace.

Repentance is not a punishment! The process of repentance and the ability to be forgiven is a gift, a blessing beyond all measure. To repent, we must have faith in the atoning power of Christ and the merciful Love of God. *Repentance allows us to partake of the fruit of the Tree of Life, which is the Love of God.*

We all sin daily.

We are all mortal human beings with weaknesses, and therefore we all sin many times every day. As the Lord does not look upon sin with any degree of allowance, we are all fallen. Any sin, no matter how "big" or "small," will keep us from our eternal goal if we don't repent. We are not "bad," we are simply weak. All of us.

Emotional illness may cause us to "sin."

This definition of sin (*any way of being, thinking or doing that is unlike God, or unlike pure love*) makes living with depression and anxiety especially hard, as inherently these diseases cause a woman to automatically think negative and fearful thoughts, and to be full of sad and anxious feelings.

Are these sins? In a way they are, because they are not like God's feelings and thoughts; they are unlike love. But are women with depression and anxiety "bad"? In spite of what they believe about themselves, and how others may judge them, of course not. They are dealing with a disease that brings weakness into their minds, thoughts and feelings.

Our past experiences often cause us to feel like we are "bad."

Sometimes there is a feeling that "If I need to repent, I must be a bad person." Often this feeling of being "bad" comes from childhood, when the little girl may have been told that she was bad, or she was criticized often, or she never felt she could please a parent, or she was abused, etc. This feeling persists even though there is much evidence that she is not bad, but that she has always done her best to "be good."

But because we are all weak and we all sin daily, each one of those sins confirm the belief that she is bad. She adds her daily sins to all of the sins she has committed in the past and she can only come to the conclusion that she is bad. So she continues to feel bad about herself, not like herself, and feels frustrated that she can't seem to overcome her weaknesses. This is a major cause of depression and anxiety.

Repenting is not evidence that we are "bad," but simply that we have weaknesses, as all do.

There were so many years when I believed I was bad. My dear mother, a very good woman who loved me with all of her heart, believed that for me to be a better person she must point out my faults. I took that and created a belief, in my own limited way as a child, that I could not please her, that I must be a bad girl. My mother loved me and was pleased with me, but I didn't believe that.

As I grew, my weaknesses proved to me that I couldn't please not only my mother, but also God, because I kept sinning. I felt like a bad teenager, even though I wanted to be good. I felt like a bad wife, and then a bad mother. I was doing my best, but my best was never good enough. I did so many things wrong every day that I really disliked myself.

It took many years and many experiences to work through this belief that I was bad. But one experience that stands out in my mind was when I was a young mother living in New Jersey. The Washington D.C. Temple had just been built, and our ward was providing a bus for us to be able to go to the dedication. There was no closer temple, and I hadn't been to the temple since we had moved to New Jersey. Also, I had never been to a dedication before, and truly desired to attend. So I arranged for a babysitter for the 12 hour trip back and forth.

However, even though I held a temple recommend, deep inside I didn't feel worthy of going. I held bad feelings at times towards my husband, and I frequently lost my temper with my hyperactive two year old son. I didn't believe I was a good housekeeper, which was one of my primary jobs as a woman, and I was very far from perfect at my church calling as Primary President. I held onto mistakes I had made as a child, a teenager and a young adult as proof that I was unworthy to be in God's house.

So I went on this trip fasting and praying. We left very early in the morning, and I prayed in my heart all of the way there that I would be forgiven of my many, many sins so that I could feel worthy to be part of this joyous occasion.

We arrived at the beautiful temple and were led into a side room, where the dedication was televised. The spirit was strong, and during one of the stirring choir songs my prayers were answered. I was filled with a most beautiful feeling from head to toe, which I took to be the Spirit witnessing the Love of God for me, and the distinct words came to my mind, "All of your sins are forgiven." I also received the feeling and inspiration that they had always been forgiven, every time I had asked, every time I had repented, and that I no longer needed to keep repenting of past mistakes.

This feeling of being loved and forgiven carried me home on wings of peace and joy. The memory of this special feeling allowed me to have a knowledge that assisted me through many rough spots in the future, when I continued to return to the belief that I was bad. This knowledge that I was loved and forgiven every time I sincerely asked carried me through these dark times until I was finally given the knowledge that our weaknesses are given to us for a purpose, and I could truly let go of the belief that I was "bad."

Each one of us is forgiven in the same way, whether we feel it or not. I am not a special case. God is no respecter of persons. The knowledge that I was forgiven whenever I sincerely repented is true for everyone.

Healing comes through repentance.

All healing comes through the Atonement of Jesus Christ. Therefore, repenting of acts that are unlike love, either against ourselves or others, and repenting of negative and fearful thoughts and feelings, whether we have the ability to control them yet or not, allows us to partake of His gift to us and begins to bring healing. Repentance allows us to partake of the fruit of the Tree of Life, which is the Love of God.

The four "R's" of Repentance are often misunderstood.

We often learn in our church meetings about the four "R's" of repentance:

Recognition that we have committed a sin.

Feel **R**emorse that we have committed a sin.

Repair the mistake, or make **R**estitution.

Resolve to never commit the sin again.

However, we often create beliefs about these steps that bring us down into anxiety and depression rather than lift us into the Love of God.

1. Recognition that we have committed a sin.

Depression and anxiety tend to cause women to think a lot about their sins and wrong-doings. This causes much guilt, which leads to more anxiety and depression. Recognizing our sins doesn't mean that we spend a lot of time focusing on them. It just means that we realize that we have done something that is unlike what God would do, that is unlike love, and then simply move on to the next step.

Obsessing over and over in our minds about something we have said or done is not healthy. It brings out the self-critic rather than the self-counselor. It brings out the beat-up stick rather than building faith in the Atonement. It is unhealthy and unlike God.

Recognizing our weaknesses causes us to be humble, teachable, and dependant on God. It is not to make us feel guilty and hate ourselves.

> *If men come unto me I will show them their weakness...* *(Moroni 27:12).*

As I worked with missionaries, I noticed an interesting process in their growth. As they worked to become closer to God and to grow in faith, they became more acutely aware of their past sins and current weaknesses. They became more humble and would go to the Lord in prayer and repentance. Because of this they were more compassionate to those they taught who were struggling, and they became more loving and more effective missionaries.

And if men humble themselves and come unto me, my grace is sufficient for all. (Moroni 27:12).

Often we blame others for the effects of our weaknesses. We blame others when we become offended or angry at someone, and hurt them emotionally or physically. We blame others when we are depressed or worried, because of what they have done or are doing. However, it is always our choice how we think and feel. Our fears may be triggered by what someone else says or does, but it is our fears and weaknesses that we get to look at, not theirs. "Why did that trigger me? Why am I getting so upset over this?"

It is important for us to recognize and acknowledge our sins and weaknesses so that we can humble ourselves and go to the Lord in repentance. As we do, His grace, or the gift of His atonement, is sufficient for all of our sins and weaknesses, for all of our fear and suffering.

The atonement of Christ is sufficient for all of our weaknesses.

I like to remember that the Lord's grace was sufficient for Saul, who severely persecuted the early followers of Christ. He became Paul, an Apostle of Christ and one of the greatest missionaries that ever lived.

The Lord's grace was also sufficient for Alma and Alma the Younger, who committed many sins and led many away from the truth. They also became prophets of God.

If the Lord's grace was sufficient for these men who had been living "wicked" lives, then certainly His grace is sufficient for me. So I pray to know my own sins and weaknesses so that I can partake of the Lord's grace, therefore growing in faith and love.

Beware of OCD.

There are those with a certain type of Obsessive-Compulsive disorder that spend *too* much time and energy on this aspect of repentance. They see everything they do as a sin and feel the need to confess every wrong doing multiple times. Yet they never feel forgiven. This is a form of anxiety and is important to get treated.

In the workbook there are techniques to assist in stopping those obsessive thoughts that create such pain and waste so much time in negativity. It takes time, patience and effort, but this type of anxious thinking can be changed.

> *Never let us be discouraged with ourselves; it is not when we are conscious of our faults that we are the most wicked: on the contrary, we are less so. We see by a brighter light. And let us remember, for our consolation, that we never perceive our sins till He begins to cure them (Francois Fenelon, 1651–1715). (38)*

2. Feel remorse that we have committed a sin.

Often we confuse the word "remorse" with feeling guilty. I believe feeling guilty and feeling godly remorse are two distinctly separate feelings that carry us in opposite directions.

There is a difference between feeling guilty and feeling godly remorse.

Feeling guilty causes us to feel like we are inherently bad. Godly remorse causes us to feel sadness about a mistake that can be remedied. Feeling guilty causes us to believe that we can't change because we aren't good enough. Godly remorse allows us to have the hope that the Atonement can cleanse and perfect us.

Feeling guilty holds us back and keeps us from feeling worthy. Godly remorse moves us forward with the knowledge that the atonement makes us worthy. Feeling guilty destroys faith in ourselves and in God. Godly remorse builds faith because, through repentance, we see the evidence that with God, all things are possible.

Feeling guilty brings forth negative thoughts and feelings, and causes depression and anxiety. Godly remorse brings hopeful thoughts and feelings, and brings peace and gratitude. Feeling guilty prevents action. Godly remorse spurs us to action.

Feeling guilty keeps us from truly repenting because we cannot forgive ourselves. Godly remorse allows us to fully repent because we have faith that Christ can heal us.

Feeling guilty causes us to withdraw from Christ. Godly remorse brings us to Christ.

God didn't intend for us to hold onto the pain of our sins indefinitely.

There is no need for guilty feelings. It causes us to get out our beat up stick and beat ourselves up. It changes nothing. That is very unlike the pain of godly remorse. It is better to allow ourselves to feel the pain and sorrow of what our sin created and then **let it go** through repentance.

God didn't intend for us to hold onto the pain of our sins forever. That is why He sent His Son, not to condemn the world, but to save the world. Rather than pull out the beat-up stick, we can bring forth our self-counselor and say, "That didn't work. How can I do it different next time?" And then pick ourselves up and work on it again, and again, and if necessary, again.

3.   Repair the mistake, or make Restitution.

This step is self explanatory, but sometimes it is one of the hardest things to do. It is often difficult to go to someone and admit our anger at them when we believe they were wrong and our anger was justified. It is embarrassing to admit our mistake to one we have harmed, especially if they don't know about it, such as from stealing or gossip. When we strive to repair the mistake we made, we fear that others will think less of us, and it is possible that they will. It takes much courage to follow through with this step in the repentance process.

However, this step is such a cleansing and healing step! It is so healing that it is part of the 12-step program for addictions. Steps 8, 9, and 10 state:

> 8. *Make a list of all persons we have harmed, and become willing to make amends to them all.*
>
> 9. *Make direct amends to such people wherever possible, except when to do so would injure them or others.*
>
> 10. *Continue to take personal inventory and when we are wrong promptly admit it.* (39)

It is very important to do our best to admit and rectify the best that we can any way that we have harmed others. Trust that this step will allow you to feel much better, even if others do judge you or think worse of you. However, generally they will appreciate your sincere admittance of wrong-doing.

Be careful that this does not become an obsessive process. People with anxiety and OCD will start to worry about every little thing and keep confessing for little things that were done years ago. Their obsessive worries can overwhelm them in this step. If you find yourself obsessively thinking about this step, recognize that this is anxiety, not a need to repent.

Of course there are things that we can't repair ourselves, and at this point we need to trust that the Atonement will make up the difference for what we can't do.

4. Resolve to never commit the sin again.

There are many false beliefs created out of this step, the most common being that if I repent and resolve not to commit the sin again, and then I do commit the sin again, I must not have really repented. Because I haven't really repented I must be bad and I will never reach the celestial kingdom.

The truth is that overcoming weaknesses is a lifetime process. We can have the desire to never do it again. We can commit to ourselves and to others to never do it again. But sometimes we do it again anyway. And then we do it again, and again.

We are forgiven every time we sincerely repent. When the true desire of our hearts is that we never do it again, we are forgiven. If we are sincerely striving to change we are forgiven.

When we make the mistake again, if the true desire of our hearts is that we hadn't made the mistake, we are forgiven. God is ever merciful. God knows our hearts. God gave His Only Begotten Son, not to condemn us, but to save us. Through the Atonement He lifts us up when we fall, and gently encourages and inspires us to work on it again. And again, and again.

However, if we do not have that true desire in our hearts and make promises to ourselves, to others and to God that we don't intend to really keep, if our repentance is just for show rather than truly heartfelt, there is no forgiveness. God knows our hearts and our desires.

Therefore, resolve in your heart to never do it again. Strive to never do it again. But if you do it again, don't give up. Repent and resolve one more time. God will support you until you learn enough to overcome this weakness.

Repenting is a process of letting go of pain.

Sometimes we feel that we have repented, but we still feel the pain of what our mistakes have caused. True repentance is letting go of that pain, giving it to Christ and allowing Him to lighten our burdens. Holding onto the pain is unlike God; unlike love.

After having felt the godly remorse, as we repent our slate is wiped clean, so we no longer need to hold onto the pain of it. As the pain comes up, keep choosing to let it go. Often God forgives us much sooner than we forgive ourselves. Let it go. Again and again. Let it go.

Repentance cleanses and perfects us.

> *Be ye therefore perfect, even as your Father which is in heaven is perfect (Matthew 5:48).*

Many of us Mormon women use this scripture verse as a beat-up stick every time we sin. The sin is proof that we are not perfect, that we can never reach the Celestial Kingdom.

The truth is, however, that on this earth, we can only reach perfection through Christ, but we can do so every time we sincerely repent, when we are baptized, and every time we partake of the sacrament with a broken heart and contrite spirit. We are cleansed of our sins and in that moment we are perfect.

The Celestial kingdom is not made up of those who have never sinned, but *"these are they who are just men made perfect through Jesus the mediator of the new covenant, who wrought out this perfect atonement through the shedding of his own blood"* (D&C 76:69) .

Partaking of the Atonement is a continual process, a moment to moment process that allows us to be perfect through it. Of course, we strive to do our best and strive to obey the commandments. But when we lose perfection because of our weaknesses, the Atoning blood of Christ perfects us again each time we sincerely repent.

Have I been forgiven?

Sometimes we have the belief that it takes years for God to forgive us of some of our wrongdoings. The truth is, we are forgiven the moment we truly turn to Christ and ask for forgiveness with a broken heart and a contrite spirit.

Consider the story of Alma the Younger. When the angel appeared to him he went into a coma-like state in utter misery, considering all of the awful things he had done. But after three days in this state, he started considering how to get out of it, and remembered his father's teachings about Christ. As soon as he turned to Christ and asked for forgiveness, he was filled with an "exquisite joy." He had been forgiven the moment he asked for it, in spite of all of the things he had done that had pulled so many people away from God.

If it is one of your concerns whether you have been forgiven or not, consider the little miracles, the small spiritual promptings, the "coincidences" or the "tender mercies," as Elder Bednar calls them, that become blessings. This is evidence that God is in your life. The Spirit does not dwell in unholy temples. Sometimes, with depression and anxiety, it is hard to feel the Spirit. However, if you are having any small gifts or tender mercies given to you, it is a sign that you are forgiven and have been cleansed.

The ability to repent is a blessing beyond measure.

I choose to repent daily, because daily I have thoughts, words or actions that are unlike Love. This is not an obsessive need because of anxiety and OCD. It is a process that cleanses me and brings me peace and allows me to move forward. I do it because I choose to partake of the atoning process constantly, as I constantly need it. I am not "wicked," but I am mortal, dealing with mortal weaknesses.

As I choose to recognize each weakness, feel godly remorse, ask for forgiveness, and ask for God's help in letting go of this weakness and the pain caused by it, and then move forward, I can feel God's love and better love myself. I am so grateful for this process of healing, which allows me to let go of the pain of all of my weaknesses and renew myself each day and each time I partake of the sacrament.

Repentance turns exceeding pain into exquisite joy.

And it came to pass that as I was thus racked with torment, while I was harrowed up by the memory of my many sins, behold, I remembered also to have heard my father prophesy unto the people concerning the coming of one Jesus Christ, a Son of God, to atone for the sins of the world.

Now, as my mind caught hold upon this thought, I cried within my heart: O Jesus, thou Son of God, have mercy on me, who am in the gall of bitterness, and am encircled about by the everlasting chains of death.

And now, behold when I thought this, I could remember my pains no more; yea, I was harrowed up by the memory of my sins no more.

And oh, what joy, and what marvelous light I did behold; yea, my soul was filled with joy as exceeding as was my pain!

Yea, I say unto you, my son, that there could be nothing so exquisite and so bitter as were my pains. Yea, and again I say unto you, my son, that on the other hand, there can be nothing so exquisite and sweet as was my joy (Alma 36:17–21).

✻ *Third Law of the Subconscious Mind: Once an idea has been accepted by the subconscious mind, it remains until it is replaced by another idea. The longer the idea remains, the more opposition there is to replacing it with a new idea.* ✻

Be patient with yourself as you work on letting go of the idea that you are bad, wrong, not good enough or evil. If it has been there since childhood it may take awhile to completely let it go. But as you work on replacing guilt with godly remorse when you see your weaknesses, and as you pray for forgiveness and give Christ the burden of your weaknesses and your pain rather than carrying them by yourself, and as you grow in faith that His atonement can truly make you perfect, over time peace and healing will be the result.

Chapter 19

Forgiving One Another: *Letting Go of Pain Caused by Others' Weakness*

We must forgive others in order to be forgiven.

One of the most important things we need to repent of are our feelings of anger and even hatred towards others, especially those we believe have harmed us.

Jesus taught us how to pray through what is now called The Lord's Prayer. A major concept in that prayer is *"Forgive us our debts as we forgive our debtors"* (Matthew 6:12). Jesus then goes on to say:

> *For if ye forgive men their trespasses, your heavenly Father will also forgive you:*

> *But if ye forgive not men their trespasses, neither will your Father forgive your trespasses (Matthew 6:14–15).*

Holding onto the pain and anger that we feel because of the acts or words of another is unlike God. It is impossible to let go of the pain that we have caused through our own "sins" until we can let go of the pain we feel because of the actions or words of others.

This can be very hard when we truly believe we have been wronged. Many wars are fought over "an eye for an eye and a tooth for a tooth." When someone hurts us, the natural man desires revenge. But forgiving another is for our own healing, not necessarily for the other person. It is the only way to feel peace and to create peace: in ourselves, in our families and in the world.

The weaknesses of others that hurt us have purpose in our lives.

We came to earth to be in a place where God wasn't, so that we could experience the opposite of what God is. Through this experience and knowledge of opposites, we are better able to learn to choose to be more like God, by increasing in our ability to love.

We experience the opposite of what God is through dealing with our own weaknesses and the weaknesses of others. Each person is accountable for their own actions. We are not accountable for what someone chooses to do to us, but we are accountable for our own feelings and actions towards that person. When someone has "wronged" us, working through those feelings allows us to better ourselves.

When Christ tells us to *"Love your enemies. Do good to those who despitefully use you,"* that process of learning to love, in power and wisdom, is for our own healing. It blesses our lives by bringing greater peace and love into our hearts. It allows us to become more like God, to have more power in love, and more wisdom in love, which is our purpose here.

Forgiving others is letting go of the pain others have caused us.

When we forgive someone, we are not saying, "What you did was ok." Forgiving is simply letting go of the pain that we felt because of what that other person did.

Holding onto the pain is very rewarding at times. It gives us our "story." It defines us. We may not even know who to be if we let go of the pain. But as long as we hold onto the pain, we cannot truly forgive. And we must forgive to be forgiven.

There is always some perceived benefit to holding onto pain, but it is never worth it.

If there is pain you are holding onto—pain caused by your mother or father, by an abuser, by a spouse, by a child, or whomever—consider why you are choosing to hold onto it. What benefit is it giving you to hold onto it? You may think this is ridiculous; of course you don't receive any benefit from this pain. But the truth is, if there is no benefit, you would have let it go long ago. Again, consider the benefit the subconscious mind believes it is receiving from holding onto the pain. It may be giving you attention, or the sweet feeling of revenge by making them feel bad, or you may be receiving pity because of it. We all do it at some time or another. Holding onto pain is usually the result of our own pride. There are many subtle causes of needing to hold onto past hurts. But none of them are worth it. That benefit is a lie. It is never worth holding onto the pain.

Being unforgiving and holding onto pain others have caused us causes health problems.

It has been shown in studies that reviewing in our mind hurts caused by others increases heart rate and blood pressure. Those who harbor hurts and offenses have also been shown to have higher rates of depression and anxiety. When forgiveness has truly happened, it improves both the body and the mind.

Letting go of pain allows us to move forward as we forgive.

Get a pen and hold it in the palm of your hand, and then grip it tight. You may think that this pen is useful to you, that if you hold onto it tight enough and never let it go you won't lose it and you will be able to use it to write with. But while you are gripping it tightly, it really is of no use to you. You cannot really write well with it while you are gripping it so tight. Now see this pen as all of your pain. See that the pen, or the pain, is not you. It does not define you. It is simply something you are holding onto.

Now, you decide to let the pen go. Just loosen your grip and let it fall. That was easy! It is simply a choice to let go. By not gripping the pen, your hands are free to do whatever you choose. Letting go of pain does the same thing. It frees you to move forward, frees your attention to better things to allow you to find joy again.

Pain is a feeling. Feelings are simply chemical releases in our body in response to thoughts or memories. They are not you. They do not define you. You are not losing a part of you if you let them go.

And if you end up having a need to hold onto the pain again, allow the pain to be there for a moment. Accept it. Feel it. Then see that it is simply a feeling, and it is not you, that it does not define you or control you, and let it go again. There may be a time when you choose to pick it up with knowledge, hold it lightly, and write with it. Pens and pain can be used as tools to improve ourselves. But we do not need to hold onto them and never let them go.

As you let go of pain, you will notice that your heart opens. You are filled with compassion. You are open to feeling more love, more joy, and more desire to serve others. Letting go opens doors that you didn't even know were there. Forgiving others is not for the other person, but truly for our own good, for our own joy. In this space it is easy for us to feel God's merciful love, to feel forgiven.

Forgiving ourselves allows us to let go of the pain of our own sins.

Forgiveness is an act of love. When we learn to love our "enemies" by forgiving them, we increase in our capacity to love. As we let go of the pain, we are more open to feeling God's forgiving love towards us, and we can more easily let go of our own pain.

Forgiving others does not mean we allow them to keep abusing us.

If there has been abuse in a relationship, and being in contact with that person would continue the abuse, there is no need to re-establish a relationship, even after forgiveness. We can love our "enemy" from afar, if that keeps us from being abused. It is important to love ourselves enough to keep from being abused.

Sometimes we blame ourselves for abuse that happened to us. There is no need for repentance for something done to us that we had no control over.

> *Your real self is eternally innocent and eternally chaste. …Nothing that anyone has ever done to you could make imperfect what God created perfect. What God has created is both changeless and forever….And the more you make conscious contact with that purity, the more quickly dysfunctional thoughts, toxic shame, and*

other buried feelings that may have arisen from sexual violation will begin to dissolve and disappear forever (Marianne Williamson). (39)

Keep remembering who you really are, beyond these mortal weaknesses and experiences. Get in touch with the pure spirit within, and feel the innocence and love that emanates from you.

When we have been hurt by church leaders:

Often women with depression and anxiety have visited with Bishops, Stake Presidents and other leaders who do not understand them, and at times those leaders say things or give advice which hurts or offends them. When this happens, remember the following:

- Even though the head of the church is Jesus Christ, the church is run by mortal men with mortal weaknesses. This is God's plan.

- As good and spiritual as they are, even prophets and apostles have mortal weaknesses. Remember how Lehi doubted when Nephi broke his bow, how Isaac wanted to give Esau the birthright blessing rather than Jacob, etc. Our priesthood leaders may be truly inspired in their callings, and inspired in much of the direction they give us, but they are not perfect. The only perfect person to live on this earth was Jesus Christ.

- We learn through serving in our positions. A bishop doesn't know how to be a bishop until he becomes a bishop and learns with his congregation. By the time he learns how to be a good bishop, he is released and given something else he doesn't know how to do.

- Most church leaders have not received professional counseling training, and many do not understand mental illness. They are often in way over their heads in the types of problems they are given to deal with, yet they do it anyway, because they are asked to, because they desire to serve, usually praying that God will bless those they are counseling.

- It is harder to receive inspiration about things that are not in our knowledge base. Often when the Spirit gives whispering advice, we (all of us, not just church leaders) compare it to our knowledge base and use only that which we know, missing some of the subtler knowledge that may have been given.

- The Spirit gives inspiration when we have a humble and open heart. Too often all of us (not just church leaders) have strong beliefs about certain things which keep us from having that humble and open heart which allows us to receive truth through the Spirit about that subject.

- We are accountable for all of our choices, whether recommended by a priesthood leader or not. I have often been counseled by priesthood leaders to go home and pray about the counsel they gave to me. It is important for me to receive my own confirmation and revelation about the path I am to take.

- Most leaders are good people that dedicate an incredible amount of time and energy, doing their best to serve without pay, because they love the Lord and have faith that God will help them through it. Just because they make mistakes at times, such as having pride (as we all do), giving bad advice (as we all do), or judging (as we all do) does not mean they are bad men. They are simply human men, doing their best in a difficult situation.

- It may be that they have given inspired advice but in our weakness we have not truly understood the nature of their counsel.

- When we forgive others we are forgiven. Not speaking evil about the Lord's anointed is for us, not for them. When we think negative thoughts about church leaders we are judging. When we judge we lose the Spirit.

• Continuing to harbor negative feelings about others causes depression and anxiety to get worse.

• Letting go of the pain caused by something someone said allows us to forgive them. Assume the best about others. Be gentle and kind and forgiving if you feel hurt by what a church leader has said. Assume they never intended to hurt or offend you. Assume they were just doing the best they could with the weaknesses they have been given, just as all of us are.

Living the Great Commandment is the true process of forgiveness and forgiving.

Jesus said unto him, Thou shalt love the Lord thy God with all they heart, and with all thy soul, and with all thy mind.

This is the first and great commandment.

And the second is like unto it, Thou shalt love thy neighbor as thyself.

On these two commandments hang all the law and the prophets (Matthew 22:37–40).

When we choose to love and trust in God in spite of all of the awful things that have happened and are happening to us, it is easier to feel His merciful love for us. When we feel His love, it is easier to forgive ourselves.

When we love God and feel His love for us, it is easier to love and forgive others. We recognize that all of our weaknesses are given to us for a purpose, and that we learn through those weaknesses. When we love God and begin to feel His love for us, we begin to have faith that

He sent His Son to bring us home again, in spite of our weaknesses and the things that have happened to us. And He sent His Son to bring those who have wronged us home again, in spite of their weaknesses.

When we love God, love ourselves and love others, and use that love in power and wisdom, we partake of the deliciousness of the fruit of the Tree of Life. This is how we live in joy and peace.

Not forgiving others, being filled with anger and hate towards others, is the greatest source of suffering in this world.

When we are having wars within our own minds towards others, we have war in our families, and incredible suffering results. When we have war in our families, there is war in our communities, in our nation and in the world. The only way to end war and suffering in the world is to begin in our own hearts, by letting go of anger and hate that we harbor towards others, even towards those we profess to love.

When we pray for world peace, we must also pray for forgiveness for how our thoughts, feelings and actions have contributed to the state of the world, and ask for God's assistance so that we may forgive those we feel have wronged us.

Again, I can not emphasize enough, the anger and hate in our own hearts has an effect on the entire world, and we must repent ourselves and forgive others in order to begin to change the world. **Our loving forgiveness is a power that can change our hearts, our health, and even the world.**

✳ *Fourth Rule of the Subconscious Mind: Each suggestion that is accepted creates less opposition to successive suggestions.* ✳

Each time we forgive a small act of unkindness towards us, it becomes easier to forgive, until we can truly forgive the major acts we feel were committed against us.

Each time we let go of the pain we have felt by another's words or acts, it becomes easier to let go of the pain from each problem that arises.

Chapter 20

Healing through Baptism and the Sacrament

Baptism is a symbolic representation of our willingness to follow Christ.

If you are reading this book, the assumption is that you have already been baptized a member of the Church of Jesus Christ of Latter-day Saints.

The act of baptism is a symbol of the covenant we are making with God. We are agreeing to take upon us the name of Christ ("I am a Christian") and become part of His family, follow Him and strive to become like him. Alma the Elder in Alma 18 explains some of the things we are covenanting when we are baptized:

- Bear one another's burdens, that they may be light.

- Mourn with those that mourn; comfort those that stand in need of comfort.

- Stand as a witness of God at all times, in all things and in all places even until death

- Serve God and keep his commandments.

In return, God covenants with us to:

- Redeem us

- Number us with those of the first resurrection

- Pour out His Spirit more abundantly upon us

Depression and anxiety seem to keep us from fulfilling our baptismal covenant.

When we covenant through the symbol of baptism to become more like Christ, we are covenanting to be willing to love as Christ loves, to take care of each other and serve each other.

Depression and anxiety cause us to become inward focused. All our thoughts become consumed with our own problems, and it is difficult to feel much for anyone else. It becomes hard to feel love, and loving others as purely as Christ does seems impossible. This often causes feelings of guilt.

When the depression and anxiety are severe it becomes hard to accomplish anything, even for ourselves, and the thought of giving service and helping others is overwhelming. We become needy and become the recipients of service rather than the givers. And the guilt that comes from not performing service for our family and others increases the depression and anxiety.

We often judge ourselves by how much we are able to serve and please others.

Often we determine our worth by how much we can accomplish; by how much we can do that will bring attention, gratitude or accolades from others. This causes us to wear ourselves out, because there is no way we can get everything done and please everyone. Others, in their own weakness, may not acknowledge or appreciate our efforts.

Depression and anxiety often come on or are exacerbated by our inability to please others by fulfilling their needs. We make mistakes in our relationships and begin to feel worthless. We become worn out trying to please others and not completely succeeding.

Service is the action form of love, but are we really serving from a place of pure love?

We often believe that in giving service we are showing our love. That is truth when we are truly giving out of a loving and wise heart, expecting nothing in return. But it is important to look at our own true motives in giving service. Are we serving out of pure love, or are we serving so that we can feel like we are worthwhile, or so that others will love us, or so that we will receive accolades, or because we are seeking for attention and appreciation?

When we serve in this way we wear ourselves out. We feel walked on and used, because often others don't appreciate our help when it is given in this way. Often others perceive us as judgmental, self-righteous or controlling when we give from this place. We may be pushing others to receive our help when they don't really want it. We cannot perceive their needs with wisdom when we are serving from a place of need ourselves.

To learn to give service from the heart, start with serving self.

Since depression and anxiety are a lack of love, especially towards self, start with serving self.

"But I should be giving more to others than I do to myself!" However, I guarantee that as you start loving yourself to be able to serve yourself, you will naturally become more outward focused and be able to serve others better.

We begin to love those whom we serve.

As you choose to begin to serve yourself in small ways, it is easier to begin to love yourself. You must love yourself as Christ does before you can truly love others as Christ does. And serving and loving others without expectation for anything in return (including acknowledgment and gratitude) increases your love for yourself. It becomes a beautiful circle of love.

Ways to serve self.

- Be kind to yourself; think kind thoughts about yourself.

- Treat yourself as you would treat one of your children.

- Forgive yourself for your mistakes as you would forgive others.

- Take an hour to do something that you've wanted to do but haven't taken the time.

- Get yourself out of the house for something fun (dinner, movie, walk in the mountains, shopping, lunch with a friend) even though you really don't feel like doing it.

- Etc.

Then begin to serve others.

As you begin to feel more kindly and forgiving towards yourself, you naturally begin to feel more kindly and forgiving towards others. Begin to reach out in small ways. It is the small expressions of love that move the world to a better place. We don't have to do grand acts of service, we don't have to become a Mother Teresa, to change the world.

Being outward focused is healing.

As we begin to learn to serve from the heart rather than from our own neediness, the inward focus that comes with depression and anxiety begins to change. We begin to be lead by our hearts to small expressions and acts of love towards others. We become more outward focused.

As we become more outward focused, from a space of love rather than neediness, healing comes. It seems so simple, and it is. But in the middle of depression and anxiety it seems impossible. But if you continue to put forth the effort again and again, change comes and healing begins.

The experience of depression and anxiety gives us greater compassion for others. By going through this experience and slowly learning how to pull ourselves out of it we are better able to serve others through their problems.

Then we are able to truly bear one another's burdens, mourn with those that mourn, comfort those in need of comfort, and love more like Christ does. Healing from depression and anxiety is part of the process of fulfilling our baptismal covenants.

Partaking of the sacrament is part of the cleansing process of repentance.

We are taught that the ordinance of the sacrament is a renewing of our baptismal covenants. And just as we must repent before being baptized, it serves us to repent before taking the sacrament.

What a powerful message is sent to our hearts and our brains as we sit during the sacrament reviewing our weaknesses of the week and asking forgiveness. How hopeful it is to contemplate during this time on how we can do each thing in a way which is more like God, which is more like love, in the coming week. And how cleansing it is to partake of the bread and water and feel our sins washed away once again, to begin with a clean slate for a new week.

> *Be ye therefore perfect, even as your Father which is in heaven is perfect (Matthew 5:48).*

This concept of "being perfect" seems so impossible to reach, but the reality is, we reach it each time we sincerely repent and partake of the sacrament. We are perfected and sanctified through the atonement of Jesus Christ because of our hope in the atoning process and our faith that He can cleanse us. What a blessing the sacrament is! We sin daily, but we can become clean weekly, if that is the true desire and effort of our hearts and lives.

✱ Seventh Rule of the Subconscious Mind: An emotionally induced symptom tends to cause organic change if persisted in long enough. ✱

If we allow ourselves to truly feel cleansed by repenting and partaking of the sacrament each week, it can cause a positive physical and mental response over time, assisting healing to take place.

Chapter 21

Healing through the Gift of the Holy Ghost

The Holy Spirit brings us to a remembrance of God and all truth.

Through the scriptures, we see that the Holy Spirit teaches about, guides us towards and testifies of God and the truth of all things. The Holy Spirit brings us to a remembrance of all things. This implies that we already know all things, and the Holy Spirit is the means to bring this knowledge back into our conscious awareness.

The truth of all things abides within us.

> *For by the water ye keep the commandment; by the Spirit ye are justified, and by the blood ye are sanctified;*
>
> *Therefore it is given to abide in you: the record of heaven; the Comforter; the peaceable things of immortal glory; the truth of all things; that which quickeneth all things, which maketh alive all*

things; that which knoweth all things; and hath all power according to wisdom, mercy, truth, justice, and judgment (Moses 6:60–61).

The Holy Spirit brings us to a remembrance of the truths we have forgotten about who we really are.

This is one of my favorite scriptures, as it confirms to me that who I really am is much more than I perceive myself to be. The veil has been drawn at birth and in early childhood, so that my condescension from light into darkness is forgotten, and I begin to believe that this darkened mortal being with weaknesses is the real me.

But this scripture confirms to me that within me is a part which knows heaven and my spiritual history, which knows the truth of all things, which has all power used in wisdom and mercy. This part of me is the true daughter of God, with knowledge and powers beyond the imagination of this mortal mind. This part of me is my spirit, which is truly connected to God.

The Holy Spirit heals by connecting us to God and the power of our own spirits.

The gift of the Holy Spirit connects me to my own divine spirit within and allows me to remember the truth: the truth of who I really am, the truth of my Heavenly Parents, the truth of the Plan of Happiness, the truth of Jesus Christ and His atoning gift.

In essence, the Holy Spirit connects me to God by connecting me to that part of me that is connected to God. In that connection I begin to recognize the glorious spiritual being that God created me to be. In that connection I am able to see that this darker piece of me on this earth is created for my spiritual learning and my spiritual growth, and all is in divine order.

The Holy Spirit connects me to that creative power within that allows me to fulfill my purpose here. It connects me with the merciful love that constantly surrounds me.

And in that connection I begin to heal from the misperceptions and false beliefs I have formed over the years which keep me in darkness.

In that connection I know Christ, and I know I am forgiven as I repent. In that connection I know God's merciful love for me. In that connection I am given peace of mind and peace of heart. In that connection I am comforted.

In that connection I am blessed to partake of the fruit of the Tree of Life, and feel the overwhelming love that God always holds for me.

It is hard to feel the Spirit when dealing with depression and anxiety.

Most often we are aware that the Holy Spirit is with us because we can *feel* it. The Holy Ghost touches our feelings and that is how we are aware of its presence, and how we know the thoughts that come with the feelings are inspired.

Because the dark feelings that come with depression and anxiety are so difficult to deal with, there is a natural, subconscious numbing of feelings in order to be able to survive. Because of that numbness, it is harder to feel the good feelings of the Spirit. Anti-depressant and psychotropic medication also may cause a numbing of feelings that makes it hard to feel the Spirit.

Depression and anxiety often cause one to feel unworthy to have the Spirit with them.

This lack of being able to feel the Spirit is often misinterpreted as not being worthy to feel the Spirit. And because those with depression and anxiety deal with low self-esteem and self-criticism, they often *do* believe they are not worthy to feel the Spirit. This is one of the lies that the overactive part of the brain tells us.

Because the Spirit dwells at the frequency of light and love, we, at a lower frequency as "the natural man," may need to work to be at that level.

Just as sound is a slower frequency than light, we, as mortal human beings, are a slower frequency than the Holy Spirit. When our thoughts, feelings and acts are unlike God, unlike love, then we are not on the same frequency as the Holy Spirit and it is hard to feel it. Even though we may have been given the Gift of the Holy Ghost and the Spirit is always with us, unless we bring ourselves into a higher state of being, or "quickened" with a higher frequency, it is hard to connect with it and be able to utilize it.

We can use many methods to be able to connect with the Spirit.

When the prophets ask us to attend our meetings, read the scriptures, pray alone, pray with our families, give service, and attend the temple, there are many reasons they do so. One reason is that these things, done in sincerity and humility, put us in a state of mind which is more like God, more like love. As we enter this state of being, it is easier to connect with the Spirit and receive comfort, answers and healing.

Other ways of achieving that enlightened frame of mind are many. Going into nature, listening to music which lifts you, watching an inspiring movie, holding a baby, meditating, thinking kind thoughts to yourself, taking time to be alone, taking time to be with those that love you, writing in a journal, creating music or writing or art or sewing or scrapbooks or whatever, and many more things, all have the capacity to lift us into a higher state of love and gratitude, which allows us to more easily connect with the Spirit.

It may take extra effort to commune with the Spirit when you have depression and anxiety.

Those with depression and anxiety, however, have difficulty entering that state of mind even when they do those things. The following are suggested ways to increase the ability to reach that elevated state of mind, no matter what you choose to do to increase your ability to feel it. For example, if you choose to go to the temple, or if you choose to take a walk in nature, bring this list and do the following:

- **Create the desire.** *"Yea, even if ye can no more than desire to believe, let this desire work in you"* (Alma 32:27). Allow the desire to connect with the Spirit and commune with God to swell within your heart.

- **Take the time.** Take the time and make the effort to do something that in the past has lifted and brightened you. Often with depression and anxiety there is little motivation to do anything, so you may choose to plan something and commit to do whether you feel like it or not.

- **Repent.** Ask forgiveness for your thoughts, feelings and actions that have been unlike God. Ask for forgiveness for your negativity, your fears, your irritability and your judgments. Be as specific as you can. Ask that God open the doors so that you can learn how to let go of the pain that causes you to be that way. Let go of the self-critic and simply express godly sorrow.

- **Ponder how you could do something differently.** If you did something that didn't work very well, and you repented of it, use your self-counselor to assist in pondering ways to do things differently if the same thing happened again. Come up with several solutions that you can do to create a more positive outcome.

- **Look at your successes.** Look at everything you have done in the last few days that have been positive. Count every little thing, even the act of getting out of bed and getting dressed when it was very hard to do so, no matter how late you did it. Keep the "buts" from taking over (I didn't lose my temper when Johnny spilled his supper all over the floor... *but* I did get angry at him later for fighting with his sister). Let go of what didn't work, and focus on what did. Be kind and generous to yourself on this step.

- **Find gratitude.** Think of at least three things you are truly grateful for and allow yourself to feel that gratitude in your heart and in your body.

- **Feel love.** Think of someone that you love and that you know loves you. This can even be an animal. Feel that love for them, and open your heart to feel the love they have for you.

- **Pray and ask for the Spirit to be with you.** Ask for the ability to feel the Spirit and have it guide your prayers and your communication with your Heavenly Father.

- **Offer your broken heart and contrite spirit.** As you repent and pray, express to God the knowledge that you have no control over the depression and anxiety, over your anger, your pain, and your weaknesses. Offer to Him your broken heart, your pain, your fears and your weaknesses. Hand over to Him your finances, your problem child, your friend who hurt your feelings, your sick grandchild, your husband who doesn't understand you, and all the other things that are worrying you. Hand them over to Him in words and even visually in your imagination. Let go of control and let God take over.

- **Listen.** After praying, expressing gratitude, communicating feelings and asking questions, take plenty of time to listen. Sit in meditation, letting go of the thoughts that keep coming, breathing through your heart space, and let your mind be quiet. If your mind continues to chatter, let it be in the background as you are quiet and listen.

- **Let go of fear.** If an answer brings fear, it is not from the Spirit. The Spirit always brings peace, even in warning. You have a peaceful conviction that this is what is important to do.

- **Allow the peace in.** Be patient, and peace *will* come. The Spirit *will* come. Whether you receive the exact answers to your questions or not (and often you will), you will receive the peace that comes with knowing that God is with you and directing your paths, that all is in divine order, and that you can trust in Him that all will work out for the best in the end.

- **Trust the answers.** If you do receive thoughts that seem to be answers in those moments of peace, trust that they are true. If you are given instructions, commit to follow them. The more you trust the answers and follow them, the more often you will feel the Spirit and the easier it will be to find those answers the next time you ask.

When seeking for healing, seek for the Holy Ghost and it will tell you all that you should do.

Do ye not remember that I said unto you that after ye had received the Holy Ghost ye could speak with the tongue of angels?....

Angels speak by the power of the Holy Ghost; wherefore, they speak the words of Christ. Wherefore, I said unto you, feast upon the words of Christ: for behold, the words of Christ will tell you all the things what ye should do....

For behold, again I say unto you that if ye will enter in by the way, and receive the Holy Ghost, it will show unto you all things what ye should do (2 Nephi 32:2–3,5).

The Holy Spirit will direct you towards those paths that will assist in your healing.

✱ The Eighth Rule of the Subconscious Mind: The greater the conscious effort, the less the subconscious response. ✱

The more effort we put into trying to figure out answers with our mind, the more difficult it is for the Spirit to teach us with its subtle, gentle voice. Let go of the thoughts of the analytical mind of the natural man and just listen and feel. The Spirit has the power to change the beliefs of the subconscious mind as it teaches our conscious mind the path towards healing.

Chapter 22

Healing through Becoming as a Little Child

Becoming as a little child allows us to enter the Kingdom of Heaven.

*A*t the same time came the disciples unto Jesus, saying, Who is the greatest in the kingdom of heaven?

And Jesus called a little child unto him, and set him in the midst of them.

And said, Verily I say unto you, Except ye be converted, and become as little children, ye shall not enter into the kingdom of heaven.

Whosoever therefore shall humble himself as this little child, the same is greatest in the kingdom of heaven (Matthew 18:1–4).

Children can often teach us more than we can teach them.

I have often felt that my children were sent to teach me rather than the other way around. Through observing their pure little personalities, and dealing with my reactions to their struggles as they grow, I have truly become more of the person I desire to be.

A little child is loving.

Consider the ways of little children who have not been hampered by abuse and/or fear. They are loving, always seeking to give and receive love and affection. They naturally love everyone until they have been hurt or are taught not to.

A little child is forgiving.

Little children are immediately forgiving, and seek hugs after we have hurt them in some way. They will forget the hurts quickly, unless it is a major trauma which changes how they view life. All they desire is to love and be loved.

A little child is joyful and passionate.

Little children are full of joy, and find pleasure in the little things of life. They live in the moment, letting go of the past and not fearing the future, unless they have been taught to fear it. They are passionate, becoming excited about things we adults often consider insignificant.

A little child loves to learn.

Little children are always curious, learning from observation, from their games, and from their environment. They aren't afraid to ask questions so that they can learn more about how life and the universe works. They love discovery, and are so excited when they reach that "a-ha" moment of grasping a concept, or gain the ability to accomplish an activity they couldn't do before.

A little child is honest.

Little children are honest, sometimes to our chagrin, as they repeat to others things we have said or done. They are not afraid to honestly express their feelings, and use their entire bodies to express them.

A little child does not judge.

Little children express themselves, not with judgment, but simply with what they observe and how they feel. They hold no judgment except in those ways in which we have taught them. They naturally expect the best from others. They desire to be friends and friendly with everyone.

A little child is humble, trusting and dependent.

Little children know they are unable to do things on their own. They are so trusting that we will be there for them and take care of their needs, and they are completely dependent on us. They trust that we will feed them, dress them, and keep them comfortable and happy. They trust that we will love them and cherish them.

Little children know that they don't know everything, and they are always open to learning more. They have open and humble hearts.

Little children love God.

I have seen over and over again how little children soak up and accept teachings about a loving God and a loving Jesus. Those that have never been exposed to God will often seek for Him. Those that know little but that there is a God come forth with profound expressions of faith in Him. They love prayer and the ability to trust that their prayers are answered. I've seen this happen in many cultures and many religions. Little children know the truth of God's love and protecting care unless teachings of fearful parents about an angry and vengeful God override that knowledge.

The mind of the natural man is the ego mind. The mind of a "little child" is the spiritual mind.

> For the natural man [ego mind] is an enemy to God, and has been from the fall of Adam, and will be, forever and ever, unless he yields to the enticings of the Holy Spirit, and putteth off the natural man and becometh a saint through the atonement of Christ the Lord, and **becometh as a child**, submissive, meek, humble, patient, full of love, willing to submit to all things which the Lord seeth fit to inflict upon him, even as a child doth submit to his father.

We cannot serve two masters. We cannot serve two minds.

For most of our lives we have been controlled by the ego mind, by the natural man. The ego mind is the source of our pain. The spiritual mind, or "the little child," brings healing.

The ego mind tells us that we are worthless. The spiritual mind tells us that we are spirits of light simply experiencing darkness.

The ego mind tells us that we can't do it. The spiritual mind tells us that with God, we can do whatever our heart inspires us to do.

The ego mind tells us that we are not loved and not lovable. The spiritual mind tells us that we are always loved and surrounded by love. The spiritual mind tells us that we are inherently lovable, no matter what our mortal weaknesses are.

The ego mind worries constantly what others think of us. The spiritual mind knows that she has no control over other's thoughts, and is happy being who she is.

The ego mind tells us that we never have enough. The spiritual mind knows that all that is important is always provided.

The ego mind tells us that others have offended us. The spiritual mind simply chooses to believe the best about others and knows it cannot be offended unless it chooses to do so.

The ego mind tells us that others take advantage of us. The spiritual mind knows that all experiences are learning opportunities and forgives.

The ego mind tells us that we are not appreciated for what we do. The spiritual mind knows that true charity is giving without expectation of anything in return. The spiritual mind chooses to do only that which is for the highest good, and sometimes that is in giving to and serving others simply because we love them and not because we want accolades from them.

The ego mind tells us to hide our true natures and passions. The spiritual mind knows that being who we really are will fulfill our purpose here on this earth.

The ego mind tells us to hide our feelings. The spiritual mind knows that loving communication is important, but lets go of expecting anyone else to change.

The ego mind tells us not to trust anyone. The spiritual mind tells us to trust in the Lord and all will be for our best good.

The ego mind tells us to dwell in the mistakes and pain of the past. The spiritual mind repents, forgives, lets go of pain and lives in the moment.

The ego mind tells us to fear the future. The spiritual mind tells us to trust in the Lord and He will direct our paths.

The ego mind tells us that everyone else and our circumstances are keeping us from being happy. The spiritual mind knows that true happiness comes from within the heart and not from outside of us.

The ego mind is afraid of change. The spiritual mind welcomes change as the learning experience that brings us Home.

The ego mind hates herself. The spiritual mind knows she is in the perfect state, the perfect place and the perfect time in her journey towards Love.

Living the Gospel of Jesus Christ allows us to become as a little child.

A little child is trusting, full of faith and dependent on us. A little child, as long as we are truly loving, is willing to submit to our will for her.

As we increase in trust and faith in the power of the Atonement of Jesus Christ, as we humble ourselves before Him and sincerely repent, as we submit ourselves to His will, as we become patient and full of love, the Holy Spirit has the capacity to fill our hearts and release the ego mind from its fearful beliefs. Thus we become as a little child.

As we become more as a little child, we become more loving, forgiving, joyful and passionate. We love to learn, become more honest and less judgmental. We become more humble, and more trusting and dependant on God. And we love God and desire to do His will more than we desire to please those around us.

Unless we fully recognize our complete dependence on God, unless we are able to let go of the notion that we have control over our weaknesses and even over our lives, unless we are willing to seek for and submit to His will for us (which is also what is for our highest good), we cannot know the real power of the Atonement in bringing us back to our Home, bringing us back to who we really are, bringing us back to the peace of mind and the wisdom of heart that is surrounded by love.

✲ *Second Rule of the Subconscious Mind: Imagination is more powerful than knowledge.* ✲

Even if the mind of the natural man, or the ego mind, seems to have a strong hold on us, our imagination can bring about change. Imagine what you would act like and feel like if you truly were living from the spiritual mind, as a pure, innocent child. Imagine how you would act and think and feel in specific situations if you were in that state of mind. The brain doesn't know the difference between imagination and reality. The same pathways are activated whether you are imagining something or doing it. Imagine over and over, and the pathways begin to change.

Chapter 23

Healing through Loving
One Another

Christ's teachings are all about how to love.

*A*nd blessed are the merciful, for they shall obtain mercy.

...And blessed are all the peacemakers, for they shall be
called the children of God.

...whosoever is angry with his brother shall be in danger of his
judgment.

...Go thy way unto thy brother, and first be reconciled to thy
brother, and then come unto me with full purpose of heart, and I
will receive you.

...Give to him that asketh thee, and from him that would
borrow of thee turn thou not away.

...love your enemies, bless them that curse you, do good to them
that hate you, and pray for them who despitefully use you and
persecute you;

That ye may be the children of your Father who is in heaven...

...when thou doest alms let not thy left hand know what thy right hand doeth;

That thine alms may be in secret; and thy Father who seeth in secret, himself shall reward thee openly.

...And forgive us our debts, as we forgive our debtors.

...For, if ye forgive men their trespasses your heavenly Father will also forgive you...

...Judge not, that ye be not judged.

For with what judgment ye judge, ye shall be judged;

...And why beholdest thou the mote that is in thy brother's eye, but considerest not the beam that is in thine own eye?

...Therefore, all things whatsoever ye would that men should do to you, do ye even so to them, for this is the law and the prophets."

For I have given you an example, that ye should do as I have done to you.

...I say unto you, The servant is not greater than his lord; neither he that is sent greater than he that sent him.

If ye know these things, happy are ye if ye do them.

...A new commandment I give unto you, That ye love one another; as I have loved you, that ye also love one another.

By this shall all men know that ye are my disciples, if ye have love one to another.

Fear and anger worsen depression and anxiety; love and gratitude heal.

Christ told us all of these things because he loves us and knows what will make us happy. He knows that fear, anger, and frustration activate the areas of the brain which perpetuate depression and anxiety.

And He knows that love, trust and gratitude produce positive chemicals in the brain which heal.

When we hold onto pain, when we allow angry thoughts towards others to ruminate and grow, when we take an offense home and allow it into bed with us, the natural consequence is an increase in negativity and bad moods.

When we go through the process of allowing ourselves to feel the emotions that come up, but then choose to let them go, let go of the pain, repent and forgive, and move forward in gratitude and love, the natural consequence is joy.

If ye know these things, happy are ye if ye do them (John 13:17).

Judgment, forcing and control are not part of God's plan.

As a parent, spouse, teacher or leader it is not our job to judge. It is not to make others do things our way. It is not to impose our values on others. It is not our job to make others feel guilty, or to point out all of their faults to make them better.

It is not our job to get perturbed with others to the point of alienation. It is not our job dispute or contend with others in anger and frustration. It is not our job to control their lives.

These are the things that were sometimes done to us by our parents or spouses or teachers or leaders. We know these ways of relating don't feel good. They don't help us. They can destroy our feelings of love towards ourselves. They bring us down and allow us to feel depressed and anxious. We don't want to do to others the same things that created the problems in ourselves.

And when we do these things towards others, it increases our own depression and anxiety as well.

Love is the best parent, wife, teacher and leader.

So what is our job in relation to others?

Our job is to teach truth and inspire others through love. Our job is to be compassionate with wisdom. Our job is to accept each individual for who they are with the right to learn through making their own mistakes, while we build morale and instill confidence in their own true nature.

Our job is to motivate through inspiration and love, and build courage in others. Our job is to let go of fear and to love and trust in the Lord, trusting that He is as involved in their lives as much or more than we are. Our job is to be the example of the pure love of Christ—to not condemn but to save through love.

> *You will observe that the most potent influence over the mind of a child to persuade it to learn, to progress, or to accomplish anything, is the influence of love. More can be accomplished for good by unfeigned love, in bringing up a child, than by any other influence that can be brought to bear upon it. A child that cannot be conquered by the lash, or subdued by violence, may be controlled in an instant by unfeigned affection and sympathy. I know that is true; and this principle obtains in every condition of life. ... Govern the children, not by passion, by bitter words or scolding, but by affection and by winning their confidence (Joseph F. Smith).* (40)

Rules and consequences can be created with love.

All of this does not mean that we do not create rules and consequences for ourselves and our loved ones. By working with guidance from the Spirit and our loved ones, we can create rules and consequences in our homes which work for the positive.

We can create rules of what we will and will not allow in our homes, and provide consequences if those rules are broken. We cannot force someone to obey the rules, but specific consequences given through love can be a very effective teacher.

God has rules, and we live with natural consequences when we choose not to follow them. *There is always a consequence to every thought and every action.* This is called the Law of the Harvest. It is through the consequences of our successes and our mistakes, added with time and patience, that we learn what works and doesn't work, what brings pain and what brings joy.

God is ever-loving, ever-forgiving, full of patience, and the Atonement of Christ takes away the most serious consequence of our mistakes, which is our eternal separation from God.

At times we desire to control our loved ones to keep them from suffering.

Like Christ, we always only want what is for the highest good for others. Sometimes true love means that we must watch those we love endure much pain without our own interference in their lives, as we cannot assist in their progress until they are ready to make the necessary changes in order to take full advantage of life's opportunities.

As humans, it is hard to stand back and let our loved ones suffer. Like Christ, we can support them through sending love and prayers, but we must allow them to learn through their own choices, becoming involved only when moved upon by the Spirit to do so.

This does not mean that we do not interfere to keep our little ones safe. If we see a little one running into the street, we all would run and stop the child, even if he wants to keep running. Use wisdom with your love.

Sometimes the best way to love is to let go of being responsible for their happiness.

Sometimes we believe we are responsible for the happiness of those we love. That is a lie. Each person is responsible for their own happiness. A good relationship can add to happiness, but not create it. True happiness comes from within.

When we spend our time in worry and fear over the suffering of our loved ones, and spend our energy in trying to make their problems better, it simply continues the depression and anxiety, and does not serve them or us.

Let go of being responsible for their feelings. Send them love instead of fear and worry. Imagine angels surrounding and supporting them. Know that God's love always showers down upon them. This is a much more effective and positive way to think about and view our suffering loved ones.

If we are in a loving rather than fearful space, we are more open to the promptings of the Spirit.

Stop wearing yourself out worrying and trying to figure out what to do for your loved ones. If there is something God has for us to do for them, we must trust that He will let us know. We are more open to feeling the spiritual promptings that guide us in what actions to take, if any, when we are in that positive, loving space rather than a fearful, worried place.

Force and control is not part of God's plan.

Controlling others' choices and forcing them to do what will reduce their pain is not what God does for us. He allows us to learn through our mistakes and our pain.

> *And in that day Adam blessed God and was filled, and began to prophesy concerning all the families of the earth, saying: Blessed be the name of God, for because of my transgression my eyes are opened, and in this life I shall have joy, and again in the flesh I shall see God.*
>
> *And Eve, his wife, heard all these things and was glad, saying: Were it not for our transgression we never should have had seed, and never should have known good and evil, and the joy of our redemption, and the eternal life which God giveth unto all the obedient (Moses 5:10–11).*

God did not stop Adam and Eve from transgressing, even though He knew it would bring suffering to them and to the world. He did allow them to experience the consequences of their mistake. However, Adam and Eve were able to see that there was purpose in their weaknesses and mistakes, in the suffering and sorrow, and that this was the process that would allow them to find joy and eternal life.

We must allow our loved ones to follow the same process. We can teach, inspire, and implore with love, but it does not serve them or us to force them to follow the path we desire for them. Satan's method of forcing all to be good does not fulfill God's plan and does not bring us or them joy.

It serves us to follow the example of our Heavenly Father.

The greatest example of all is when our Father did not interfere with the spiritual, emotional and physical suffering of His Son. He allowed His Only Begotten to suffer because of His love for us. He allows us to suffer for the same reason. He is always there for us to turn to and receive comfort. He always loves us, but He does not interfere with our choices or the consequences of those choices, except as we repent, come unto Him and partake of the Atonement. He knows that this is the only way for us to eventually find true joy and become like Him.

We can do the same for our loved ones. We can always be there for them to turn to, we can be forgiving, we can always love them and send the power of love their way, but when they are suffering from the consequences of their choices we do not interfere unless moved upon by the Holy Spirit to do so. It is not our responsibility to "teach them a lesson" by withholding our love. It is our responsibility to follow the Spirit in how we choose to be there for them and serve them or not as they are learning their lessons by the results of their choices.

And when we let go of worry and fear over them, we can better see how all of this is in divine order and part of their learning experience on this earth. As we let go of worry and fear, we can follow the Spirit's promptings in how to care for them, if there is anything we can do. And thus we can find peace through love.

We can learn to love ourselves in spite of our weaknesses.

We are each on this earth doing the best we can do with the experiences we have had and the weaknesses that have been given to us. We are learning to make choices so that we can eventually choose to be like God. In our learning, we at times make choices which bring pain to ourselves and to others. This does not mean we are bad, we are worthless, or we are stupid. It simply means that we have fallen down and it is time to have faith in the Atonement of Christ, repent, let go of the pain, make things right the best we can and pick ourselves up again.

Part of the Plan of Happiness is falling and learning how to get up again.

We will fall in one way or another throughout our lives. When we learn how to overcome a weakness at one level, it will often pop up at another time in our lives so that we can learn how to deal with it at another level. When something that was hard becomes easy through our efforts and the grace of God, something new will come up to challenge us. This is the Lord's plan if we are desirous of becoming the best we can be. This life was created for our learning, and if we desire to continually progress, we will be given every opportunity to learn.

This is the Plan of Happiness. This is what we rejoiced over before we came here. Sometimes it is hard to believe that we chose this life of pain and suffering, but we did, because we knew that the outcome would truly be joy.

When we learn to love ourselves in spite of our earthly weaknesses, we begin to find joy.

The joy comes as we learn how to love ourselves as God loves us, and as we learn to love others as God loves them, by experiencing the opposite of what God is. The joy comes as we experience the peace that comes from knowing we are always loved, and that we are cleansed and perfected each time we truly repent.

As we accept this, and accept that our weaknesses are simply part of this earth life and not because we are inadequate and not good enough, we begin to allow God's Plan to unfold in our lives. As we accept and love ourselves as we are, in effect, loving the God who created us to be this way at this time.

Loving ourselves is loving God.

There are no teachings from God that tell us to hate ourselves, to disapprove of ourselves, to speak negatively in our thoughts and out loud about ourselves. There are no teachings that say we should constantly feel guilty and ruminate over our past misdeeds. There are no teachings that say we should hate our bodies or the way we look. When we do these things we are lacking in faith, and in essence we are rejecting God's eternal and perfect love for us. When we hate ourselves it is impossible to truly love our Father who created us.

As we learn to love and accept ourselves the way we are in this moment, we are loving God. If we love and accept ourselves as glorious in our strengths and in our weaknesses, knowing we are doing the best we are able to do with the experiences and the weaknesses we have been given, knowing that if we were able to do things in a better way we would be doing it, knowing that if our hearts truly desire to be better, Christ does heal our weaknesses, either in this life or the next, then we are able to follow the first and great commandment: to love God with all our hearts. We can love God because we accept and love all His creations, including that creation called "me."

Truly loving ourselves allows us to truly love others.

When we truly love and accept ourselves, then it naturally follows that we love and accept our fellow men in their strengths and weaknesses, using wisdom and power in how we choose to relate with them. (We can love and still refuse to be abused. We can love and still know that it does not serve us to associate with someone who constantly berates us, misuses us, betrays us or tempts us to do what is not for our highest good.)

When we truly love God and the way He created us, when we love ourselves just the way we are, and when we love others the way they are, our hearts are healed, and there is no more depression and anxiety.

True charity is a spiritual gift.

Be aware that this is not always as simple as it sounds by just saying the words. Pathways have been created in the brain, creating over-activity in parts of the brain which make it more difficult to love. It takes a lot of work to change thoughts and feelings. But, with God, all things are possible.

True charity, the pure love of Christ, is a spiritual gift. We can prepare ourselves for that gift by doing all that we can to change our patterns of thought and behavior, but it is important also to pray and ask for that gift. Charity is a gift given to all who truly seek for it, though it often takes time, patience, and lots of learning experiences.

✻ *First Rule of the Subconscious Mind: What is expected tends to be realized.* ✻

Expect that what others do is the best they can do in their current circumstances and weaknesses. Expect that what you do is the best that you can do in your current circumstances and weaknesses. Expect that others are inherently loving and good, and any offense was unintended. Expect that you are inherently loving and good, and that you are inherently worthy of every blessing that is given you. Expect blessings and miracles.

Chapter 24

Women Are That They Might Have Joy

Joy comes when we truly understand that the "opposites" of earth life are part of Heavenly Father's Plan of Happiness and for our highest good.

And now, behold, if Adam had not transgressed he would not have fallen, but he would have remained in the garden of Eden. And all things which were created must have remained in the same state in which they were created; and they must have remained forever, and had no end.

And they would have had no children; wherefore they would have remained in a state of innocence, having no joy, for they knew no misery; doing no good, for they knew no sin.

But behold, all things have been done in the wisdom of him who knoweth all things.

*Adam fell that men might be; and **men [and women] are, that they might have joy** (2 Nephi 22–25).*

Joy comes when we understand that we chose to be on this earth and go through our experiences here, as Job did.

*Where wast thou when I laid the foundations of the earth?...When the morning stars sang together, and all **the sons of God shouted for joy**? (Job 38:4, 7).*

Once when I was quite depressed I sought for and was given a beautiful blessing, which in part stated words which I believe are true for all of us:

*You were there when the plan of Mortal Life and Salvation was presented to the host of Heaven, when the Morning Stars sang and the Sons of God shouted for joy at the opportunity of coming here. You were anxious to come. You were not forced to come. You came of your own free will and choice. Before you came here you were a spirit child of God. You saw the perfection of your Heavenly Parents. You desired to be like them.... You saw the glorious perfection of God. You wanted to be in his likeness. Spirit and body inseparably connected receive a fullness of joy. This you are here to prepare for. The more opposition and trials you endure and overcome the greater will be your reward in the life to come....**Go on your way rejoicing** and know that the Lord is conscious of the trials that comes to all His children, and sees the acts of everyone....*

Joy comes when we truly have faith in the redemption which Jesus Christ brings to us.

*And the angel said unto them, Fear not: for, behold, I bring you **good tidings of great joy**, which shall be to all people (Luke 2:10).*

We are so blessed to be able to have the knowledge that we learn from all of our experiences, and that when we are weak, even though our hearts desire strength, Christ will make up the difference for us. We are judged by the desire of our hearts, and if our desire is for love, wisdom and righteous power, His atonement makes everything good in the end, and brings us into the Celestial Kingdom.

Joy comes when we know that the gospel of Jesus Christ is meant to bring peace and joy, not suffering.

> *These things have I spoken unto you, that **my joy might remain in you**, and that **your joy might be full** (John 15:11).*

> *For the kingdom of God is not meat and drink; but righteousness, and peace, and **joy** in the Holy Ghost (Romans 14:17).*

The purpose of this earth life is not to suffer, though we may suffer as we are learning by experiencing the opposite of what God is. *The purpose of this life is to find peace and joy through learning to love.* Jesus is the great example and teacher of wise and powerful love. As we turn to Him and continually repent, we can feel His love and become filled with peace and joy.

Sometimes we experience suffering in order to reach the point where we truly learn that kind of love, however, suffering isn't the end, but the beginning. When we learn that suffering comes more from the conflict within us than circumstances outside of us, suffering can end. Through giving our burdens to Christ, as Jean did, our burdens become our treasures, and we have the opportunity to feel joy not only after this earth life, but even on this earth, even now.

Joy comes when we recognize that our temptations and weaknesses are for a purpose.

> *My brethren, **count it all joy** when ye fall into divers temptations; Knowing this, that the trying of your faith worketh patience. But let patience have her perfect work, that ye may be perfect and entire, wanting nothing (James 1:2–4).*

Contrary to popular belief, perfection does not come from being perfect in this life. Perfection, as stated here, comes with temptations, the trying of our faith, and patience with our weaknesses. Remember, the Celestial Kingdom is not made up of people who were perfect in this earth life, but of those who have been *"made perfect through Jesus the mediator of the new covenant, who wrought out this perfect atonement through the shedding of his own blood"* (D&C 76:69).

> *Be ye therefore perfect, even as your Father which is in Heaven is perfect (Matthew 5:48).*

We cannot be perfect in our actions while on this mortal earth with a mortal body and a mortal brain. We can strive always to improve ourselves, but that is not perfection. We are perfect when we have repented and are baptized. We are also perfect each time we repent and partake of the sacrament, renewing our baptismal covenants. That perfection is reached through the grace of the Atonement of Jesus Christ, given to us as a gift, the gift that brings joy.

Joy comes when we repent and turn to Christ.

> *…I cried within my heart: O Jesus, thou Son of God, have mercy on me, who am in the gall of bitterness, and am encircled about by the everlasting chains of death. And now, behold, when I thought this, I could remember my pains no more; yea, I was*

*harrowed up by the memory of my sins no more. And oh, what **joy**,
and what marvelous light I did behold; yea, **my soul was filled
with joy** as exceeding as was my pain! (Alma 36:18–20).*

It is not good to dwell on the mistakes we have made and feel guilty
over them, but it is good to recognize them, feel godly sorrow, and
repent from them. When I recognize that I have been thinking thoughts
of fear, of judgment, of pride, of self-righteousness, or of negativity
towards myself or others, I repent right then, and ask that God bless me
with the ability to love myself and others more fully. I know that
thoughts unchecked lead to actions. I choose to repent if I can recognize
the thoughts before they become actions. I express gratitude that He
allows me to see my mistakes and turn them around.

When I keep a watchful eye on my thoughts and my actions, when
I repent as soon as I realize my mistake, when I turn to God and ask for
His eternal mercy, when I express gratitude for this life and all the
opportunities I am given to learn, my heart fills with peace and I can feel
God's love for me. When I do this I feel joy.

Joy comes when we seek for the Spirit and release the pains of the flesh to Christ.

*Now the works of the flesh are…these:…hatred…wrath, strife,
envying,…and such like…But **the fruit of the Spirit is love, joy,
peace, longsuffering, gentleness, goodness, faith** (Galatians
5:19–22).*

When I am in this world I think and act from the mind of the
natural man, which is the ego mind. I feel fear, anxiety, depression,
anger, irritation, worry, and envy. It is easier to fight with others, and I
fight within myself and dislike myself.

But when I am in my spiritual mind, I feel peace inside. I accept myself and others. I know what is for the highest good for me to do. I feel love for all, including myself, and I desire to serve God and my fellow man from that love. I am patient, and I trust and have faith that God is directing my path, even if I can't see where it is going. When I am in my spirit, I feel joy.

Joy comes when we share truth with others.

> *…ye have desired that ye might bring the souls of men unto me, while the world shall stand. And for this cause ye shall have fullness of joy; and ye shall sit down in the kingdom of my Father; yea, **your joy shall be full**, even as the Father hath given me **fullness of joy**… (3 Nephi 28:9–10).*

> *…he that receiveth the word by the Spirit of truth receiveth it as it is preached by the Spirit of truth. Wherefore, he that preacheth and he that receiveth, understand one another, and **both are edified and rejoice together** (D&C 50:21–22).*

You do not need to be an ordained missionary, a counselor or a church leader to share truth. Truth brings joy. When we are given a spiritual prompting to share a truth that has lifted us with another person, and we do so, both of us are lifted and given joy from the knowledge of that truth.

Joy comes when we sing and dance our praises to God.

> *For **my soul delighteth** in the song of the heart; yea, the song of the righteous is a prayer unto me, and it shall be answered with a blessing upon their head. Wherefore, **lift up thy heart and rejoice**, and cleave unto the covenants which thou hast made (D&C 25:13).*

*If **thou art merry**, praise the Lord with singing, with music, with dancing, and with a prayer of praise and thanksgiving (D&C 136:28).*

One of the things I love to do the most when I am feeling down is turn on the music and dance and sing. I am always lifted and feel much better when I do this. This is not easy to do when the depression or anxiety is strong, but it is definitely worth the effort!

Joy comes when we pray always and ask for the inspiration and knowledge that will bring us peace and joy.

*If thou shalt ask, thou shalt receive revelation upon revelation, knowledge upon knowledge, that thou mayest know the mysteries and peaceable things—**that which bringeth joy**, that which bringeth life eternal (D&C 42:61).*

*Pray always, and I will pour out my Spirit upon you, and great shall be your blessing... Behold, canst thou read this without **rejoicing and lifting up thy heart for gladness**? (D&C 19:38–39).*

*If thou are sorrowful, call on the Lord thy God with supplication, that **your souls may be joyful** (D&C 136:29).*

Joy is a gift. Don't forget to ask for it. Prayer will always bring an answer. If we ask for the gift of joy, doors will open so that we can learn the knowledge that will bring us joy. Be open to watching for and recognizing those doors of opportunity while you pray. Trust that all of your prayers are heard and answered, and that the opportunities to learn those answers are there.

Joy comes as we turn to the Lord, repent, partake of the sacrament and fast on the Sabbath Day.

> *But remember that on this, the Lord's day, thou shalt offer thine oblations and thy sacraments unto the Most High, confessing thy sins unto thy brethren, and before the Lord. And on this day thou shalt do none other thing, only let thy food be prepared with singleness of heart that thy fasting may be perfect, or, in other words, that **thy joy may be full** (D&C 59:12–13).*

There have been many times when my heart has been low and I have not wanted to do anything spiritual. When Sunday comes, there have been many times when I have not wanted to go to church. But I always prayed and asked if it was for my highest good to go to church, and usually the answer has been "Yes." So I go, knowing that there must be a purpose for me to be there.

When I go to church knowing that there is a purpose for me to be there, I feel more desire to repent and express gratitude for Christ while I partake of the sacrament. Because my heart is open I feel the cleansing and sanctification that comes from my repentance and the covenant of the sacrament.

When I go to church knowing that there is a purpose for me to be there, my heart is more open to hearing what the Spirit wants me to hear, and to saying what the Spirit wants me to say. Because my heart is open I receive answers to my prayers, and come home grateful that I went, feeling peace and joy.

When I fast, I learn to depend on the Lord for my strength rather than on food. When I fast, my body is rested from its labors of digestion, and the spirit can become stronger than the body. When I fast, I become more spiritually tuned, and I more easily receive answers to my prayers.

Joy comes when we let go of the fears of and about the body and remember that we are a Spirit of Light.

> *Wherefore, fear not even unto death; for in this world your joy is not full, but **in me your joy is full**. Therefore, care not for the body, neither the life of the body; but care for the soul, and for the life of the soul (D&C 101:36–37).*

Depression often causes us to hate our bodies and how they look. Anxiety often causes us to fear the symptoms of our bodies, to fear illness, physical suffering and death. We often spend an inordinate amount of time worrying about and caring for our physical bodies.

Our bodies are simply tools for our learning. They have weaknesses so that we can experience the opposite of the perfect body of godhood. They are our greatest teachers. When we recognize that our earthly mortal bodies are not who we really are, we can more easily come to know our spiritual selves, and care for and focus on that part of us more than our physical bodies.

We can let go of fear and accept what we are experiencing with our bodies as being for our highest good. When we can truly express gratitude for what our bodies are teaching us and how they are serving us, our spiritual mind will let us know what is important for us to do for our physical bodies.

Joy comes when we give service and gifts out of love, with no expectations, rather than out of obligation, expectations attached or resentment.

> *...if a man being evil giveth a gift, he doeth it grudgingly; wherefore it is counted unto him the same as if he had retained the gift, wherefore he is counted evil before God (Moroni 7:8).*

...He which soweth sparingly shall reap also sparingly, and he which soweth bountifully shall reap also bountifully. Every man according as he purposeth in his heart, so let him give, not grudgingly, or of necessity; for God loveth a cheerful giver (2 Corinthians 9:6–7).

As women it seems to be easy for many of us to become "martyrs," to feel like we are giving and giving and no one appreciates us. It is easy to feel used and manipulated into fulfilling everyone else's needs when no one is fulfilling our own. We find it hard to say no, because we don't want anyone to think badly of us, but then resent doing what we were asked to do.

After reading these scriptures when I was younger, I decided that if I was giving service and I resented it, I had better change my attitude or not give the service. I realized that if I felt obligated to do something, or if I was doing something so others wouldn't think poorly of me, I usually resented having to do it. I chose to either make this act of service my own choice, coming from my heart because I desired to do it out of love, doing it cheerfully, or say no to whomever was asking me to do it.

Because, if I gave from a grudging heart, it was counted as if I never gave.

I had a patient once that had a lot of physical symptoms created by stress. When asking what her stressors were, she told me that she was on a city beautification committee, and no one else was doing their job, so all of the work was on her shoulders. She was angry and resentful to the other committee members, and felt like they were using her. She was very stressed about it all.

I counseled her to go home and pray about this volunteer job, and feel if it was in her best interest or not. I counseled her that she either needed to give up the job or change her feelings about it, because the stress of how she felt was destroying her health. She came back later much happier. She had decided that she really did enjoy doing the work, and that it was worth it to her even if the others did nothing. She let go of worrying about what the others weren't doing and just gave of herself the best she could, enjoying the gifts she was able to give to the city. Her physical symptoms improved fairly quickly after that.

Joy comes when we focus on our gifts and talents rather than our fears and weaknesses.

> *… Lord, thou deliveredst unto me five talents; behold, I have gained beside them five talents more. His lord said unto him, Well done, thou good and faithful servant: thou hast been faithful over a few things, I will make thee ruler over many things: **enter thou into the joy of thy lord** (Matthew 25:20–21).*

We have learned that our weaknesses on this earth, in our mortal bodies, have a purpose, part of which is to assist us in learning to be more like God, in learning to love more like God, and in being humble and depending on God and the Atonement of Jesus Christ.

It is important to recognize our weaknesses, repent of them and strive to improve, but it is important to *not* focus all of our time and attention on our weaknesses. That which we focus on becomes stronger. When we focus on our weaknesses and hide our talents, as did the servant that was given one talent, then our weaknesses become stronger, and our talents lie dormant or we may even lose them.

When we focus on our gifts and talents, as the servants with five and two talents did, then those talents become stronger and we are given more.

We are given weaknesses to learn, and we are given gifts and talents to fulfill our purpose here on this earth. God has given each one of us different gifts and talents. God put in us a special gift that allows us to recognize those talents and causes us to use them, and that gift is joy. When we feel joy when we do something, not simply worldly pleasure, but true joy, we are receiving the message that this is something good to do, and there is purpose for it in our lives.

We women tend to feel guilty when we do things that bring us joy. For some reason we believe that we must do the things that are most distasteful to us to feel like we have accomplished something. We feel that we must sacrifice the things we enjoy and spend our time doing those things we don't enjoy in order to overcome our weaknesses and serve others the best. If we enjoy it, then we are being selfish.

This is, for the most part, a lie that we are telling ourselves.

When I was a young mother, I hated to do housework. However, I loved to work outside in the yard. Both needed to be done, but for some reason, when I was working outside, I felt guilty that I wasn't inside doing the housework. So I would leave undone the yard work that I loved to do, and spent my time doing housework, which I didn't enjoy.

After a time, I learned that when I worked outside while the children played out there, they were happier. I realized that there was purpose in the joy that I had in my yard, even more than creating the beauty of flowers that I craved. I didn't need to feel guilty that all of my housework wasn't done, because while I was creating outdoor beauty, my children were enjoying my presence nearby while they were playing.

My talent wasn't in housework. I felt guilty for years that I wasn't able to keep my house as clean and orderly as other women could. I found great joy in books and in learning, but I felt guilty when I spent my time reading and learning rather than doing the never-ending job of housecleaning.

I wanted to go back to school, which brought me joy, but how could I do all that I needed to do as a wife and mother and go back to school? So I focused on my weakness, which was trying unsuccessfully to keep a clean and organized home. I disliked myself because I couldn't seem to do it.

Then I started learning that my weaknesses are for a purpose, given to me by God to learn from, and that my gifts were given to me to fulfill my purpose. As I pondered on my gifts, circumstances came that made it important for me to return to school. As I followed the path that enhanced my gifts and talents and brought me joy, rather than the path that focused on my weakness and brought me pain, I eventually became a doctor. The things that brought me joy led me to the place where I am fulfilling my purpose.

I still work on keeping a clean house because I like a clean house, but I don't feel guilty anymore when it is not as clean as I would like it. And if doctoring or grandchildren or friends take me away from my cleaning, I no longer feel like I'm not good enough because my house isn't clean.

Many women feel great joy in housekeeping, and have a gift for keeping a clean and orderly house. That is fulfilling part of their purpose. Other women find joy in spending time with friends. Possibly part of their purpose is in their ability to lift others through their friendship. Others enjoy creating music or art. Others enjoy serving. Others enjoy their jobs. Each of us is given gifts that bring us joy. Improving and using those gifts not only brings us joy, but fulfills our purpose. Creating time to build on and use our gifts while we are busy as mothers and wives is not easy, but it is important.

Joy comes from loving ourselves exactly the way we are in this moment.

All things can be seen as a symbol of Christ. One thing most of us don't realize is that each of our lives is symbolic of the Only Begotten.

Our birth is but a sleep and a forgetting. Not in entire forgetfulness, and not in utter nakedness, but trailing clouds of glory do we come (William Wordsworth). (41)

Like Christ, we came from Heaven, full of glory, condescending ourselves into this mortal, dark and weak body.

Like Christ, we suffer temptations, and suffer the pains of this world, and because of Christ we can overcome them.

Like Christ, and because of Christ, our mortal, "natural man" can die and those dark parts of us can be resurrected into something better.

We are symbolic of the cross. Imagine yourself as a cross, the head being the top, the feet being the bottom, and the outstretched arms as the beam.

The head symbolizes heaven. The feet symbolize earth. We are of both heaven and earth. The head symbolizes spirit. The feet symbolize the mortal body. We are of both spirit and flesh.

The right hand symbolizes light, the left hand dark. The right symbolizes good, the left evil. The right love, the left fear. The right is strengths, gifts and talents, and the left is weaknesses. We are each of us all of that.

The center of the cross is symbolic of our hearts, our own power within. It symbolizes the place where all comes together through love and through Christ into at-one-ment, into One.

Each part of the cross is necessary to fulfill our purpose here. It is important that we accept all parts of us as one: heaven and earth, spirit and flesh, light and dark, good and evil, love and fear, strength and weakness. Each one of us is all of these, and to fulfill our purpose here we accept it all, and bring it through our love into the One that is Christ, that we may truly be One.

Joy comes when we accept all of who we are, every part of us, the head and feet, the right hand and the left, and through the at-one-ment become One with Christ and the Father.

Depression and anxiety seem to keep us from experiencing joy.

When we suffer from depression or anxiety, it is hard to find joy in anything. There is often a belief that we have no gifts, but that is a lie. Sometimes the depression or anxiety came partly because we focused on our weaknesses rather than on our talents and those things which brought us joy. Possibly we even denied ourselves the things that brought us joy because we felt guilty and selfish. Possibly we felt that because we didn't do something perfectly, even though we enjoyed doing it, that we were no good and that we had no talent.

Pray to find that which brings you joy.

However, it is possible to remember the things in the past that used to bring us joy. Make a list of them. Pray that you will be inspired to remember and to find them. Add to that list things you have thought of that might possibly bring you joy, even though you might not yet have experienced them.

Start doing one or two of them, little by little, even if you feel that you aren't doing them well, or that you aren't really enjoying it. Trust that by focusing on your talents, using them and improving them, you are on the path to fulfilling your purpose here on this earth and in the eternities.

Women are that they might have joy. It is possible and desirable to find joy in this life. It is good to do the things that bring us joy. With depression or anxiety it is difficult to find the motivation, but every little effort towards creating joy is a baby step towards healing. Even by using baby steps we can eventually climb a mountain, the mountain of healing.

✱ *The Eighth Rule of the Subconscious Mind: The greater the conscious effort, the less the subconscious response.* ✱

Let go of trying so hard to change. Let go of trying so hard to be happy. Just know that it is possible. Allow yourself to simply be, allow yourself to be okay just the way you are. Allow yourself to have kind thoughts towards yourself, to let go of judgment of yourself. Put away the self-critic and allow the self-counselor to work in kindness and gentleness with you, and you will find joy in yourself.

We each have very difficult and painful things happen to us. Rather than fight them, accept them for what they are—opportunities to grow in light and love. See the hand of God in how you work through them, in the small blessings given to you on a daily basis. Focus on the good rather than fight the negative, find things to be grateful for daily, and you will find joy in situations you never believed you could.

Imagine the future as being good, successful, and full of blessings. Imagine over and over again in your mind that you are happy. See yourself in situations where you are feeling joy, feeling excited, feeling so grateful, feeling delighted, feeling loved. Just imagine and feel, and allow your subconscious mind, the angels, and Jesus Christ to do the work. Act on the good feelings that come. Act on the inspiration that comes. Act on the things that bring you joy.

And joy will come.

One Woman's Healing Journey

y husband is a member of the Church, but he is inactive and critical of many things about the church. Even though I felt God's confirmation in marrying my husband, it was the beginning of all my troubles. We did not get married in the temple because my husband was not able to go. This was a source of worry and grief for me for many years. I struggled alone trying to teach my children the gospel and to nurture them spiritually.

I did not receive any spiritual support from my husband in teaching the gospel in our home. I gave up on family home evenings. We had no regular family prayer or scripture study. I silently resisted my husband's complaints that I was splitting up the family every Sunday. Whenever I went to church I would be filled with guilt because I would be reminded of the things I was not doing. Many times I would come home on Sunday and instead of being uplifted I would feel heavy and depressed about my life, my marriage, and my family. It was not what I had dreamed of; it was not what I had wanted.

I continued to go to church because I felt a need for it in my life. Even though I was spiritually strengthened by going to church, there were many things that hurt me: things that were said, the way people behaved toward me and my family, the way I felt judged by others, which seemed evident in their conversations with me. It was not enough that I already felt bad about my family, that I already judged myself, that I felt like we were one of the least worthy families in my ward.

Many times I would sit in church looking enviously at couples and families sitting together. Did anybody understand how I felt? But I did not even dare to speak about it. Was I not responsible for my own problems? Had I chosen to marry the wrong person? Had I not heard a hundred times to marry in the temple? Why would I even ask for anyone to understand when I had brought this upon myself?

I tried so desperately to be perfect, but what I did not understand was that I couldn't do it through my own strength, ability, or power. The focus on works in our church had made me completely miss the importance and power of God's grace.

In church I had heard it over and over again, all the things that I need to do to be able to go to the celestial kingdom, the long "To-do-Lists" that kept overwhelming me. *'It is by grace that we are saved, after all we can do'* (2 Nephi 25:23). It seemed that in church we had always focused on the second part of this scripture. I was always encouraged to focus on what I can do to be better, and I had come to believe that I had to do it all to be saved. I did not really understand the grace of God because I had not heard it really talked about in our church.

Often I felt hopeless and fell into depression and despair. I thought I needed to earn my place in heaven through my own diligence and effort. But I had come to a point in life where I had run out of energy and realized that I could not do more and needed help. Of course, there were times when Heavenly Father had clearly guided and inspired me and I was able to do exactly the right things and make the correct decisions. I could feel His love in those moments and at those times. But I would usually fall back into my self-doubt, into my depression or sadness, into my busy life and into just struggling along.

Through all my struggles, difficulties and challenges I had come to discover many of my weaknesses and shortcomings. And I just could not overcome them, no matter how hard I tried. In addition I was so concerned about my children. I was not only trying to save myself, but I felt that I needed to save my children too. Whenever they did something wrong I felt responsible. I was carrying a great responsibility and a great burden. My depression continued to worsen.

One summer I began to feel a nudging feeling in my heart that I needed to correct two things in my life. One was to pay tithing. Due to my husband's feelings about paying tithing to the church I had stopped paying tithing. I had justified myself because I did not have a job and was not earning any money. However, I came to feel that my work at home was worth something and that a part of my husband's income was my earning. So I decided that I would pay my tithing from the money that my husband gave me to run the home.

The other thought that was in my heart was concerning the temple. I had received my endowment as a young adult a few years before I met my husband. After marrying my husband I had stopped going to the temple for many reasons. But this summer I felt the urging inside my heart to go to the temple. I resisted it for a while but it would not go away and so finally I decided to just go.

After I corrected these two things in my life I was almost immediately blessed. The struggle that I had for over 20 years with the church, my ward, and Utah Mormons; my struggle with feeling misunderstood, rejected and not fitting in was simply gone. It was not in my heart anymore. I was amazed. I also immediately knew that it was the atonement of Jesus Christ that had healed me from this pain and had taken that burden from my soul. That is when I realized for the first time in my life that I had partaken of the atonement of Jesus Christ. I comprehended for the first time how important it is and I began to understand it.

For now I had learned the importance of keeping covenants. There are those commandments that may seem easy to do, such as prayer, scripture reading, partaking of the sacrament, paying tithing, keeping the word of wisdom, going to the temple, and others. They are a matter of choice, a matter of deciding to do it. They are clearly defined. Making a change in keeping one commandment is a good starting point in moving forward and a safe plan to fall back on when we struggle with life, or when we struggle with the other commandments that seem so much harder; such as loving our Heavenly Father with all of our heart, loving our fellowmen including our enemies and those who are so hard to love, or especially loving ourselves. However, in spite of the blessings of keeping those covenants, the depression continued.

I had focused all my life on loving my Heavenly Father and loving others, and yet I discovered over and over again that I was not able to do so perfectly. I also struggled with loving myself. About two years after repenting from my two covenant breaking sins and being healed by my Savior from my personal struggles with the church, He would teach me the next lesson.

After a summer in which I had overworked myself, I became ill. That is when I found Dr. Moore and saw her for my physical problems. At that time I did not know that she also helped people with their emotional problems. After several visits I discovered that she had written a book called *Healing from the Heart*. At first when I read it, I thought it was interesting that our emotions make us ill. But I also kept a protective wall of skepticism.

Then I listened to the CD included in her book and made a discovery about myself: I did not like myself! On my next visit I did not intend to tell her, but somehow it just all spilled out. I was really surprised about myself afterwards. How could I have lost my composure and control over myself and shared my deepest, darkest secrets with a stranger? But I felt okay. I felt totally fine, a little scared and frightened, but at least it was out. I had told someone else.

The next few visits with her helped me to open my heart and discover the reasons why I did not like myself. She helped me to discover what had hurt me in life and what wrong conclusions and beliefs I had drawn from my experiences, which were keeping me literally tied up in chains. These chains kept me from improving in the ways that I wanted to. As I opened my heart and asked myself many questions, why I felt about things in certain ways, I began to discover more and more false ideas that I had formed, often in childhood, and continued to hold on to.

But I was still not able to love myself. That was something only my Heavenly Father could change and heal me from. Over time, seeking with my heart open, I began to feel His love for me. I was able to be healed by our Heavenly Father's unconditional and incredible love for me. I felt His love so strongly that I was amazed. It was the most healing, the most beautiful experience I have ever had. My Heavenly Father knew me personally and not only that, He loved me. He loved me despite of all my weaknesses, my failures, and my past mistakes.

I discovered that all along I had already done what He wanted me to do even though it was not perfect. He loved me and had accepted my efforts. But I was still not able to love myself. I still struggled with that. Finally I gave up and decided to trust in His love for me. My Heavenly Father loved me. Without any doubt He had clearly made me feel His love in my heart. If He loved me so completely then I could accept myself. I was okay—warts and all.

After accepting myself, I was able to do something that I was not able to do before. When I had experienced my Heavenly Father's love for me, it had filled me also with an overwhelming desire to only do His will. I did not want to live for myself anymore but just for Him.

And so by resting in the security of His love I asked Him: 'What am I doing wrong?' I was never able to ask that question before. I was too fragile, too insecure, too self-critical and had not been able to face myself completely. Instead, I had to constantly do all kinds of foolish things to help me feel better about myself.

We all do these things: compare ourselves to others, be critical of others and put other people down to make ourselves feel better, feel arrogant and prideful, hide our problems or the things we are ashamed of, not do something good because we could make a mistake which would make us feel miserable; and I am sure many other things.

But I had enough of the struggles with myself and was finally ready to get better. And so I asked my Heavenly Father in my prayers: 'What am I doing wrong?' I wanted to know and I wanted to do better. That is when my Heavenly Father showed me my pride, my fear – of which I had a lot, my anxieties, and my need for self-importance. He did not show them to me all at once. He showed me one at a time. And not only did He show me but He healed me from these things.

My fear and anxiety was my biggest problem. For a couple of months I felt it, I was aware of it, I mentally struggled with it trying to convince myself that I did not need to fear, trying to make myself have more faith. But I could not. I told myself how many times Heavenly Father had helped me out of my troubles. I reminded myself of the miracles that He had done in my life. I tried to convince myself by reading in the scriptures about God's many and mighty miracles. There was no reason for me to be afraid. It was not right for me to have so little faith. I did not want to be like the people of Moses who had witnessed the ten plagues poured out on Egypt, the cloud and pillar of fire, and the miraculous rescue through the Red Sea; and still they had so little faith.

But no matter how hard I tried I could not make myself have more faith. After my own pep talks I would fall straight back into fear. And so I did the only thing that so often is the only thing we can do. I prayed continuously to my Heavenly Father asking Him to forgive me for my fear, my lack of faith, to forgive me my weakness and to help me to overcome it, to heal me from it. It took about two months of praying and repenting and just holding onto my covenants, doing all the things I was able to do, going to the temple, to church and reading scriptures daily, because though I couldn't have faith, I could do those things. But then one day, miraculously, the fear was simply gone.

I have learned since then that there are many things that we truly cannot overcome ourselves. I have learned that when we come unto Christ He will heal us, in His own time frame, when it is for our highest good. He is the only one who can. We cannot heal ourselves. That is a humbling discovery but also the most glorious one. All we must really do is believe in our Heavenly Father and in our Savior Jesus Christ. They have the power to perfect us. We do not have this power. We can totally rely on Jesus Christ's strength, love, and guidance. Without my Heavenly Father, without my Savior I am nothing. But with them, I am everything and I can do anything (Alma 26:12). These are not just empty words for me anymore because I have experienced it and experience it every day.

I am still not perfect. I still make mistakes. I still mess up and fall short of my own expectations. Sometimes I have thoughts of pride, sometimes I judge, at times I doubt and am afraid I will fail or I worry about my image and what others think of me. But now I recognize these things almost right away and I know what to do. I run into my Heavenly Father's arms and tell Him that I am sorry. I confess it all and ask for His forgiveness and I let His love wrap around me and hug me and hold me very tight. I imagine Him saying to me: "It's okay, I know you are working on it. Don't give up. You can do it. I am always there to help you. I will never forsake you and I will never stop loving you.

No longer am I ashamed of myself. I am not ashamed of my family, of my children, or the fact that I am not married in the temple. Heavenly Father knows my desire. I know that He is perfectly able to bless me with everything. I also know that He knows what is best. He works in everyone's life and His purpose is to teach His children. He is totally in control. I can completely trust in His plan for me and my family.

The best way that I can help Him and thank Him is by trusting Him. I do not need to take matters into my own hands and get worried and anxious and pushy with my husband or my children. I just need to love them and pray for them. I trust that my Heavenly Father will prompt me when He wants me to say something to them or do something for them. I just need to trust my Heavenly Father and do His will.

I like to use two phrases that help me to more completely surrender and submit to my Heavenly Father and to more completely trust Him. These are the words of Jesus Christ and they reflect His love and trust in His Father: "Father, into Thy hands I commit my spirit" (Luke 23:46) and "Father, glorify Thy name" (John 12:28). Focusing on my Heavenly Father's love for me fills my heart with peace and overwhelming gratitude for His plan and what He has done for me and is doing in my life. It is this gratitude that makes me want to praise Him forever and give all glory to Him.

Many times I have asked myself: Who am I? That is a question that goes much deeper than the general answer that "I am a child of God" can satisfy. Why am I the way I am? Did I choose myself, did I choose how I wanted to be? If so, maybe I would have made myself more beautiful, more righteous, wiser; I would have made myself better than I think I am. But that is not wise because God in His great wisdom and love created me the way I am for a purpose. The purpose is for me to learn and grow and also to teach and help others. If I can fulfill the purpose of my creation by being willing to accept and love myself as I am, and by being willing to learn and strive to do my Heavenly Father's will in serving Him and others, then I will have done all that He wants me to do. Then I can be satisfied with myself and I know that Heavenly Father will rejoice over me.

I do not understand so many things. I do not understand why I so much desire to do what is right and others seem not to care. There are so many mysteries, things that we do not understand right now because we walk by faith and not by sight. But our Heavenly Father will teach us what we need to know and when we need to know it.

For now, I choose to believe that He created me exactly the way I am with the strength and weaknesses and personality that I have. When I believe that, together with the knowledge that He loves me and that all that God creates is good and has a purpose, I can feel peace inside of me. I am able to accept myself and focus on what my Heavenly Father wants me to do instead of worrying about myself.

We are all broken from the moment we enter this world. We are not able to fix ourselves through our own strength or willpower. All these years I have struggled to become perfect and have been weighed down by my own failures and by my circumstances and the world around me. When Heavenly Father filled my heart with His love, my eyes were opened to the scriptures in new ways.

One of the most beautiful scriptures that have touched me deeply is Jesus Christ's words as recorded in 3 Nephi chapters 9 to 11. Jesus invites the people to come unto him and *be healed*. I have learned that I come unto him by entering into covenants and doing my best to keep them, doing all that I can do, but then, most importantly, by having faith in Him and inviting Him to heal me from my weaknesses and all those things that I am not able to do.

The most transforming and life changing experience that we can have is to experience God's love personally for us. That is what will truly heal us from pain and sin. And it is something that we can all experience, not just the prophets. For many years I had been praying that God would fill my heart with His love without really understanding what I was asking for. I just wanted to be able to love better. Well, God loves us with a love that we all long for and do not find on earth. And I believe that He desires to reveal His love to all that ask for it.

—Yvonne Mughal

Medications: To Take or Not To Take

*M*any people question if they should take a medicine or not. There are so many viewpoints on this and everyone is different. Some depend completely on medication and others feel like a failure if they have to resort to a medication. Many with anxiety are afraid to take medication, and others with anxiety are afraid not to, even when it doesn't seem to be helping.

There are a few things to remember about medication:

1. Medicines can be seeming miracles from God or they can be seeming curses from Satan.

There is no way currently to tell how someone is going to be helped by or react negatively to a medication. It is all experimentation. Some people feel a positive difference right away, and some feel sick and horrible right away. Some lose their suicidal ideation, and some have an increase in their suicidal thoughts. Some may get addicted to anti-anxiety medication, and some can stop as soon as their anxiety improves without any negative effect. And in many cases there is no change at all. A high percentage of people never have complete relief of their symptoms, even when on two or more medications.

It is important to recognize that there is no right or wrong concerning taking medication. Medication in and of itself is not inherently good or evil. This is a matter between you, your doctor and the Lord. Ask the Lord if it is for the highest good for you to take medicine or not. Trust the answer. Yes, it is hard to feel the Spirit and receive answers when you suffer with depression and anxiety, but do it anyway and do the best you can.

2. Anti-depressant medications work no better than placebo except in severe clinical depression. However, in severe depression, it makes a significant difference. (42)

If you have mild to moderate depression, the placebo effect of taking a medication can be quite strong. Just the act of doing something allows you to feel better. This doesn't mean medication would not work for you, but the chances are that a placebo pill would work just as well. The mind is very powerful, and if it believes it is being helped, then it is being helped.

If you have severe clinical depression, you have an increased chance of being helped by medication. However, studies have also shown that good counseling and cognitive behavioral therapy can work as well as medications.

3. Medication should not be used as the only treatment, but as a band-aid to help stop the emotional bleeding as the cause is being dealt with.

In my experience, the majority of people who are prescribed a medication and do no counseling or other work to deal with their issues end up needing more or different medication in the future because it "stops working." I believe that the issues, if not dealt with, keep resurfacing even through the medication.

Medication can be very useful when a person is really struggling, but make sure it is used with other methods to deal with the many things, both physical and emotional, that may be adding to the depression and anxiety.

4. Going off of a medication and subsequently having symptoms is not proof that you need the medicine.

Many people coming into my office already on medication say that they have tried to go off, but they cry all the time or become very irritable, etc. They feel that they cannot come off of their medicine because of it.

"Antidepressant Withdrawal Syndrome" has been proven to exist by double blind placebo controlled trials. (43) The body and brain can become dependent on the medication and there are withdrawal symptoms when the medication is interrupted or the dose reduced. Physical symptoms may include problems with balance, dizziness, electric shock-like sensations, sweating, nausea, insomnia, tremor, vertigo, post-SSRI sexual dysfunction, gastrointestinal symptoms, flu-like symptoms, and sensory and sleep disturbances. Psychological symptoms include anxiety and/or agitation, crying spells, irritability and aggressiveness.

If a person feels ready to come off of their medication they can choose to wean down over a period of two to six months, or in some cases even longer, to avoid withdrawal symptoms. Even so, there may be, at times, some symptoms with each drop in dose, which may take 5 days to 2 weeks to resolve. For most people the withdrawal symptoms don't last over 2–3 weeks even if weaning more quickly, but in some the symptoms may be more severe.

Not everyone has symptoms coming off of antidepressant medication. But many people do. Just be aware that having symptoms as you come off does not mean you need the medication. You must be off for at least a month or two to determine if the medication really made a difference for you or not.

Appendix 2

Do Diet and Supplements Make a Difference?

*T*he following is not intended to be used as medical advice. Please seek the advice of your health care practitioner before using supplementation. Supplements and medications can have interactions. If you are taking medication it is important to consult with a practitioner knowledgeable in medication-supplement interactions before you start taking them.

Supplements have been shown to improve mood.

Vitamins and minerals

Vitamin deficiencies can aggravate or even cause depression and anxiety. A good multivitamin-mineral supplement has been shown to improve symptoms more than placebo.

The B-complex vitamins are essential to mental and emotional well-being. They cannot be stored in our bodies, so we depend entirely on our daily diet to supply them. B vitamins are destroyed by alcohol, refined sugars, nicotine, and caffeine, and used up more quickly in stress, so it is no surprise that many people may be deficient in these.

Subclinical deficiencies of vitamin C can produce depression. Supplementation is particularly important if you have had surgery or an inflammatory disease. Stress, pregnancy, and lactation also increase the body's need for vitamin C, while aspirin, tetracycline, and birth control pills can deplete the body's supply.

Deficiency of magnesium can result in depressive symptoms, along with confusion, agitation, anxiety, and hallucinations, as well as a variety of physical problems such as muscle tension and spasms. Most diets do not include enough magnesium, and stress and eating sugar also contribute to magnesium depletion.

Calcium depletion affects the central nervous system. Lower levels of calcium cause fatigue, nervousness, apprehension, irritability, and numbness.

Zinc inadequacies result in apathy, lack of appetite, and lethargy. When zinc is low, copper in the body can increase to toxic levels, resulting in paranoia and fearfulness. A high copper-zinc ratio is associated with mood disorders such as bipolar disease, can cause estrogen dominance, is associated with eating disorders, and can increase the risk of cancer.

Depression can be a symptom of chronic iron deficiency. Other symptoms include general weakness, listlessness, exhaustion, lack of appetite, and headaches.

Manganese is needed for proper use of the B-complex vitamins and vitamin C. Since it also plays a role in amino-acid formation, a deficiency may contribute to depression stemming from low levels of the neurotransmitters serotonin and norepinephrine. Manganese also helps stabilize blood sugar and prevent hypoglycemic mood swings.

Potassium depletion is frequently associated with depression, tearfulness, weakness, and fatigue. Lower levels can also cause muscle spasms and heart arrhythmias.

I recommend SuperMulti Plus by SpringTree Health for my patients. By way of disclosure, I formulated this product and own the company. I did this because most multivitamins on the market do not have enough B-vitamins, calcium, magnesium and trace minerals, and therefore people have to buy them separately, which costs more.

Amino acids

The current fad belief that "meat is bad" has caused an increase in amino acid deficiency, especially if the protein isn't replaced by eating good combinations of vegetarian foods. The modern American diet is high in simple carbohydrates and low in good healthy protein.

The amino acid tryptophan uses B6 to metabolize into serotonin, a mood-elevating neurotransmitter. Phenylalanine is converted into norepinephrine, which can energize the mind.

L-Tyrosine and/or DL-Phenylalanine can also create dopamine. Dopamine is the thinking neurotransmitter. It creates energy and allows you to focus and concentrate. ADD is a symptom of a dopamine deficiency. Becoming quickly bored with the routine and having a hard time focusing are classic symptoms of ADD. Dopamine deficiency can also be the cause of depression. People with dopamine deficiencies tend to start a lot of things and then don't finish them. They work on a lot of different things at once. Forgetfulness, a sluggish mind, low motivation and fatigue are signs you need more dopamine. (Parkinson's disease results in an almost complete lack of dopamine. Parkinson's patients deal with depression because of that.)

L-threonine is an amino acid that is calming, often used for anxiety. GABA is an amino acid that is also a neurotransmitter, and is also used to treat anxiety.

If you don't know which specific amino acids to use, even a general essential amino acid supplement will often help.

Herbs and glandulars

There are different herbs and other supplements that can improve depression. Some of those that have been studied are St. John's Wort, SAM-e, and Rhodiola Rosea. For anxiety, chamomile, lemon balm, and kava kava are used, among others. Generally these herbs and supplements are safe for use. However, some of them, such as St. John's Wort, increase serotonin levels, and if you are taking an anti-depressant medication, can increase the risk of "serotonin syndrome." Be sure and work with a doctor knowledgeable in the interactions between herbs and medicines.

Anxiety and depression often cause adrenal stress or adrenal fatigue. A good adrenal supplement with adrenal glandulars and herbs can help support the adrenals to reduce fatigue. I formulated Adrenal Stress Relief from SpringTree Health (see www.springtreehealth.com).

Sugar has a profound effect on the brain.

Many of us have been brought up being rewarded with sweets, thereby associating sugar with love and "being a good girl or boy." It is a reward because it can act like a drug in our brains. Sugar leads to the release of powerful chemicals like serotonin, the opiod-like beta-endorphin and the reward chemical dopamine. There are scientific signs that sugar can be addictive, with tolerance, withdrawals syndromes, and cravings.

Almost all processed foods have sugar, processed sugar substances or high fructose corn syrup in it—meatballs, pickles, even french fries. Willpower is not the main reason for our obesity epidemic. It's more about how sugar affects our physiology. It not only makes us feel good, but it can confuse the brain into thinking we're still hungry even after we've had plenty to eat. When our food makes us more hungry instead of satisfied, of course we'll keep eating. We'll keep eating until we gain weight, get sick, and get anxious and depressed because of blood sugar swings and the effect of sugar on the brain.

In the short-term, a high-sugar diet can lead to headaches, indigestion, joint pain and imbalanced gut flora. Imbalanced gut flora can cause chemical changes that affect the brain (see below). But it gets worse over time. A high-sugar diet over many years can feed inflammation and therefore lead to health problems like heart disease, metabolic syndrome, Type 2 diabetes and even cancer.

A treat or dessert every once in a while is one thing, but relentless cravings are another. Cravings are messages from your body. Non-stop sugar cravings may mean something physiological is going on in your body, including stress, hormonal fluctuations, insulin resistance, food sensitivities, systemic yeast, low serotonin levels and consumption of excessive acid-forming foods.

But there are also psychological causes of sugar cravings. Just like any addiction, often sugar is used trying to fill an empty hole inside. However, like any addiction, it is like filling a hole in the earth with water—it may fill up and we feel better, but it quickly disappears. It gives a false feeling of love which keeps us from the true Source of Love.

Going off sugar, or dramatically reducing sugar intake, and replacing it with a good healthy diet with healthy snacks between meals has consistently helped improve moods in my patients with depression and anxiety.

Be careful with artificial sweeteners. The majority of them have their own health concerns and can affect the nervous system, increase diabetes, etc. Xylitol does not have the brain effects and can reduce tooth decay, but some have increased gas and bloating with it. Stevia, an herb, is the only sweetener than seems to have no negative effects.

The intestines and the brain are very connected.

It is often said that we have two brains, one in our skull and one in our intestines. Our intestines and brain originate early in fetal life from the same clump of tissue. This tissue divides, and one section turns into the central nervous system (the brain and spinal cord) and the other into the enteric nervous system (the nervous system inside the intestinal tract). They are connected through the vagus nerve, the longest of the cranial nerves. Half of all nerve cells are found in the intestines!

That is why anxiety can cause stomach pain, nausea, or abdominal pain and upset, or irritable bowel syndrome. It produces "gut feelings." The state of the intestines can have a profound effect on our mental and physical health. And the brain can have a profound effect on our intestinal health.

Besides genetics, there is something very important the mother in passes to her child: her unique intestinal micro-flora. An adult, on average, carries 4½ pounds of bacteria in the gut. There are more microbial cells in the intestines than there are cells in an entire human body! It is a highly organized micro-world, where certain species of bacteria have to predominate to keep us healthy physically and mentally. Their role in our health is very important.

Healthy intestinal flora assists in absorption and digestion of food and nutrients, so those with improper gut flora often have low grade nutritional deficiencies. The flora also actively synthesizes specific nutrients such as vitamin K, most of the B-vitamins, and various amino acids and proteins. Pathogenic bacteria consume iron, which can cause anemia. Healthy gut flora actually provides energy to the intestinal tract, so those with dysbiosis (an unhealthy imbalance of intestinal bacteria and yeast), usually have digestive problems.

Healthy intestinal flora is very important to the immune system. The beneficial bacteria ensure appropriate production of different immune cells, immunoglobulins and other parts of the immune system. They also keep the immune system in the right balance. Intestinal dysbiosis causes two major arms of the immune system, Th1 and Th2, to get out of balance. Dybiosis causes an underactive Th1 and an overactive Th2. As a result the immune system starts reacting to most environmental stimuli in an allergic or atopic kind of way. Eczema, allergies, and at the worst, autoimmune diseases, can result. A compromised immune system can also cause reactions to immunizations.

One of the major functions of the good bacteria is controlling about 500 different species of pathogenic (disease causing) and opportunistic microbes. When the beneficial bacteria get destroyed the opportunistic pathogens get a special opportunity to grow into large colonies and occupy large areas of the digestive tract, especially yeasts such as Candida species, and bacteria from the Clostridia family. As these pathogens digest the food passing through our intestines, they produce various toxins which can affect the neurons and neurotransmitters in the intestines, and are also carried through the bloodstream to the brain. These toxins can cause neurological and psychological changes in the brain. It is very common for people with depression, anxiety, ADHD, dyslexia, bipolar disease and schizophrenia to have severe intestinal dysbiosis. When their intestinal tract is healed, their symptoms will often dramatically improve.

A typical modern mother had quite a few courses of antibiotics in her childhood and youth for various infections. Antibiotics have a serious damaging effect on the intestinal flora because they wipe out the beneficial strains.

Often the mother used contraceptive pills, which change the flora to less positive strains. A modern diet of sugar, processed and fast foods provides perfect nourishment for these pathogens. Non-steroidal anti-inflammatory medications such as ibuprofen, and other medications, also have a negative effect on the intestinal flora.

As a result of all these factors a mother may have seriously compromised intestinal flora by the time she is ready to have children. The infant's intestinal tract, after the first 20 days or so of life, becomes populated with intestinal flora, mainly from the mother. Clinical signs of intestinal dysbiosis (abnormal gut flora) are present in almost 100% of mothers of children with neurological and psychiatric conditions (ADHD, autism, dyslexia, anxiety, bipolar and schizophrenia). The most common health problems in mothers are digestive abnormalities, allergies, auto-immunity, PMS, chronic fatigue, headaches, skin problems and mood disorders. Many of these children, as infants, had thrush or yeast diaper rashes, which is a sign of intestinal dysbiosis.

The children then go through their own courses of antibiotics, junk food, etc., and increase the problem of gut dysbiosis. Each generation has the possibility of getting worse physically and psychologically unless changes in diet and medications are made.

Clearing up severe dysbiosis requires a strict sugar-free, grain-free, and chemical-free diet, often medication to kill yeast, healthy food, nutritional supplements and lots of probiotics. It seems hard because we are so used to the ease of the processed foods and the taste of our modern diet, but it can be very effective, and once it is learned, not as hard as it seems. One website that provides good information on this type of healing is www.gaps.me. I highly recommend a good period of time for intestinal cleansing.

Appendix 3

For the Family: Dealing with a Wife or Mother with Depression or Anxiety

$\mathcal{T}$racy Izatt, who suffered from generalized anxiety disorder, depression, fibromyalgia, and SAD (seasonal affective disorder), and her husband, Ted, describe how her problems affected him and her children:

"My anxiety and depression were very severe for many years. At every change of season, I would start feeling the symptoms of either extreme anxiety in the spring or heavy depression in the fall. During this period I would anticipate my children beginning their summer activities or the beginning of another school year. Either way, I was overwhelmed and wondered how I would deal with something that loomed over me like a heavy load rather than seeing it as an opportunity to learn and enjoy life with my children. My husband was often travelling, and I saw myself as alone and unable to be the super mom or even the half way normal mom that I truly desired to be.

"There were weeks at a time that my daily routine was to stay in bed all morning and most of the afternoon. I did not shower or brush my teeth or hair. I did not get dressed. I wore my robe most days.

"I feel as though I somewhat neglected my children. I would take naps in the afternoon, after they came home from school. I would instruct them to not awaken me unless it was an emergency. My daughter definitely felt responsible for me and my challenges, my comfort, and even sometimes my decision making. She often had to take care of me and her own problems and issues because I wasn't emotionally or physically available.

"It was frustrating for my kids. While coping with the constant aches and pains of fibromyalgia I would often ask a child to pick up things off the floor and hand the item to me or put it away. I always felt I had to remind them that it helped my aching back when they'd pick up after me. They'd complain, "Why don't you do it yourself, Mom?" This was a constant conflict and I held a lot of guilt.

"My kids had friends over to our home less often than they normally would have if I had been well. My son very seldom invited friends to our home. He was embarrassed for them to be around me. Sometimes (in front of his friends) I would say totally random things or I would dance to a song on the radio. This was unacceptable to him.

"I would be gone from home a lot, either seeing health practitioners or doing other things to rescue and heal myself, such as developing my talents or attending the LDS Addiction Recovery Program (I felt I had an addiction to my negative thoughts, and the meetings really did help). Often my husband would be traveling. At that time, my daughter and sons would usually be alone, as they were old enough to stay home and be in charge of themselves.

"I was not very dependable when it came to time. If I said I would be gone for an hour, it could easily turn into 3–5 hours. This, I am sure, made

my children feel uneasy and insecure. They could not always count on me. Sometimes if my daughter was home alone in the evening, she would turn on all the lights in our home. She was frightened and this helped her feel a little safer.

"*Another challenge was keeping up with household chores. Housework was a dreaded task. I would rather take my children out to eat than face shopping, cooking, and cleaning up after a meal. My husband requested help from the Relief Society on several occasions. In one instance, a group of sisters seemed very judgmental. I perceived them as judging after they said there was not much for them to do that I could not handle myself. They did not understand how my emotional illness and back pain kept me physically drained and non-functioning. I looked good, so all they could see was an able-bodied woman. I imagine they felt that I was taking advantage of their good hearts. I do not judge them now. I know they did not fully understand what I was going through. And my needs were more overwhelming than they could take care of. On the other hand, in another situation years later, another set of sisters definitely assisted me with tasks that I was too afraid (or too paralyzed) to follow through with—for example showering or packing for a family trip.*

"*Laundry was the most daunting task of all. Finally, when the basement was filled with mountains of dirty laundry and there were almost no clean, unwrinkled clothes for any of us to wear, my thoughtful, understanding, and loving husband stepped in. He taught each of our children when they were between 8 and 10 years old how to wash, dry, fold and put away their own laundry. I appreciated this. I could have taught them, but this did not even occur to me at that time. My husband spent much time and effort taking care of me when he was not caring for our children.*

"*Our children had to deal with my ebb and flow; my darkest moments. Sometimes they had to hear me yelling at them, or crying and yelling at my husband, or begging my siblings or parents to listen to me and my challenges, talking and crying long distance from the home phone.*

"I did not hide this or go in another room. It was all out in the open, which probably was not the best choice on my part. I wish I could call a do over. Fortunately, my now adult children realize that my choices, my behaviors, and most of all my condition and situation were not my fault. They also know I love them with all my heart, and now we are blessed to enjoy a healthier and truly loving relationship. Thank God!

"If I could do it over again, I would have done more for my children. On the other hand, they did learn some valuable skills such as how to deal with other adults, how to do their own laundry, cook their own meals, and even plan their own birthday parties some years.

"I believe that even though at times I was not always physically or emotionally there for our children, they still benefited from my efforts to cheer them on, to praise them, and to teach them even when I could not be very positive at all with myself. Most of the time they loved to be with me, their imperfect mother.

"I am forever grateful to have my life back, to be able to see my strengths as well as other's strengths and talents so much more clearly now. I give thanks to God, to my husband, to my children, and to a few caring individuals and professionals, who have completely and unconditionally supported and loved me. Thankfully, I am able to love, be loved, and even feel lovable now and eternally. Praise God!

"Never, never, never give up! The Lord is always there, even when it seems you are all alone. I am a living modern miracle of a woman who never gave up. I truly appreciate Dr. Moore for seeing past the person who walked into her office several years ago and realized that the anxiety was not the true me."

—Tracy A. L. Izatt

From Tracy's husband:

"We all have wonderful dreams of what our married and family life will be like. Even when someone comes from a challenging background, they are still able to imagine a better life when they get married. It is that faith and hope that drives us to build relationships.

"However, the dreams we have for our future rarely include what it might be like to live with a partner that has chronic health problems. One is forced to make fundamental decisions about his or her life purpose and direction when dealing with a spouse with chronic illness.

"I have learned that it is normal for people that have a spouse or partner with chronic health problems to frequently experience intense feelings of disappointment and fear that the dreams they held for their own life may no longer be met. They often have fear that they will be unable to care for the spouse, that the children will be hurt, that the financial burdens will be too high, or that co-workers or friends will have negative responses.

"They may have anxiety about how to deal with all the new realities of life, they may experience feelings of guilt at not being able to solve the problem, or they may want to escape and resort to behaviors of avoidance. Experiencing feelings of being alone and misunderstood can compound all of this.

"While chronic physical and mental health issues are both extremely difficult to deal with, I believe chronic mental health issues add an additional burden on the spouse that is not discussed enough. People can readily understand chronic physical problems. If someone has a surgery, heart disease or diabetes, then outsiders can readily understand and accept the illness. The ward rallies around them and often gives service for them.

"In the case of mental challenges, however, the person may look and act normal and people may think any problems are just temporary or that simply an attitude adjustment is needed. This denial of the reality of the

illness by outsiders adds to the burden and negative feelings that the caretaker has.

"In my case, I have gone through all of these emotions. I have tried to deal with friends, family and co-workers that frequently didn't seem to understand or want to understand the issues and challenges that my wife and I have faced.

"In the nearly three decades that my wife and I struggled with her problems, I have had to make critical decisions that I believe others face as well. The first is whether to stay in the marriage. I have known numerous people that have chosen to leave a partner when a partner has faced serious physical and/or emotional problems. The reason frequently given is that by leaving, the spouse can better pursue his or her dreams. This willingness to leave is frequently accompanied by the belief that the sick person has a poor attitude. They may believe that the problem is their spouse's fault and they can change if they want. Or it may be that their spouse, in their illness, has become verbally or even physically abusive. I cannot judge people who make the decision to leave because I understand how challenging it is to deal with chronic illness at the same time one is trying to pursue a career, raise children and live a fulfilling life.

"In my case, critical factors in the decision to stay with my wife were faith and the fact that my wife never gave up. Faith was important because it gave the perspective that there is a higher good and a purpose in keeping an intact family. As strong a factor faith is, I readily admit that it may not have been enough for me. The other critical factor was the attitude of my wife. She never gave up on seeking for a solution. I believe if her attitude had been one of "this is the way I am, just accept it," then I might have made a different choice. Instead, she was always trying to find an answer and this gave me the confidence that we could work together on solutions.

"Another critical decision spouses need to make is how deal with children and career issues. In my case, I believe I made some mistakes and

did some things well. On the positive side, I tried to structure my job in a way to spend as much time at home as possible and I cut back on other outside commitments (community and Church). I also spent as much time with my children as I could. Having said this, I believe I spent too much time commuting and should have lived closer to my work.

"I also failed to fully understand the impact of everything on my children. I believe that I frequently allowed decisions to be made based on my wife's anxiety rather than on what was best for everyone. I did this because I wanted peace in the family and felt I could only deal with a certain number of issues at a time.

"However, in the end, I believe we had a fairly happy family life. I attribute this to our willingness to work together and the fact that my wife maintained a good overall attitude towards others. The children could see that she really loved them and was doing her best in spite of her severe anxiety over them and about everything she did. I also believe our family life worked because I tried to spend time with my family and because we all got fully involved in the medical treatments.

"After many decades of struggle, we finally found a solution and my wife has been very healthy over the past few years. For us, this has been a miracle and we are thankful daily that we stuck with it and worked together. I still worry about what will happen if she ever falls back into her previous health problems. I realize that I may have to face these challenges again in my life. However, I also realize that I may have no control over whether I do. So, that leads to what is perhaps the most important thing I have learned through this whole experience. I have learned that we need to live each day to the fullest, be appreciative for what we have and express our love to family and friends."

—Ted Izatt

Living with a depressed, anxious or other emotionally ill spouse, parent or child is always challenging, often scary, and frequently frustrating. The person with depression and anxiety has a mind that is so inward focused, it seems that they are very selfish and can think of no one but themselves. They have little emotional support to give, and often aren't able to care for other family members. They can be very needy and may seem demanding. They may seem overcritical because of their constant negativity.

Dealing with any serious illness in a family member will often cause the steps of grieving (see chapters 12 and 13). Some of the feelings a family member may experience would be:

- *Disbelief*—it couldn't be that bad. It is just a phase. She will snap out of it soon. She's been under a lot of stress and she will be fine.

- *Guilt*—what did I do wrong? Was I too harsh, too weak, did I cause it in any way? It's my fault. I should be able to solve this and I can't. Etc.

- *Anger at the person*—what did they do wrong? They are just too negative. They created it. They can stop it. It's their own fault. They are just selfish. Etc.

- *Anger at the system, at the person's parents, at the person's friends, at the church, at God*—if it weren't for _____, this would never have happened. It is their fault.

- *Need to control*—if I control everything they do, then they will get better. I know what is better for them than they do. If I control them, then my own life will be in better control. I am responsible to fix this family, and I need to fix my spouse, or my child.

- *It is my responsibility to save her*—I need to do everything for her, make her decisions because she is afraid, take care of her, make sure the children don't aggravate her, find solutions for her, etc.

- *Depression and/or anxiety*—what is going to happen today? Is she going to commit suicide? Estrange the kids? Do something stupid? Is she going to get out of bed? Where is my companion, my mother, my daughter? How can I do it all? I don't have any support, I have to do it all alone. I'm so lonely. My life is out of control. I can't do the things I want to do. My life is hindered and I can't succeed. She takes too much of my time. Etc.

- *Avoidance*—It's too hard. I need to bury myself in a book, TV, escape with friends, sports, addictions, affairs, go into my "cave" and not interact, divorce, run away. It's easier to ignore her and distance myself from her.

- *Acceptance*—it is what it is. It is no one's fault. It is an illness of the brain that none of us have control over right now. We are all doing our best. The Lord will support me and give me the strength to bear my burdens through all of this.

These feelings and others are all normal and natural, but the goal is to move towards acceptance, which allows the patient and family members to be in a space where healing can happen more easily.

Sometimes the illness is bad enough that the person is out of control and may be too abusive for the family members to be safe. It is not a sin to leave temporarily or permanently, with inspiration from God, to protect yourself and family members from severe abuse. Sometimes it is necessary to love from afar until there is safety.

The following are some of the things family members may choose to do to reduce problems for themselves and the person with the emotional problem.

1. Set boundaries.

Each one of us lives with a different capability of being able to deal with stress. It is important to talk together about the things that go beyond your ability to handle, and set boundaries about what you can and can't do.

For example, your spouse may have a lot of anxiety and be afraid to drive. She may want you to drive her everywhere or do all of the things yourself for the family that a car is needed for. You may be willing to assist her, but doing all of the errands and driving her to everything cuts into your work time, and your boss is not happy. You may have to set boundaries about what you can or cannot do to assist her. Then she will have to make the choice of whether to do it herself or to not do it at all.

Remember, a person who has anxiety is stressed when things aren't done that they believe need to be done. But if they can't do it themselves, and it something that is not that important to you, that may be where you set your boundary. They probably won't like it, but they can work that issue out with their counselor.

It is also important to set boundaries with behavior. People who are not well may become irritable, angry, defensive and critical. They can be emotionally, and sometimes physically, abusive when they lose control of themselves. They often tend to blame others for their own negative feelings. They often believe that their depression or anxiety is caused by someone else's behavior, most often their spouse, but often a parent or even a child.

If a family member who is emotionally ill criticizes you, calls you names, and is disrespectful, it is okay to look at yourself to see if what they are saying is true about you. If it is true and you can change, then do so. If it is true and you still seem unable to change because of your own weaknesses, or if it is not true and it is just their perception, then let go of their anger and criticism towards you. It is not personal. It is not even really about you, whether it is true or not. When they are angry at you or criticizing you, it is really simply about their own pain.

Defending yourself will not work. They are going to believe what they see from their own perspective no matter what you say. An example of what you may say or do follows, but nothing works all of the time, and sometimes it is necessary to remove yourself when they cross boundaries, so they know what you will and will not deal with.

Rather than defending yourself, it works better to simply acknowledge their feelings and your own. You may choose to say something such as, "I can understand how you may feel that way, but I see it differently (or, I am working on it but I am unable to change that behavior at this time, or I am doing the best I am able to in this situation). If you want to change the subject I will be happy to keep talking with you. If you keep criticizing me (calling me names, swearing at me, disrespecting me, yelling at me, etc.), I choose to leave the room." They may not like it. They may choose to follow you around complaining. You must find a way to separate yourself from the things that increase your stress and your own anger.

It works best if you can set the boundaries together when you are not in the middle of a crisis, or in the middle of the problem. However, since you don't know all of the problems that may come up, you may end up using different things until you find something that works. Don't give up. There are always an infinite number of possibilities. If one thing doesn't work, keep doing something different until you find what works.

2. Let go of absolute control.

Even though you may need to set boundaries, it is very tempting to feel the need to control the person in order to control your own life and your fears about the situation. You may feel the need to fix the person or fix the situation. You may feel like you are supposed to save the person, and you need to control their life to be able to do that. You may be embarrassed by their behavior and feel the need to force them to change because you worry about what others will think. It is very stressful to watch a loved one go through pain, and we may want to control them to help stop that pain.

There are obviously situations where safety is at risk and you need to control the situation. But you can never really control another person. Controlling the person, even when they may believe they want you to, because of their own anxiety and fears or lack of motivation, will usually eventually make things worse.

In spite of the emotional illness, people really do not like to be controlled. Free agency is of utmost and eternal importance, even with emotional illness. When people feel controlled, they naturally rebel and feel angry and resentful. And they usually will get more depressed and/or anxious. That is why people struggle being in a mental hospital, because it is an atmosphere of absolute control.

Again, controlling the situation may be necessary for safety of the person and/or the family, but controlling the person themselves may actually cause the problem you are trying to control.

Even people with emotional illness need to learn from their own mistakes. They need to be able to learn how to care for themselves in the best way that they can. They need to learn to make their own decisions, even though they may be extremely fearful to do so, and even though their decisions may lead them on a path you don't like for a while.

The more control a person can have in their own life, even if they make mistakes, the more they are fulfilling their own purpose in life (which may be simply to learn how to control and heal themselves, which is a huge purpose).

In learning how to be gods, we get to learn how to inspire rather than force and control. Yes, their mistakes may have a profound effect on our own lives. But that is true of everyone, emotionally ill or not. It is part of the Plan of Happiness, so that we may each get to experience "the opposites" through our own weakness and the weakness of the people in our lives.

We get to be there with love and support as the person learns how to deal with their illness, even when it takes much longer than we think we can handle, and even when they make mistakes which cause them, and us, pain.

We get to set boundaries and have loving but firm consequences for crossing those boundaries. We get to let go of judgment of what their path in life is supposed to look like. Their life path may be exactly what they came here to learn, and we cannot judge that. Their path may be teaching us lessons that we came here to learn as well.

There is a fine line between setting boundaries and control. Mistakes will be made, and that is part of life. Just let go of what didn't work and do something different, until you find what works. The movie "Benny and Joon" is a movie about a brother taking care of his emotionally ill sister. It deals with the matter of learning to let go of control through mistakes that were made, as the brother was trying to keep his sister safe. It can be very scary to let go of control, but in the end, over time, the results will be worth it.

3. Create time for yourself and your own needs and desires.

An emotionally ill person often either hides away so you have to do everything or demands a lot of time and attention dealing with their issues. Make sure that one of the boundaries you make is your own personal time and space. You may possibly be accused of being selfish, because of their own insecurities, or you may feel guilty to spend time doing something you enjoy, but your own sanity is as important as hers is.

4. There is no excuse for abuse. Do not use mental illness as an excuse for their abuse of others.

When a spouse, parent or child has an emotional illness, some of them may lose control and become verbally, emotionally or even physically abusive. Frequent loss of control that includes yelling, name calling, severe criticism, put downs, blaming, breaking things and/or hitting becomes abuse. Do not allow yourself to be abused. Do not allow your children to be abused. Keep yourself and them safe, even if it means leaving.

There is often a belief among spouses that they are honoring their temple and eternal marriage by not standing up to the abusive person. Or they believe they should not argue or show lack of support in front of the children. However, if your spouse is abusive to you or the children, it is important to stop it in the moment it is happening, even if it causes a worse crisis, even if it is in front of the children. Love yourself enough to not allow yourself to be abused. Love your children enough to not allow them to be abused. You and your children should not have to walk on eggshells to keep from upsetting your spouse. It is very damaging to not be able to be yourselves.

There is never any excuse for abuse, even emotional illness. The emotionally ill person may not have as good control over their mental processes and actions, but they can do what it takes to stop their outbursts, such as medication and/or good counseling. They always have a choice. If you do not allow it, eventually they will chose something different.

5. There is no excuse for abuse. Do not allow your own frustrations at the person turn into abuse.

Living with an emotionally ill person can be very frustrating, and it may be easy to lose control of yourself and start yelling, name calling, giving severe criticism, give put downs, blaming her, breaking things and/or hitting. These things are considered emotional and physical abuse. Your abuse will not change her, but will generally make her worse. There is no excuse for abuse, no matter how the other person is acting or how frustrating and difficult they are.

6. Consider what you are learning and how you are growing as a result of this relationship. Strive to find gratitude for being in this relationship.

I firmly believe that in the pre-existence we chose our parents, spouses and children knowing what weakness they would be given, because we knew how we would grow and become better by learning to deal with that weakness in the way we desired to grow on this earth. God is no respecter of persons. One of you is not "better" than the other. He loves each of you equally. He knows each of you intimately. He knows the weakness that each of you was given, and knows that it is temporary for this earth experience. Consider what you desired to learn by being in this relationship.

Using Neurofeedback to Treat Depression and Anxiety

*N*eurofeedback is one of the most potent treatments for chronic anxiety and depression to come out within the past few decades. The treatment is beginning to make its way into mainstream medicine, but it's surprising that neurofeedback is not better known. My experiences using it on clients over the past five years have been remarkable.

Neurofeedback is based on the principle that the brain, as a learning organ, adapts and optimizes itself to the influences around it. This is called "neuroplasticity" of the brain. This learning ability is a core part of how we survive and thrive in such a large variety of circumstances (consider the contrast between the Australian aboriginal peoples and the corporate executives on Wall Street). Our brains shift and change to support our ability to function among the influences arising from these circumstances, positive or negative. The more we expose our brains to these influences (in either time or intensity), the more entrenched those changes become.

Let's take an example. A man living at home with his family will usually experience a full range of brain activity. But when the military sends him off to the front lines in a war, in Europe or Vietnam or Iraq or Afghanistan, threats to his life flood his environment. As he spends more and more time in "fight or flight" mode his brain begins to optimize around extreme brain patterns such as intense awareness, reflexive defenses, light sleeping, and aggression. These extreme arousal states become his new "normal," helping him survive and thrive in a state of war. When he comes back home however, that same extreme arousal state, combined with vivid memories, is labeled *post-traumatic stress disorder* (PTSD), and is a very *unhealthy* state to be in.

Soldiers are not the only people subject to unhealthy influences. Others include those who have experienced emotional or physical abuse, the loss of a loved one, rape or another violent crime, the loss of a job or income, or experiencing extreme physical and/or emotional demands over an extended period of time (many mothers fall into this category). In general, anyone who experiences significant physical or emotional pain may experience brain optimization around unhealthy influences. These negative adaptations often show up in people as chronic anxiety and/or depression.

Neurofeedback unravels these unhealthy adaptations. After testing the brainwaves through a Quantitative Electroencephalogram (qEEG), a protocol is developed to assist the brain in improving its ability to shift into a healthy state. The neurofeedback equipment painlessly interacts with the brain using an EEG[1] device, providing targeted audiovisual stimuli that the brain adapts to with *healthy* activity. As with unhealthy influences, the brain system is exposed to these healthy stimuli over an extended period of time (one half hour twice a week, usually for three to six months). This draws the brain out of its negative "ruts"

---

[1] An electroencephalogram (EEG) measures the activity of the brain, just as an electrocardiogram (EKG) measures the activity of the heart.

(optimized, reinforced neural pathways) and into healthy functionality again. Unless the brain is exposed to unhealthy influences again, the shift is permanent once the neurofeedback is completed.

The concept is simple, but the effect is powerful. As I work with Dr. Moore's patients, many who have been struggling with a variety of mental, physical, and emotional issues for *decades* see marked improvement within a short period of time. Frequently, within three to six months, though sometimes longer, we have been able to reduce or even eliminate these people's need for medication, see them move out of survival mode, and begin engaging and contributing in life.

Of course, neurofeedback is no panacea. Dr. Moore uses a variety of treatments in any healing process—mental, physical, or emotional. However, again and again we have found that the brain plays a significant role in the problem. Anxiety, depression, PTSD and other emotional illnesses are just the tip of the chronic symptom iceberg; issues as wide ranging as ADHD, fibromyalgia, chronic allergies, traumatic brain injury and irritable bowel syndrome have all been linked to unhealthy brain activity. In these cases neurofeedback can significantly accelerate healing; in many instances it has proven to be the key factor in successful recovery.

I invite you to take a closer look at neurofeedback as a part of your healing process. There are a variety of books and magazine and newspaper articles about it available on the web and at your local bookstore. For more information on how to take advantage of the benefits neurofeedback offers, feel free to visit our website.

—Jason Moore
Vanguard Center for Neurological Medicine
www.VanguardCenter.com

Notes

Preface

1. *Teachings of Presidents of the Church: Joseph F. Smith* [1998], 184.

2. Spencer W. Kimball, "The Role of Righteous Women," *Ensign,* Nov. 1979, 102.

How to use this book

3. Dag Hammarskjold, Swedish diplomat, Secretary-General of the United Nations 1953–1961, when he died in a plane crash in Northern Rhodesia flying there to negotiate a cease fire. His journal writings were published after his death in *Markings* (1964). This quote is taken from that book.

4. *Ibid.*

Chapter 1—Depression and Anxiety are Real

5. See http://www.nami.org/Template.cfm?Section=depression

6. Kessler RC, Chiu WT, Demler O, Merikangas KR, Walters EE (June 2005). "Prevalence, severity, and comorbidity of 12-month DSM-IV disorders in the National Comorbidity Survey Replication." *Arch. Gen. Psychiatry,* 62 (6): 617–27. doi:10.1001/archpsyc.62.6.617. PMID 15939839.

PMC 2847357. http://archpsyc.ama-assn.org/cgi/content/full/62/6/617.

7.   "Abraham Lincoln to John T. Stuart," 23 January 1841, *Collected Works of Abraham Lincoln,* 1:229–30.

8.   "Sweet Is the Work: Gordon B. Hinckley, 15th President of the Church," *New Era,* May 1995, 8.

9.   Dallin H. Oaks, "He Heals the Heavy Laden," *Ensign,* Nov 2006, 6–9.

10.   David O. McKay, "The Mission of Brigham Young University," BYU address, April 27, 1948. Printed in *Church News,* May 16, 1948.

Chapter 2—Depression and Anxiety: What are They?

11.   Martje H. L. et al. "Psychiatric nurse; member of the HF management team?" *European Journal of Cardiovascular Nursing.* 2005. 99–100.

12.   Kessler, R. C. et al. "Sex and depression in the National Comorbidity Survey I: Lifetime Prevalence, Chronicity and Recurrence." *Journal of Affective Disorders.* 1993. 85–96.

13.   http://www.amenclinics.com/clinics/professionals/how-we-can-help/brain-science/deep-limbic-system-thalamus-dls/.

14.   Hastings RS, Parsey RV, Oquendo MA, Arango V, Mann JJ, "Volumetric analysis of the prefrontal cortex, amygdala, and hippocampus in major depression." *Neuropsychopharmacology.* 2004 May; 29 (5):952–9.

15. Arnold E. Eggars, "Redrawing Papez' circuit: A theory about how acute stress becomes chronic and causes disease," *Medical Hypothesis,* volume 69, issue 4, Pages 852–857 (2007).

16. Joseph A. Lieberman III, MD, MPH, "Assessing the Symptomatic Overlap Between Anxiety and Depression: Impact on the Patient," supplement to *Psychiatric Times Reporter,* Apr. 2009, 2–6.

17. http://www.amenclinics.com/brain-science/cool-brain-science/a-crash-course-in-neuroscience/basal-ganglia-system/.

Chapter 3—The Brain of a Woman

18. Most of the factual information in this chapter was derived from: Louann Brizendine M.D. *The Female Brain,* Morgan Road Books, 2006.

19. M. Russell Ballard, "Mothers and Daughters," April, 2010 LDS General Conference.

Chapter 4—The Origin of Our Beliefs

20. "Adverse Childhood Experiences Reported by Adults—Five States, 2009," *JAMA,* Feb. 16, 2011, vol. 305, No. 7, 666.

Chapter 5—Physical Causes of Depression and Anxiety

21. *Eur J Cancer Prev.,* Oct; 11, 2002, (5): 481–8.

Chapter 6—Who Can Find a Virtuous Woman?

22. Dieter F. Uchtdorf, "The Love of God," Oct. 2009 LDS General Conference.

23. Julie B. Beck, "And upon the Handmaids in Those Days Will I Pour Out My Spirit," Apr. 2010 LDS General Conference.

Chapter 7—Unfulfilled Expectations

24. Rex Lee, Janet Lee, Jim Bell, *Marathon of Faith,* Salt Lake City, Deseret Book Company, 1996.

25. Keith N. Hamilton, *Thoughts & Reflections of a Black Mormon,* Salt Lake City, UT, Ammon Works, LLC, 2011, 86–87.

Chapter 8—Why Do I Have So Many Weaknesses?

26. Dieter F. Uchtdorf, "You Are My Hands," Apr. 2010 LDS General Conference.

27. Mike Dooley, *TUT…A Note from the Universe,* daily email newsletter, Nov. 12, 2010.

Chapter 10—False Beliefs about Fear and Love

28. Joseph F. Smith, "The Love of Mother," *Improvement Era,* Jan. 1910, 278.

29. David A. Bednar, "And Nothing Shall Offend Them," *Ensign,* Nov. 2006, 89.

Chapter 13—The Only Way Around Grief is to Go Through It

30. President Gordon B. Hinckley, "Rise to the Stature of the Divine Within You" *Ensign,* Nov. 1989.

31. Ann M. Dibb, "Hold On," LDS General Conference, Oct. 2009.

Chapter 15—Healing through the Gospel of Jesus Christ

32. Dallin H. Oaks, "He Heals the Heavy Laden," LDS General Conference, Oct. 2006.

Chapter 16—Healing through Faith in the Lord Jesus Christ

33.   *Teachings of the Prophet Joseph Smith,* sel. Joseph Fielding Smith [1976], 121.

Chapter 17—How to Grow in Faith

34.   http://www.amenclinics.com/cybcyb/brain-health-club/seven-ways-to-optimize-your-brain-and-your-life/3-kill-the-ants-that-invade-your-brain/.

35.   Wallace Goddard, "A Little Known Debate in Heaven," *Meridian Magazine,* Oct. 21, 2010

36.   Andrew Newberg MD, Mark Robert Waldman, *How God Changes Your Brain: Breakthrough Findings from a Leading Neuroscientist,* Ballantine Books, New York, 2009.

Chapter 18—Healing through Repentance: Letting go of Pain Caused by our Weakness

37.   http://www.thefreedictionary.com/Sin

38.   http://www.bookrags.com/quotes/Fran%C3%A7ois_F%C3%A9nelon

39.   http://www.aa.org/en_pdfs/smf-121_en.pdf

Chapter 23—Healing through Loving One Another

40.   *Gospel Doctrine: Sermons and Writings,* Salt Lake City: Deseret Book, 1939, 294.

Chapter 24—Women Are that They Might Have Joy

41. William Wordsworth "Ode: Intimations of Immortality from Recollections of Early Childhood," *Poems, in Two Volumes,* 1807.

Appendix 1—Medications: To Take or Not to Take

42. Jay C. Fournier, MA, "Antidepressant Drug Effects and Depression Severity: A Patient-Level Meta-analysis," *JAMA,* 2010; 303 (1):47–53. doi: 10.1001/jama.2009, 1943

43. Oliver J. S.; Burrows G. D.; Norman T. R. (September 1999). "Discontinuation Syndromes with Selective Serotonin Re-uptake Inhibitors: Are There Clinically Relevant Differences?" *CNS Drugs,* 12 (3): 171–7. doi:10.2165/00023210–199912030–00001.

About the Author

~

Dr. Judith Stay Moore is a family practice physician who is also Board Certified in Integrative and Holistic Medicine. She owns the Diamond Springs Wellness Center in Midway, Utah. Dr. Moore has extensive training and experience in emotional illnesses, and co-authored Marie Osmond's book *Behind the Smile: My Journey Out of Postpartum Depression*. Dr. Moore has six children and 19 grandchildren, and attributes her many experiences with her family as her greatest education. She served a mission as the Area Medical Advisor in Buenos Aires, Argentina in 2005–2006, caring for the health of over 2,000 missionaries, and loved it!